Coaching Physicians and Healthcare Professionals

This important volume applies the practice of professional coaching to the hospital setting specifically, imparting the authors' rich experience of coaching healthcare providers to other coaches working within the field.

The book details how coaches can tailor their skills to the complex world of the modern hospital where physicians, nurses, medico-technical staff, managers, and administrators must carefully coordinate their efforts to be successful in high-stakes situations. It moves through the various stages of coaching, starting from the initial contact with management to the different applications of individual and team coaching, addressing common client issues including failing leadership, crisis, conflict, violence, and burnout. Each chapter includes clinical vignettes and theoretical ideas supported by field-specific research and literature. The book's final reflection proposes changes to be considered to improve the functioning of hospital care teams, job satisfaction of healthcare professionals, and, ultimately, patient outcomes.

Coaching Physicians and Healthcare Professionals is essential reading for professional coaches and mentors active in the hospital setting, as well as coaches in training, consultants, and all hospital professionals.

René Chioléro is an independent coach and business consultant, primarily focused on healthcare providers (mainly executive, life, and group coaching). Until 2009, he was professor and head of the Critical Care Medicine Department at the University Hospital of Lausanne, Switzerland.

Véronique Haynal is a psychotherapist with a Freudian and eclectic background; she is also a life and professional coach. She specialized in non-verbal communication, emotion management, and psychosomatic disorders. She worked in liaison psychiatry as a researcher and was a supervisor in a crisis unit in the Geneva University Hospital (Department of Psychiatry).

Coaching Physicians and Healthcare Professionals

Supporting Workplace Wellbeing and High-Quality Care

René Chioléro and
Véronique Haynal

Routledge
Taylor & Francis Group

LONDON AND NEW YORK

Cover image: © Sang Eui Kim

First published 2022
by Routledge
4 Park Square, Milton Park, Abingdon, Oxon OX14 4RN

and by Routledge
605 Third Avenue, New York, NY 10158

Routledge is an imprint of the Taylor & Francis Group, an informa business

British Library Cataloguing-in-Publication Data
A catalogue record for this book is available from the British Library

Library of Congress Cataloguing-in-Publication Data
Names: Haynal, Veronique, author. | Chioléro, René, author.
Title: Coaching physicians and healthcare professionals : supporting
workplace wellbeing and high-quality care / Veronique Haynal
and René Chioléro.
Description: Milton Park, Abingdon, Oxon ; New York, NY : Routledge,
2022. | Includes bibliographical references and index. |
Identifiers: LCCN 2021058351 (print) | LCCN 2021058352 (ebook) |
ISBN 9781032272139 (hardback) | ISBN 9781032252001 (paperback) |
ISBN 9781003291831 (ebook)
Subjects: LCSH: Medical personnel--Management. | Communication in
medicine. | Leadership.
Classification: LCC RA971.35 .H39 2022 (print) | LCC RA971.35
(ebook) | DDC 610.69--dc23/eng/20211222
LC record available at https://lccn.loc.gov/2021058351
LC ebook record available at https://lccn.loc.gov/2021058352

ISBN: 978-1-032-27213-9 (hbk)
ISBN: 978-1-032-25200-1 (pbk)
ISBN: 978-1-003-29183-1 (ebk)

DOI: 10.4324/9781003291831

Typeset in Bembo
by MPS Limited, Dehradun

Contents

13 Viewpoints, perspectives, and conclusion   305

RENÉ CHIOLÉRO AND VÉRONIQUE HAYNAL

Preface

Coaching meets our moment

Coaching is the oldest of professions, and also the youngest. Ever since the dawn of humanity, the Shaman, or Priest, or Tribal Elder has coached each new generation on proper communal behavior and individual problem solving. But coaching, as academic discipline and defined profession, is remarkably young—having been introduced by a university program in Australia just two decades ago.

Coaching is an effective performance enhancer for individuals, teams, corporations, educational systems, government agencies, and all sorts of other organizations. Its phenomenal growth in so short a time reflects the many gaps in previous services that needed filling. The international appeal of coaching proves that it is tapping into something basic to our human nature and fundamental to our interpersonal relationships. The exponential increase in numbers of coaches and clients proves that both of these roles are attractive and deeply satisfying. And the rapid creation of methods, training programs, standards, accreditation, associations, and journals demonstrates that coaching has an extremely energetic and savvy leadership pool.

The word "coach" originated as a slang term among students at Oxford University in the 1830s, to praise tutors who were particularly helpful in getting them through exam periods. "Coaching" was first used as a sports term in the 1860s. The systematic application of psychological principles to improve athletic performance began in the 1920s.

The new discipline—"Coaching Psychology"—integrates lay coaching techniques with those derived from the research and practice in psychotherapy.

Coaching Psychology differs from psychotherapy in its goals and the needs of its clients. It aims to help well people perform better, rather than reducing symptoms in people with mental disorders. It differs from simple coaching by systematically adapting the techniques of the different schools of psychology and psychotherapy.

Because of reimbursement rules imposed by third-party insurance, psychotherapy (unless it is self-paid) requires that the client be given a DSM–5 diagnosis of mental disorder. The diagnoses used to justify payments are often exaggerated and inaccurate—the worried well-being up-diagnosed to qualify for the insurance coverage. This is stigmatizing and also regressive—the client filling the sick role assigned to him. And, in the current world, a mental disorder diagnosis can all too often lead to the use of inappropriate medication.

Coaching has the great advantage of not medicalizing everyday psychological distress. It emphasizes the clients' strengths and personal resources, not his deficits and symptoms. Usually briefer and less expensive than psychotherapy, coaching is far more accessible within the self-pay system.

The coronavirus pandemic has highlighted the value, and greatly increases the scope, of coaching. The illness itself, combined with the economic and social consequences of the physical distancing required to contain it, has created enormous emotion distress in a high percentage of previously well-functioning people.

It brings us to this wonderful book. Its publication is especially timely as we face the worldwide disruption of health systems by the coronavirus plague. In the epic battle between mighty modern medicine versus a tiny virus, the virus clearly won in most countries. This pandemic has been the ultimate stress test of our medical system, and we flunked badly.

I have worked in hospitals throughout my professional career and can say with great confidence that they just don't work very well. The organizational structure of a typical hospital is much more geared for its convenience and profit than for the medical needs and wants of its patients. Hospital bureaucracies have grown almost exponentially and almost always self preferentially. Inefficiencies abound; lethal and potentially lethal mistakes are frequent; the less sick are over-treated; the really sick often under-treated; and everything is way over-priced. Hospitals have too many moving parts, usually moving out of synchrony with one another.

The pandemic is an inflection point that may lead to reform. Coaching can play an important role both in improving the performance of the individuals working within the system, and also in helping to identify the system dysfunctions and improve its overall performance.

The authors know everything about hospitals; everything about coaching; and how best to apply the latter to improve the performance of the former. They systematically deal with all the ways coaching can be used in hospitals; what are the opportunities and potential pitfalls. Their noble aspiration is to promote more effective and humanized care, for the benefit of patients, professional staff, administrators, and the system as a whole. They succeed admirably.

Allen Frances M.D.

Acknowledgments

Writing a book together is not a natural and easy undertaking, even for two colleagues who have known each other for several years. However, this is what we, Véronique and René, attempted to do, after Véronique received a request from an editor to write a book in French on *careproviders' coaching*. Composing with four hands requires an active learning on the part of two persons with such different professional experiences (a coach and former chief physician and a psychotherapist-coach). There were sometimes divergent opinions, be it for the development of the concepts, the construction of the book, and much more. We thank the fortunate coincidence of being coaches: we undertook this endeavor like a coaching project with its purpose, the book. The whole process led to a co-construction based on trust and sharing, avoiding any sterile opposition: each one's questions, oppositions, and doubts resulting in a development and learning process for both authors.

We are very grateful to our friend, the painter Sang Eui Kim, Ph.D. and B.F.A., for allowing us to feature his beautiful work on the cover (www.sangeuikim.com).

Sarah Wang's generosity of her time, concern and excellent advices have launched us to the endeavor of not only translating but also improving the French edition of our book. As a specialist of the healthcare world, Geneviève Ley, M.D., has been a moral and financial support all along. May they be warmly thanked

We would like to thank all the clients, coachees, and supervisees who have worked with us; indeed, they have shown their confidence in us, and have shared with us their concerns, doubts, joys, hopes, as well as their secrets. They are present throughout the chapters of this book and constitute the living part of it.

Marlyne and André, our spouses, have been our inspiration and resilience. Their patience and tolerance have allowed us to complete this long undertaking. May Marlyne receive our deepest gratitude. André's death leaves us with a wonderful memory of support.

Introduction

René Chioléro and Véronique Haynal

Why write a book on coaching in hospitals?

Why a new text on coaching? What contributions could we make to healthcare sector and coaches by describing our practice and experiences in these fields?

We have been active in hospitals for many years: first as health care providers and then as coaches. This experience has provided us with compelling, authentic, and surprising experiences *under different guises*: the white coat of the physician or the psychologist and the suit of the coach. In these contexts, we have worked with doctors and nurses from diverse disciplines, as well as other health care professionals and administrators. Most importantly, we have realized the necessity for change at many levels of the hospital organization, and efficient coaching can be the catalyst for positive change.

Today's hospital resembles a small city, active day and night, with its diversity and innumerable, ever-changing challenges. Hospitals bring together many professions, for example:

- Physicians: In the United States in 2018, there were 40 specialties and 87 subspecialties recognized by the American Board of Medical Specialties.
- Nursing staff (e.g., advanced registered, registered, licensed, specialties).
- Allied health care workers (e.g., diagnostic medical sonographers, dietitians, medical technologists, occupational therapists, physical therapists, radiographers, respiratory therapists, speech-language pathologists, and dental hygienists).
- Computer scientists and information technology specialists: The number of these workers is increasing exponentially as their contribution becomes critical in all clinical, research, and other institutional fields.
- Psychology professions (e.g., clinical psychologists, psychotherapists, child and adolescent psychologists, neuropsychologists, health psychologists).
- Research physicians and students: In university hospitals, these searchers are a large segment of the population (e.g., at the Mayo Clinic in 2019, full-time scientific faculty: 252; physicians actively involved in research: 794; full-time research personnel: 4,221).[a]

DOI: 10.4324/9781003291831-1

- Teaching staff: Many hospitals are in charge of the training of various professionals.
- Logistics (e.g., transport, security, kitchen, janitorial employees).
- Support staff (e.g., lawyers, chaplains, ethicists, mediators).
- Administration (e.g., managers, financiers, bookkeepers, human resource employees).

These professions have grown and diversified steadily over the decades, along with the development of the hospital system.

This non-exhaustive list demonstrates the great complexity of a modern hospital. Coaches who penetrate such a structure and wish to work effectively need to know and understand the basic elements of hospital operations. These coaches need information and insight to fully understand the nature of their mission and its environment.

This book draws on our ten years of coaching experience in this environment, to give coaches some knowledge of the situation and hints to adapt their practice. The text is also intended for care providers in managerial positions who wish to broaden their awareness of the human problems faced by themselves, their staff and care teams, as well as the administrators who lead and/or collaborate with these health professionals.

A change of perspectives

Working as a care provider is quite different from being mandated as a coach in a hospital setting, indeed.

Care providers are immersed in the hospital environment and are subject to the constraints and sometimes the weakness of its governance. If the organization of the departments and the management of the team are adequate, their work is facilitated, and the interpersonal relations are gratifying. If not, tensions and conflicts emerge that affect the care providers' well-being and the quality of care. In the "hot" sectors of the hospital (e.g., emergency room, intensive care, operating room), the care providers will be affected by the normal daily stress of work, their day and night shifts, as well as by team life. If, in addition to those burdens, physicians are middle managers in clinical departments or divisions whose organizations suffer from chronic conflict, their task becomes unnecessarily difficult, when employees transfer or simply burn out (30%–50% in the most exposed divisions).

Hospital hierarchies are cumbersome, and many senior physicians have insufficient autonomy in their activities. The implementation of a real shared leadership system is yet insufficient in many departments, which is a frequent cause of frustration among care providers executives.

The multiple specialties and subspecialties of hospital medicine cause fragmentation of the medical practice. This growing diversification, combined with a misunderstanding of each other's practice, affects patient care. Ensuring effective communication within interdisciplinary teams, essential for patient care and medical education, is painstaking and involves co-ordinating the collaboration of physicians and nurses from different backgrounds, cultures, and hierarchical levels. Thus, communication flaws and conflicts are common.

Coaches working with department heads on their leadership or with a group of care providers in resolving conflicts must initiate—as always in coaching—a privileged relationship with the recipient(s) to establish over time mutual trust and understanding. For this to happen, coaches must become embedded observers in the many cultures of the healthcare hospital environment, which differ significantly from the cultures of other professions. In addition, coach should become familiar with the significant differences in the cultures of various care professions (e.g., doctors, nurses, psychologists) to gain the multi-storied picture many professionals and aids might have on a particular patient case, for example.

Coach must manage the triangular relationship between the prescriber (medical director), the beneficiary (executive physician), and himself—the coach—which often proves tricky. As described in this book, we were repeatedly confronted with coaching requests presented as professional development projects that were in fact a "last chance" coaching for leaders who had been insufficiently evaluated and mentored by their superiors. The lack of knowledge of coaching by the medical profession, which often recognizes it as exclusive to the sports world, should also be considered.

The practice of team coaching is often problematic in hospitals for several reasons: the scheduling constraints and many duties of group members make holding meetings for the entire crew difficult; groups uninterested in team life are unwilling to participate in group work, and collaboration with a reluctant department manager can be trying.

Coaching is mostly applied in difficult situations and does not focus on the departments or divisions that function well: when assessing the hospital, the coach has a view inevitably biased by this reality. We still had the satisfying experience of bringing about stimulating change and improvement to willing leaders or teams who wanted to progress. This book does not describe the entire health care institution, but it does identify specific circumstances that required and benefitted from the intervention of a coach.

Our philosophy, conviction, and approach to coaching

Coaching aims to offer effective, efficient support in the hospital environment, something we have verified many times during our years of practice. However, the effectiveness of this program is subject to several conditions:

- Coaching is conducted by experienced professionals in accordance with the standards of practice: coaches should have a university degree (or/and a great reputation) to be successful in coaching doctors and nurses, administrators, and other professional staff (our recommendation).

This is particularly important in coaching physicians, due to their common "dominant" posture.

- Coaches possess sufficient knowledge of the hospital environment and the professional culture of the care providers they assist. Many factors influence these two factors, namely, the type (private or public) and size of the institution, the mission of the hospital and the departments (academic, nonacademic, medical specialties), the type of careers (doctors, nurses, others).
- Coaches have absolute respect for confidentiality and transparency, which is crucial in prescribed coaching, although these objectives are difficult to maintain.

Book design and construction

The text includes three main sections: the first is devoted to the fundamentals of coaching; the second to the practice of coaching in the hospital field; the third is more reflexive, focused on coaching learning and on the necessary changes to humanize the hospital work conditions. Included in this section are descriptions of practical cases to help contextualize and reinforce the connections between theory and practice. All the vignettes are drawn from our observations and were modified or included several situations to ensure anonymity. Notably, we were careful to preserve the messages and emotions conveyed by these stories. Additionally, these illustrations were deliberately shortened to emphasize their signification in the context of this book. The book is based on cited material; thus, each chapter ends with a bibliography and a list of recommended literature to deepen the subject. The information is presented in a logical progression, but each of the 13 chapters can be read separately.

We wish to encourage coaches to enlarge their field and deepen their knowledge in the health care professional world.

What does the book contain?

Part I: Fundamentals of coaching

The first four chapters describe some of the basic knowledge about the practice of coaching in the hospital setting.

Chapter 1 draws a picture of coaching that we encounter in the hospital environment: external coaching, practiced by a licensed professional; *internal coaching*, practiced within the framework of the hospital; and *in-hospital mentoring*, common in the academic setting. The differences, similarities, and caveats of life coaching and psychotherapy are also discussed.

Chapter 2 discusses what relationship is and its specificities for coaching. Indeed, the relationship is the main tool for coaching success. We compare the relationship of healthcare providers with patients with that of coaches with their clients. We develop four pillars of relationship: trust, communication, empathy/compassion, and "active" or "benevolent" listening. We then present some models showing what can be put in place.

In chapter 3, we describe the reasons why supervision should be regularly practiced; its benefits and the desirable qualities of a supervisor. We then present a specific and valuable model for group supervision.

Part II: Practice of hospital coaching

These chapters are devoted to the work of the coach in the hospital field and describe numerous aspects of this practice.

Chapter 4 gives an introduction to the professional culture of health care providers: contact with suffering and death; dominant positioning of physicians; symbols and rituals like the white coat and medical jargon; culture of care and compassion in nurses. These socio-cultural characteristics influence the leading of coaching from the start.

Chapter 5 describes some essential elements of establishing and carrying out a coaching in a hospital context. It begins with a simple description of the basics of hospital organization, which can be highly complex. The consecutive stages of care providers coaching are delineated. The caveat of coaching prescribed by management is emphasized.

In chapter 6, the practice of physicians executive coaching is depicted, often caused by weak or failing leadership. Notably, the selection of most department heads is mainly based on their professional and academic skills, while their managerial and leadership skills are hardly considered. Leading executive coaching is significantly influenced by the culture of the different medical specialties.

Chapter 7 aims to describe the specific elements of life coaching and reports the experience of the authors in this field, including the professional and life transitions of executive physicians.

Chapter 8 describes some fundamental elements that determine the functioning of medical teams and hierarchies. Coaching in these teams is often difficult, due to the highly individualistic medical culture, resistance to prescribed coaching, and the frequent presence of team conflicts.

Chapter 9 delineates the most common crisis that occur in the hospital setting, particularly when the ability of care providers is overwhelmed. This lack of adaptation can lead to deteriorated work conditions, high stress, exhaustion, and burnout when prolonged. Crisis coaching requires proper management and specific strategies, especially at the onset, which require adequate training and experience.

Chapter 10 is focused on coaching among care providers suffering from their arduous work condition, a common situation in at-risk departments. Such pressure can result in mental health problems, such as burnout, and even mental health issues, which are more frequent in the medical profession than in other professions. At low or moderate intensity, burnout can be improved by coaching, which requires specific competences. Severe burnout requires specialized care.

Conflicts and violence are addressed in chapter 11. They are often hidden and undetectable, affect all areas of medical and care activities, including academic setting. Addressed effectively by coaching, conflicts become opportunities for change, development, and growth. Two environments conducive to multiple antagonisms are described: the operating theater and the intensive care unit.

Part III: Views on coaching learning and avenues to humanize the hospital environment

Making the transition from hospital care provider to professional coach, a manifest change, is reported in chapter 12. The authors' journeys, including coach training, and discovery of hospital coaching are related. Successes, difficulties, emotions, critical moments, and failures during the first years of coaching practice are described.

In chapter 13, the two authors report some leading observations they made during their coaching interventions in the world of care providers. They conclude that the overall functioning of many hospitals of the twenty-first century has yet to adapt and become more *humanized*: many areas deserve change, and when made, the achievements should be promising.

Note

a https://www.mayoclinic.org/about-mayo-clinic/facts-statistics (viewed on 10.2.2020).

Part I

Fundamentals of coaching

1 Coaching-related methods at hospital

Véronique Haynal and René Chioléro

Introduction

This presentation is intended mainly for healthcare providers, not necessarily for coaches, although we do give some hints about caveats and requirements for coaching in the healthcare world.

Coaching is a profession classified as a *helping relationship* and promotes the resources and qualities of another person, such as growth, development, maturity, adaptability, knowledge, professional skills, and physical and psychological well-being.[1] The word "coach" appeared in the Oxford Dictionary in 1930 as a slang word for "carrying" (from the coach's name: car) someone from where he is to where he wants to go. The example given is that of a tutor who "carries his student through his exam." As early as 1861, this word was used in sports. Then, with the industrial revolution, management, as well as questions of leadership, became important. Coaching is thus used to support and assist organizations, to *succeed*.

There is no universally accepted definition of coaching. The International Coach Federation (ICF) defines professional coaching as "partnering with clients in a thought-provoking and creative process that inspires them to maximize their personal and professional potential."

The ground covered by such professions has increased considerably over the last decades in many domains of professional and daily lives. It is part of a broad movement of humanistic psychology, initiated in the United States by Carl Rogers, among others, based on the belief that people have vast resources to understand and constructively change their lives and ways of being and behaving.[1] Under this movement, many forms of assistance, such as individual and group coaching, as well as life coaching and other forms related to coaching like internal coaching and mentoring, have been introduced in medical and nursing practices. Nowadays, the specifications of coaching are becoming more diverse. The American Nurses Association recently recognized a new role—the nursing coach—focusing on coaching related to care. In addition, a relatively new profession—health and wellness coach—is growing, and the International Consortium for Health and Wellness Coaching has worked with the National Board Certification for Health and Wellness

DOI: 10.4324/9781003291831-3

Coaching (NBC-HWC) to establish standard requirements for levels of training, practice, and essential skills, that is, a clearly defined and more demanding certification for these health and wellness coaches.[2,3]

Essential characteristics of coaching and elements of method

Coaching is based on structured interactions between the coachee (the beneficiary) and the coach (the supporter). To this end, coaches use action strategies, methods, and techniques to manage the changes and achieve the goals *desired by recipients*.[4]

- *Coaches* assist individuals wishing to make changes in various areas of their lives, such as improving performance in sports or other activities, developing professional skills (management, management of team), carrying out transformations in life, and following a technique of personal development. The coach is responsible for managing support processes such as the development of objectives, widening of consciousness, search for "buried" knowledge, skills, and resources to mobilize them, management of the coaching relationship, cognitive aspects, and reframing. She provides tools to the coachee. The management of the relational process plays a key role in the dynamics of coaching and is a crucial factor determining the success of coaching. The coach must assess her own competences to engage into a coaching (as in a new environment or with a "difficult person").
- *Coachees* play an active role in the coaching process: they are the masters of their lives, develop their goals and objectives, and make their own decisions. They must have sufficient psychological resources to participate actively in the process and to accept the discomfort stemming from queries regarding the conduct of their lives, professional activities, behavior, and, sometimes, personal values and identity to achieve their goals.

Coaching is a fundamentally nondirective approach: coachees are led to rediscover their reality, which is reconsidered and reinterpreted to modify it. Additionally, the coach encourages them to highlight their skills, resources, and knowledge acquired throughout their lives to identify and use them in projects wherein the change is required. Apprenticeship plays a key role in the conduct of coaching: acquiring a new skill or capacity is part of the cognitive, affective, and psychomotor domains of learning.

In the healthcare system and culture, a collaborator rarely asks for a coaching. Most of the time, it is suggested or prescribed by the hospital management (general, medical, human resources, or nursing directions) to remedy a failure of leadership or management or a personal crisis. In this situation, the external coach is not an employee of the institution as per management orders and only makes available his capacities mentioned in a defined contract. Barring the mandate with the institution, the external coach is completely independent and supports the collaborator who is prescribed coaching or who solicits it to help coachees develop and broaden their skills and performances and reach their goals. Coaches are bound by strict confidentiality, which applies to all personal aspects of their relationship with clients (coachees).

Knowledge, skills, and competences

The skills required of a coach are described by the International Coaching Federation (ICF) and summarized in 11 *core competencies* (Table 1.1).[5]

These 11 competencies constitute the fundamental foundation on which coaching activity is built. Despite their apparent simplicity, their mastery

Table 1.1 Eleven core competencies according to the International Coaching Federation

Setting the foundation
1 Meeting ethical guidelines and professional standards: understanding coaching ethics and standards and applying them appropriately in all coaching situations (this point combines two distinct competencies)
2 Establishing the coaching agreement: understanding what is required in the specific coaching interaction and coming to an agreement with a prospective and new client on the coaching process and relationship

Co-creating the relationship
3 Establishing trust and intimacy with the client: creating a safe, supportive environment that produces ongoing mutual respect and trust
4 Coaching presence: being fully conscious and creating spontaneous relationships with clients by employing an open, flexible, and confident style

Communicating effectively
5 Active listening: focusing on what the client says and does not says, understanding the meaning of what is said in the context of the client's desires, and supporting the client's self-expression
6 Powerful questioning: asking questions that reveal the information necessary for maximum benefit to the coaching relationship and the client
7 Direct communication: communicating effectively during coaching sessions and using language that has the greatest positive impact on the client

Facilitating learning and results
8 Creating awareness: integrating and accurately evaluating multiple sources of information and making interpretations that help the client gain awareness and, thereby, achieve the expected results
9 Designing actions: creating with the client opportunities for ongoing learning during coaching and in work/life situations and for taking new actions that will most effectively lead to the expected coaching results
10 Planning and goal setting: developing and maintaining an effective coaching plan with the client
11 Managing progress and accountability: focusing on the client's priorities and enabling the client to take action

requires a long learning process during practical training and personal work, which allows young coaches to position themselves in front of a client and manage this relationship with respect and humanity (chapter 12). How will a coach develop a relationship of trust with a client without first working on self-confidence; without mastering all the ethical aspects and the main reference frames in the field of human sciences; or without feeling kindness and compassion in all circumstances? The same questions arise for other competencies such as for *creating awareness*. How will coaches support clients and assist them in opening their consciousness in a process of change, if the coaches have not performed this personal work to open up their own consciousness and free themselves from a priori beliefs likely to disrupt clients' elaborations?

Based on this questioning, we propose to add another competency that we believe is indispensable for a respectful practice: *coaches should be aware of their own limits and pass the hand to another professional when the situation requires such change* (e.g., another coach, a psychologist, a doctor, or another professional). This recognition is essential to provide clients appropriate, efficient, and respectful support and protect them from what could be counter-productive or harmful to their projects, professional activities, and life conduct. Such a requirement is self-evident in medical practice (i.e., how to imagine an orthopedic surgeon proposing surgical operations that she has not mastered?) but not in coaching. If we consider coaches to be their own working tools (similar to a psychotherapist), we propose to make them aware of this aspect of their practice by offering them this new 12th core competency: identifying their limits, according to their specific knowledge and experiences, characteristics and expectations of the client, and course of the support.

Limitations of the coach

Megan is a 48-year-old woman seeking coaching to resolve what she calls her "social phobia." The coach is surprised by this request because Megan arrives relaxed, smiling, and apparently sure of herself. Megan describes her phobias as causing shame and guilt when she is confronted by significant people: "I'm terrified when I'm in front of colleagues I perceive as intrusive, I'm afraid, sometimes in panic. I indulge in avoidance and it started at school. I undertook multiple trainings, development courses as well as brief passages at the psychiatrist, but without effect. It's an endless beginning." Megan has been successful in her professional life and is a bookseller appreciated by her customers. By contrast, her family life is complicated, she reports unstable relationships with her partners, and cannot establish a prolonged relationship.

Analysis: This case is a borderline case for coaching, given the life story. Favorable elements are present: the client is autonomous, runs her bookstore without problems, and is able to make relevant requests. However, the adverse elements are heavy: a long history of suffering, sometimes exacerbated and sometimes absent for prolonged periods. The coach is surprised by the paradox of a client who reports that she is suffering but remains smiling and relaxed throughout the first coaching session. The coach proposes a trial of three to four sessions before the first evaluation and requests supervision from a psychologist, who confirms the assessment of the situation: this person wants to move forward but has been blocked for more than 30 years by psychic disorders. In the third meeting, the coach notes that Megan is obviously disturbed; she reports that her suffering is sometimes intolerable and was exacerbated for a few days. The coach evokes the possibility of interrupting the process to seek psychiatric assistance. Megan appears relieved: "It's really too hard for me, I cannot do it despite all my efforts." Three months later, she sends a word of thanks to the coach and writes that she has restarted psychotherapy and is improving.

Ethical aspects

Since ancient times, ethical reflection has accompanied all fields of human action. Ethics answer the fundamental questions of life, death, good, and suffering, which people face either individually or collectively. Originally part of philosophy and then theology, ethics expanded from the beginning of the twentieth century to be incorporated into the corpus of most professions. Concerns of professional morality (or deontology) have led to the development of rules to ensure good professional practice and compliance with the standards of the profession and rights of the client. This case applies to professional coaching, wherein the practice raises many specific ethical questions.[6] Professional associations and training institutions, for instance, the ICF; several associations of coaching in the United States; and the European Mentoring and Coaching Council proposed standards of practice and codes of professional behavior to promote an ethical practice of coaching.

The main points of deontology are focused on the following fields:

- **Respect for the *person*.** This obligation covers several elements. First, respect for the autonomy of the person who in the context of coaching defines his/her objectives and makes all the decisions that concern him/her. This point implies that the coach uses his expertise to establish a relationship of trust and create a productive, peaceful, and calm work environment to help clients discover their needs and objectives of change.

This also concerns the behavior and posture of the coach—benevolent, available, and attentive—who will always strive to promote the development and emergence of the client's autonomy.

Respect for the individual implies the delivery of complete information to the client to avoid power relations at all levels and ensure confidentiality, absence of conflict of interest, and independence of the coach. These ethical rules are sometimes difficult to apply in situations of prescribed coaching, where the coach is mandated by the hospital management and not by the client. In such context, coaches must notify the prescriber (e.g., the medical director) of the rules of confidentiality and the impossibility of having a "hidden agenda," not known to the beneficiary.

- **The protection of the *person*.** It implies avoiding any damage to clients in all the fields of their existence and to promote their well-being as much as possible. This obligation relates first to the professional issues of the beneficiary, due to which coaching is being conducted. This obligation also relates more indirectly to an individual's physical and mental health. When coaches discover overwork, burnout, serious conflicts, and alterations in clients' mental health, they should help clients find solutions; if necessary, coaches should seek help from other professionals. This was a case that we experienced several times in our hospital business. In one instance, we had to inform the medical director of the exhaustion of a department head, with the approval of the latter, a situation previously unknown to the management.

The obligation to protect clients may oppose the protection of interests of the organization with which the contract is established and the coach's duty of diligence. This case may apply when hospital management plans to sanction the beneficiary of coaching, for instance, a dismissal, a situation we have encountered. Such conflict of interest is difficult to manage and may lead the coach to break the contract.

- **Confidentiality.** It is a basic obligation of all professionals in the helping relationship. It should be always respected, except sometimes in prescribed coaching, wherein the coach receives information from multiple stakeholders who are entitled to confidentiality. In this situation, rigor is required, which is not always easy. When setting up coaching, it is necessary to define with all the parties the main boundaries that delimit the duty of confidentiality. For example, the objectives set with management represent elements shared between management, beneficiary, and coach. By contrast, the work performed on the personal objectives of an attending physician is confidential as is the private information that he/she transmits to the coach. In any case, the consent of the beneficiary of the coaching must be solicited for any information that the coach would provide to the management.

Unfortunately, coaches are not trained in true and complete confidentiality. For instance, coaches discuss sometimes their coaching clients in a restaurant—a public place. In addition, the ICF asks its candidates (who must certify a certain number of hours of practice) for a list of their coachees, including name, address, and telephone number—"in complete discretion"—as a means to validate a candidate's statements. Indeed, nothing morally prevents a sports coach from publicly praising the merits of his coachee. However, in any care provider coaching and in life coaching particularly, this lightness of secrecy is problematic, difficult to understand, and should be the subject of new prescriptions. Thus, there is an ethical attitude of discretion which, if not respected, will affect the reputation of the coach (clients will hesitate to go to him) but without legal issue, unlike healthcare professionals who meet a possible legal conviction in the form of a fine, a ban from the professional association, and the loss of licensure in case of breach of confidentiality.

- **Honesty and transparency.** These are among the essential ingredients for establishing a relationship of trust with the coachee. This is particularly important during prescribed coaching wherein the coach establishes a link with the coachee and hierarchy. This "double" potential loyalty implies complete transparency; otherwise, the relationship of trust between the coach and coachee will be undermined.

Transparency requires not only informing the beneficiary of the coaching of everything that concerns him/her but also sending the management the information that concerns him/her, such as the finalization of objectives, intermediate assessments, and institutional problems encountered during coaching. Promoting transparency implies defining a clear framework of work at the beginning of coaching, thus delimiting the zones of confidentiality and sharing.

- **Independence of coaches.** It is indispensable in all aspects of their activities, particularly in the context of business coaching. When coaching is prescribed wherein this independence is not guaranteed, the coach may be in a difficult situation. Thus, it is up to him/her to negotiate with management a framework that fulfills this condition.
- **Qualifications and experience.** These are necessary to exercise a coaching mandate (competencies and skills). In countries that have a recognized training curriculum for coaching, this requirement should not be an issue. To be recognized and credible in the medical profession, the coach should attest to basic education at the university level, in addition to specific skills and many years of experience. Notably, physicians consider

themselves professionals in the human relationships in the context of care and often place themselves in a dominant position, which complicates the role of assisting, especially at the beginning of coaching.

- **Irreproachable behavior and professionalism.** These imply loyalty and flawless integrity, in addition to the aforementioned characteristics of honesty and transparency. The more vulnerable the coachee, the more important are the respect for and rules of ethics. Indeed, the coach enjoys a privileged position based on the trust shown by coachees and institutional clients, bonds that are formed, and an intimacy created by the confidence offered. This relationship could lead the coach to exercise manipulative power in complete opposition to the attitude required of assistance. In situations where power games are possible, such as prescribed coaching or when the hidden intentions of the prescriber are unfavorable to the coachee, they offer skid opportunities to a coach who would like to use his privileged position for purposes other than supporting the client, for example, to establish authority or strengthen links with management, i.e., to gain power.

- **Conflicts of interest.** It may occur in hospital coaching. They mainly concern the possible privileged relations of the coach with the medical or human resources director or with the head of department when individual coaching precedes team coaching. All potential conflicts of interest that concern the coach must be announced to all the interested parties, and a work proposal must be refused when there is an obvious conflict of interest. Likewise, it is impossible to lead mediation if the coach knows one of the two parties. In the prescribed coaching, the coach, who has often had relations with the hospital management for other coaching requests, is in a situation with a potential conflict of interest that must be declared to the coachee before coaching begins. By contrast, the regular contact of a coach with his/her client is likely to initiate a privileged relationship associated with conflicts of interest not present at the beginning of coaching. This link inevitably leads the coach to support clients during disagreements or tension with management.

- **What to do when the ethical framework is not respected?** This brief summary of deontology highlights the many professional rules of conduct and morality that all coaches should follow. Respect and protection of the coachee are the essential pillars, given the potential vulnerability of the beneficiaries of coaching. This is particularly the case when they suffer from burnout, go through a crisis (personal or family), or are threatened in their jobs. During prescribed coaching to a coachee, who often is wary of coaching initially, absolute respect for deontology is essential to preserve the legitimate interests of the beneficiary and of the paying prescriber.

When working in a framework where guarantees of respect for the principles and rules of ethics are impossible, the coach must first be aware of it to resolve it. Supervision may be useful for reviewing the framework and analyzing the roles and behaviors of the recipient, coach, and possibly prescriber, if any. If respecting the ethics is impossible, the coach must consider giving up the mandate or interrupting it.

Usefulness of coaching

Objective demonstration of the benefits of external coaching in the business context is difficult. A recent review analyzed the available literature by focusing on the effectiveness of executive coaching (i.e., executive, business, and leadership coaching) in an institutional context.[7] Of the 732 published studies, 52 were selected on the basis of the following criteria: (1) quantitative data on the effectiveness of coaching and (2) coaching performed by professionals in a nonacademic institutional context. The results demonstrate a beneficial effect on well-being, resilience, self-efficacy, career satisfaction, goal attainment, and stress management. At the company level, a positive impact of coaching on the attitudes and behaviors of leaders as valued by their subordinates was observed and the well-being of the closest employees improved.

A study conducted by the American Academy of Family Physicians demonstrates the positive effects of the support of family physicians by change facilitators and trained external experts.[8] This study was realized as part of a vast project of practical change initiated in 2006 by this academy. Of the 337 family medicine practices that agreed to participate in a feasibility study of the new project, 36 were selected to form one representative group. This group was then randomized into two groups, both of which applied the change of practice: a group assisted by three external facilitators trained to support doctors (three months of training) from various non-care environments (finance, management, psychology of organizations); and an unassisted control group. For two years, intensive coaching was provided by the facilitators (four learning sessions, monthly conference calls, three to six support visits to the medical offices). The overall results show that both groups put at least 70% of the goals of change to practice. Physicians in assisted practices performed better on several parameters: adaptability and change capacity (adaptive reserve) and number of practice changes. The authors emphasized the positive effect of external support at the individual and group levels. Notably, facilitation did not change the patients' assessment of medical practice.

Various types of coaching

Internal coaching

All over this book, we write about *external* coaching, where an outside coach is mandated by the hospital or health institution for a specific coaching. However, we want to mention internal coaching which has progressively developed in companies in recent years and is growing in the hospital setting for supporting care providers. Coaching of *patients* by care providers is more common, especially for those suffering from chronic diseases that require therapeutic education or prolonged follow-up (e.g., diabetes mellitus, cancer, rehabilitation).

Internal coaching is normally practiced by trained employees of a company (internal resources), usually under the auspice of the human resources department. This type of coaching concerns four main activities:

- A *manager-coach* assists executives (administrative branch of health-care providers) of an institution in improving their management skills. The coach can also be a department or division head who has completed basic training in coaching, which can be applied to the said department.
- *Crisis coaching* is an aid developed in some companies to cope with the personal crises of their collaborators, particularly in cases such as family issues, mourning, alcoholism, psychotropic substance abuse, depression, and exhaustion.
- Coaching for *management of change* is general, extended support to facilitate major changes within a structure or its operation (merger, closure, opening of a new division, reorganization) or to promote innovations.
- *Employee development coaching* is similar to the field of external coaching.

To be effective, internal coaches must have completed certified training, equivalent to external coaches. In many large companies, internal coaches benefit from field experience. However, the ethical aspects of this practice are crucial. Indeed, an essential part of this process is that internal coaches can work independently of the hierarchies and management to ensure the confidentiality and neutrality of their support. A study published in 2010 evaluated the practices of 123 internal development coaches from 40 UK-based organizations.[9] They described the most common ethical dilemmas confronted in their practice: requests for confidential information, role conflicts, parallel relations, inability to use the information disclosed, personal issues affecting work performance, privileged information about the beneficiary, and beneficiaries' attempts to use coaching for their personal gain or to leave an organization. This list illustrates the importance of (1) the exchanges transmitted between the client and coach as part of coaching and (2) rigorously organizing internal coaching practices to avoid any drift. Thus, this framework is inappropriate for life coaching.

Supervision during internal coaching is essential to ensure respect for the interests of the coachee and to maintain a consistent ethical line. When conducted by an external coach in complete independence, such supervision increases effectiveness and credibility.

Mentoring at hospital

Mentoring has been practiced in human groups since ancient times. A mentoring relationship exists when a peer mentor in an expert role with skills, knowledge, and experience provides advice, guidance, and support to a colleague (mentee) to promote the mentee's professional and personal development.[10] Notably, in contemporary practice, mentoring includes working methods similar to those of coaching, such as active listening, questioning, and reframing, and represents a form of personal development. For some experts, there is little difference between mentoring and coaching.[11] Mentoring plays an increasingly important role in training physicians, nurses (care and introduction of new techniques), and researchers, and in academic medicine; it is not by definition an activity for external coaches at hospitals.

In the current academic field, mentoring can be a decisive factor in the choice of career and throughout it as well as in the acquisition of leadership and research skills.[12] This support encourages mentees to discover the determining elements of their environment, experiment with new functions, learn to progress, and develop their confidence. A review published in 2006 showed that 20%–84% of medical teachers in various North American university hospitals participated in mentoring programs to support younger colleagues and students' academic progress.[10] In this context, mentorship is now considered unanimously to exert a positive influence on personal development, choices, and career management and productivity in medical research. Some medical institutions encourage the emergence of mentor coaches trained for this purpose.

One of the advantages of such internal support is linked to the mentor's knowledge of the field, professional culture, and institutional rules. In terms of potential disadvantages, the inexperience of some mentors and risk of confidentiality breach is relevant. In our opinion, mentoring should involve basic training to particularly develop the active listening, acceptance, empathy, ethics, and congruence skills of mentors. Here, supervision by external coaches is recommended.

External coaching

The requests for *individual coaching* at the hospital mainly involve medical and nursing executives, and less commonly the members of the health care teams. The demands cover numerous fields of hospital functioning and life, for example:

- Problems of leadership
- Improving team leading and functioning
- Management problem
- Exhaustion and burnout
- Individual crisis
- Team crisis
- Conflicts within teams or between teams

The coaching work is in principle structured. The initial phases of coaching that precede the effective start of the coaching work with the beneficiary are described in detail in chapter 5. From the beginning of the process, the client develops *goals and objectives* of change that constitute an essential part of the process. Each session is then guided by "day objectives," which will frame the work of that session. Developing goals to change is often a difficult task. The coach first helps the client to perceive her needs and desires. Next, it is the client's task to list real goals of change that should be identifiable and recognizable. In addition, the efficient goals of change should respect the ecology of the system, namely, the benefits of change should outweigh the disadvantages. Toward the end of the process, the coach verifies the achievement of each goal: "How do you know that you have achieved your goal(s)?"

Life coaching, also called "existential coaching," is in principle not part of the services that the coach provides in the context of the hospital. As its name indicates, it does not directly cover the problems of a person at work, but rather her personal, private, or existential problems, as well as her personal development. Concretely, although executive coaching focuses on the performance of the leader (or any health care provider) in her various fields of action, life coaching aims to initiate lasting changes and will probably be part of all areas of existence; it can contribute to improving the functioning of the person and her well-being.[13] In North America, the medical profession commonly hires a coach to solve personal problems and finding solutions. A substantial "market" has thus developed for this activity, mainly occupied by psychiatrists or psychologists and more rarely by coaches from other horizons.[13] The case is different in European countries, where life coaching remains largely ignored by the doctors.

However, any real coaching, even when focused on the work setting, is associated with minimal changes in the person, caused by the work and interaction with the coach (and possibly with the group). It therefore contains, in essence, profound modifying factors that could be assimilated to existential coaching. In addition, personal problems are commonly discussed in the coaching of an executive, even when prescribed by hospital management. Although not the subject of coaching, these problems cannot be ignored because they are a current concern of the client and will probably influence the course of coaching. If personal problems enter the field of coaching and take the forefront, it is necessary to explain to the client that they are outside the scope of the prescribed coaching and must be the subject of private sessions.

My wife threatens to leave home

Oliver is a super-busy department manager: "I do a lot of things: I run all the time, but I like this dynamic and rich life." He accepts the medical director's proposal to initiate a coaching to improve the department organization and set priorities in management and team management. After a difficult start because of his low availability, he gets to work and actively prepares his coaching goals. Addressing the management of priorities, the coach questions Oliver about his work–private life balance: He responds straight away that it is not ideal, particularly his family life.

Oliver: One of my sons has problems at school, but I do not have time to take care of it.

Coach: What do you want to do to change this situation?

Oliver: Certainly, I have to do something. Additionally, my wife Christiane complains too; I sometimes have tense relations with her. She tells me that she feels abandoned and does not understand my excessive commitment to the department, which she endures with difficulty. In summary, family life is rather difficult.

Coach: And what about you, what do you feel?

Oliver: It's difficult for me but drives me to work harder, rather than face her recriminations.

Coach: I'm coming back to your concern, are you ready to make changes in the organization of your work? How do you imagine the changes in the organization of your work?

Oliver: Actually, I do not have much choice because Christiane threatens to leave home.

Oliver decides to add to the list of his objectives work–family balance. During the following sessions, he returns several times to his marital difficulties and actively asks the coach to help him find solutions to these issues and the sometimes painful loneliness he feels. After discussions with the coach, Oliver wants to focus the work on this work–life balance, starting with the list of his tasks and their priority; he also understands that the coaching proposed by the medical director is an inappropriate place to solve his family problems.

Six months later, the prescribed coaching is over. Oliver then requests a life coaching for himself. He feels the need to be supported to continue the development work initiated by coaching and resolve his family problems.

This situation illustrates the need to practice coaching in a manner open to all fields of life, even in a professional setting. How can the problems of this doctor at the hospital be resolved without addressing the familial aspects of his existence? In this situation, it is essential to leave the purely professional framework to explore the interactions between family and professional problems. These can be hidden at the beginning of coaching and may appear only afterward, after the relationship is established and the process is outlined.

Life coaching and psychotherapy

What are the differences?

The main goal of psychotherapists is to assess and assist people in their psychological, physical, and social pain and sufferance to improve their well-being through the power of interpersonal relationship, dialogue, and sometimes bodywork.

Then, what is the difference between life coaching and psychotherapy? When and why should one be chosen over the other? To these often-asked questions, there are no simple answers.

Tom Henschel, an executive coach, published an excellent metaphor in Forbes[14] that perfectly illustrates the difference between both methods. It is briefly summarized here: we were all marked in our childhood by events that sometimes hurt us deeply. Some of us have managed to develop strong, callous scars that do not interfere with our lives. On the other hand, in others, these wounds remain sensitive, even almost open; they give rise to self-protective behaviors, necessary at first, but which, in the long run, often turn into repetitive, limiting, self-sabotaging attitudes. Metaphorically, these vulnerable people have potholes in their private path. To make the road usable, the client asks his coach to accompany him to approach the pothole, without falling over it, and to see how to avoid it. In a relatively short time, they together find the tools that allow the coachee to circulate again more safely.

Psychotherapists however suggest to their patients to go with them to the edge of the hole and to look inside. They then help their patients to descend. While psychotherapists remain at the top, they illuminate the bottom to help the patient fill this gap from the bottom, in successive layers. To go to the edge is very worrisome, to descend into it is even more so, and to rebuild is difficult, especially at the beginning. But ultimately, the road is repaired, and the hole is no longer visible. In conclusion, both methods make it easier to circulate on the way. The first is faster than the second. However, after coaching, the hole still exists, and depending on events, it may eventually reappear. After a completed psychotherapy, however, the quagmire remains closed.

History

The two approaches have different origins and developments, which have influenced their practice.

Psychotherapy has existed since the end of the nineteenth century and was created in opposition to psychiatry, which "locked up the sick." In the beginning, psychotherapy was mainly practiced by doctors and members of religious circles (the "cure of soul" or counseling). The role of this vocation has always been to care for people who present psychic or psychosomatic disorders and have difficulties living in families and society. Notably, it is not true that coaching is intended for the "healthy" and psychotherapy is destined for the "mentally ill," but, as Henschel said in his metaphor, each of us has quagmires which deserve to be taken into consideration to become free.

Over time, both coaching and psychotherapy have become much more diverse, and their similarities have increased. Under the current professional pressure, mobility, and the enormous speed of change in our society, the two fields often overlap. Life coaching is becoming closer to, for example, cognitive behavioral psychotherapy, which is more focused on learning processes than other forms of psychotherapy are. Certain training courses also relate to care, such as health coaching or nursing coaching.

Notably, coaches work with "clients" (in Latin, *cliens* means servant) and psychotherapists treat "patients," which indicates the latter's closer links to the disease (in Latin, *pati* means to suffer). Their approaches differ and examining them is interesting.

Differences between coaching and psychotherapy training

In the United States, as in many countries, the prerequisites for beginning a psychotherapy training are an M.A. for social workers, a Ph.D. for psychologists, and an M.D. for doctors. Most therapists must complete personal therapy to be recognized by the *professional association* corresponding to their school of psychotherapy. In the United Kingdom, candidates must prove a minimum of 100 hours of supervision; at least one year of full-time postgraduate clinical experience (or the equivalent in part-time experience) for doctoral-level applicants, and at least two years for others; and a minimum of 100 hours of personal psychotherapy.

Everywhere, psychotherapists must demonstrate continuing education, which is certified each year, including supervisions, courses, readings, personal training, and others. These requirements far exceed those for coaches.

We observe an important difference between the countries where coaching is (UK) taught at universities as a major field of study and those where coaching is a non-university training. The gold standard is delineated by the International Coaching Federation (ICF), the leading coaches' organization. ICF offers three *credentials:* Associate, Professional*, and* Master Certified Coach. The average number of training hours remains low and mainly relies on practice; there are no prerequisites to undertake training other than high school graduation. Continuing education—after certification—for coaches is only mandatory if they are part of the ICF and amounts to 40 hours every three years; it does not require supervision or work on oneself. Coaches are encouraged to obtain higher and diversified trainings.

Differences and similarities between life coaching and psychotherapy

In life coaching, the *contract* is more formal than in psychotherapy. In both practices, the place, time, and price of the sessions are established. Some psychotherapists (of the cognitive behavioral orientation) will, like the coaches, offer to work during a predefined number of meetings and complete tasks between sessions, but the resemblance is most often limited to this. A coach and his coachee define goals and establish a work plan; in principle, the contract is written and signed; demonstration of results is often requested; sometimes payment is made in advance.

In therapy, the contract is vaguer. It is, undoubtedly, legally and ethically regulated, but a patient is often unable to define a goal or take action. In the beginning, the patient and therapist decide which problems should be treated. However, to use the metaphor described in the beginning, in repairing the quagmire, they often observe that under a weak layer, there remains one or more others that deserve fixing. In other words, the course of the treatment can take detours, as the patient and therapist discover difficulties to be addressed that were not considered in the beginning.

For each of the two roles, the *positioning of control* is different. In coaching, in principle, the coachee knows from the start, or quickly, that she is in control, and that the coach is accompanying her to offer or allow her to find and test new tools to achieve her goal. By contrast, patients in therapy must often learn to take their place at the helm of their life. Sometimes, the real therapeutic work is just that.

Practitioners of both methods posit that an answer to a self-made question from the inside is much more powerful and transformative than if it is imposed from the outside (from the coach or the psychotherapist). This control belongs to the patient or the coachee. In the everyday reality of work, however, things do not always occur so clearly, in either method.

In coaching, the coachee is expected to define her *objective(s) and goal(s)* from the start. "Know where you are and where you want to go" is the coach's mantra. In psychotherapy, the persons are often unable at the beginning to clearly see where they are or where they want to go. They are too caught up in conflicts, difficult events, and a deficient, oppressive, sometimes violent entourage to determine themselves. They are in a fog. They must first be supported and helped to distinguish their position and their environment.

Roughly, we assert that coaching focuses on action and the future, whereas therapy focuses on self-observation in relation to others in the past and present (and future). However, both approaches aim to improve the life of the accompanied. In coaching, we design "action plans," we want to move forward, we want to make projects that stimulate us and that carry us forward, we have tasks to accomplish between sessions and these bring us closer to our goal. In therapy, we attempt to observe the base of the quagmire, such as trauma or abuse, to repair it. In coaching, these pains should be heard with compassion when the client discusses them, but the coach should not dwell on them. This is easy to say, but not easy to do.

Client feedback at the end of each session is customary for coaching and allows the coach and coachee to readjust their interaction and direction. In addition, the contract ends with a balance sheet. In psychotherapy, however, where the relationship is at the forefront, scheduled feedback at each meeting could suggest that the client should provide nice, polite responses to "satisfy" his therapist, preventing authenticity and the beneficial emergence of conflicts. Moreover, this request for frequent feedback can be interpreted as the therapist's desire to reassure herself. The patient's satisfaction or dissatisfaction is more complex, and the therapist will perceive it during the joint work. What is necessary is to wait for the end of treatment to assess the distance traveled, with its strengths and its faults, in other words, we assess if the quagmire is completely invisible.

As the relationship is one of the foci of attention, as well as a discovery tool in psychotherapy, the psychotherapeutic *framework* and *limits* are better defined than in coaching. In the first situation, the interlocutors do not socialize outside the sessions, and distance is necessary to maintain their concentration on the course of the therapeutic process. By contrast, in coaching, the limits are less clear. Contacts are more informal and usually less emotionally charged. Coaches sometimes work with people close to them or develop friendships that they cultivate after the end of coaching.

The *duration* of coaching typically varies between five and twelve sessions. However, the duration of life coaching can, similar to psychotherapy, be much longer because emotional problems are not always resolved by a series of action plans. This fact raises the question of the dependence that the coachee develops on the coach, a dependence that the latter is generally not equipped to manage. Only supervision can probably allow a healthy separation at the end of the coaching.

In coaching, the *length of sessions* varies according to the habits of the coach and the needs of the coachee. In psychotherapy, we find again more formalism: the duration of sessions is between 50 minutes and 1 hour according to the therapists, and the time is the same throughout treatment.

A profound difference between both professions is demonstrated in *confidentiality* as already mentioned before. For the psychotherapist, there is a legal obligation, which is linked to a possible legal conviction. For coaches, confidentiality is often considered as a matter of reputation.

The attitudes of clients/patients in mentioning their accompaniment are also dissimilar. In general, coachees are open about working with a coach, whereas patients are very discreet in this regard, except in certain circles, for fear of being stigmatized.

Alarm signals

Hart et al.[15] published an investigation of 30 practitioners from the United States who were in or have been in both professions. They identify several differences between coaching and psychotherapy, including *alarm signals*. The coaches–psychotherapists interviewed[2] noted that the coaches do not receive the necessary training to notice the red flags in the behaviors, speeches, and nonverbal communication of their clients, denoting emotional states, mental disorders, and psychiatric disturbances that require sending the client to consult a psychotherapist. These signals are, for sure, difficult to detect. Indeed, clients often ignore what prevents them from carrying out the action plans defined in sessions, why their emotions take up all the space, why they forget sessions, why they do not come out of their chaos, and how to get rid of their physical symptoms. The coach can then be caught in empathy or antipathy full of his own "potholes" or unresolved problems that intertwine. All of these factors remain misunderstood and risk doing more harm than good. The clinician, by contrast, taking advantage of his knowledge and pursuing his introspection, uses these subtle messages as material to advance in a process leading to well-being.

We do not list the "red flags" but do present as an example the trap of flattery (or seduction), in which it is so easy to fall. For example, when a client tells you that he has already worked with other coaches or psychotherapists, but that *only you* can help him, it is extremely tempting to believe the coachee, and it is a terrible challenge. However, there is a good chance that you are only the Xth and not the last person consulted. The only way to possibly stop this person's repetitive behavior is to confront him/her directly, but gently, with this way of acting, at the time of the contract.

Handle with care

Henry requests supervision for his coaching with Aurelia. She said that she was in treatment with a psychiatrist*; she has been hospitalized two or three times** and should take medication* (the coach does not know which medications); she says she feels much better without these "unhealthy drugs" and that coaching would be the only solution to her problems. Henry believes her because he is opposed to drugs in general. Aurelia does not want Henry to contact his psychiatrist, whom she does not want to see too much anymore, at the moment, because "he wishes her evil," like many other people**.

Henry is correct to refer the situation to his supervisor; the latter notices that Henry takes Aurelia's side, which is quite natural; however, Henry does not realize that he is involved in a paranoid relationship with a psychiatric patient. Henry should not support the client's desire to stop the drugs without collaborating closely with the doctor nor encourage the distance taken by Aurelia from the psychiatrist because she may risk a relapse and a new hospitalization. Henry is torn between his legitimate desire to see Aurelia as a woman who really wants to get out of it; that she chose him and prefers him to the psychiatrist; and an acknowledgment of the psychic reality of the coachee, which he does not have the skills to understand and measure.

In this case, Henry can continue "light," concrete, organizational, and tactful coaching but without exploring Aurelia's emotions and personal problems or her reports of other people.

Regular supervision is indispensable.

*: red flag; **: big red flag

In such a case, an experienced psychotherapist would quickly notice that the anamnestic data raise a signal of caution (to be confirmed in subsequent sessions). One red flag means that there is something to watch; the more flags there are, the closer we are to severe psychic issues. A coach, however, has no or little knowledge of psychopathology and often cannot realize the seriousness of mental illness and the suffering the person endures. Henry could not detect these red flags. Only regular supervision could help him continue his coaching and avoid a breakdown of the client.

As coaches do not have the necessary training to undertake psychotherapy, psychotherapists also do not have the skills to offer coaching without having completed a certified course. Without these qualifications, they do not have the tools necessary for the practice or, above all, the "posture" of the coaches. Moreover, switching between these roles is difficult without real learning and introspection. The psychotherapists who do this best are probably those whose psychotherapy methods most closely resemble coaching.

Conclusion

Coaching is a profession classified as a helping relationship based on structured interactions between the coach and the beneficiary. Coaching differs from other methods of support because of its purpose, management of relationships, respective roles of coaches and clients, and the structured conduct of the work. To this end, coaches use their own action strategies, methods, techniques, and tools to promote the changes and goals desired by the recipient. Several modes of intervention are possible: while some are led by an external coach mandated for specific individual or team coaching, others are led by hospital executives and heads of departments in internal coaching and mentoring. Life or "existential" coaching is often chosen by medical professionals outside the institution in periods of transition or in all kinds of difficult situations. As one of the most commonly used means of improving individual or team performance and managing change in companies, coaching shows its large potential for healthcare providers.

We also describe the growing similarities and important differences between life coaching and psychotherapy. This comparison stresses the main points to consider in both approaches and gives a glimpse into the unfolding of these processes.

There are many ethical issues in the practice of coaching, concerning the protection of clients, particularly their defense and interests. Thus, the requirements such as specific competencies and skills, their training, and the identification of and respect for the coach's limitations and professionalism are underlined.

Bibliography

1 Rogers CR. The characteristics of a helping relationship. *Pers Guid J* 1958; 37(1): 6–16.
2 Jordan M, Livingstone JB. Coaching vs psychotherapy in health and wellness: overlap, dissimilarities, and the potential for collaboration. *Glob Adv Health Med* 2013; 2(4): 20–27.
3 Jordan M, Wolever RQ, Lawson K, Moore M. National training and education standards for health and wellness coaching: the path to national certification. *Glob Adv Health Med* 2015; 4(3): 46–56. Published online on May 1, 2015. www.ncbi.nlm.nih.gov/pmc/articles/PMC4424935/
4 Bachkirova T, Cox E, Clutterbuck D. Introduction. *In*: Cox E, Bachkirova T, Clutterbuck D. *The Complete Handbook of Coaching*. SAGE Publications, Los Angeles, London, New Delhi; 2010, pp. 1–20.
5 https://coachfederation.org/app/uploads/2017/12/CoreCompetencies.pdf
6 Brennan D. Ethics in coaching. *In*: Cox E, Bachkirova T, Clutterbuck D. *The Complete Handbook of Coaching*. SAGE Publications, Los Angeles, CA, London; 2010, pp. 369–380.
7 Grover S, Furnham A. Coaching as a developmental intervention in organisations: a systematic review of its effectiveness and the mechanisms underlying it. *PLoS One* 2016; 11(7): e0159137.
8 Nutting PA, Crabtree BF, Stewart EE, *et al.* Effect of facilitation on practice outcomes in the National Demonstration Project model of the patient-centered medical home. *Ann Fam Med* 2010; 8(Suppl 1): S33–S44.
9 Maxwell A. Supervising the internal coach. *In*: Bachkirova T, Jackson P, Clutterbuck D. *Coaching and Mentoring Supervision. Theory and practice*. Open University Press, Milton, Keynes, UK; 2011, pp. 183–195.
10 Sambunjak D, Straus SE, Marušić A. Mentoring in academic medicine: a systematic review. *JAMA* 2006; 296(9): 1103.
11 Garvey B, Cavanagh M. Mentoring in a coaching world. *In*: Cox E, Bachkirova T, Clutterbuck D. *The Complete Handbook of Coaching*. SAGE Publications, Los Angeles, London, New Delhi; 2010, pp. 341–354.
12 Sambunjak D. Understanding wider environmental influences on mentoring: towards an ecological model of mentoring in academic medicine. *Acta Medica Acad* 2015; 44(1): 47–57.

13 Grant A, Cavanagh M. Life coaching. *In*: Cox E, Bachkirova T, Clutterbuck D. *The Complete Handbook of Coaching*. SAGE Publications, Los Angeles, London, New Delhi; 2010, pp. 297–310.

14 Henschel T. www.forbes.com/sites/forbescoachescouncil/2017/02/07/the-difference-between-coaching-and-therapy/#51aaf5683417; February 7, 2017.

15 Hart V, Blattner J, Leipsic S. Coaching versus therapy: a perspective. *Consult Psychol J Pract Res* 2001; 53(4): 229–237.

2 The coaching relationship

Véronique Haynal

Introduction

Who has not experienced, at least once, the mesmerizing effect of dancing in perfect harmony with a partner when you do not notice who is leading and who is following? And suffered the opposite: trying to count the steps, guessing where the clumsy partner will put his/her foot so as not to be crushed, colliding, and turning in the wrong direction at the wrong time?

This chapter attempts to answer the questions that every coach probably asks: what is required for such attunement to occur? What makes it possible to understand one another, to twirl around together in a creative manner, swept by the music with the coachee?

The Oxford dictionary defines a relationship as "the way in which two or more people or things are connected, or the state of being connected." This definition is basic. To qualify a relationship as "good," *essential ingredients* are necessary to create the chemistry that develops between two or more people. We present the fundamental "good relationship" here, which can be experienced in any context, for instance, with family, friends, and colleagues; between coaches and coachees; or between care providers and care receivers. Individuals recognize being in a good relationship when feeling *truly understood, listened to,* or *respected in their identity*, and this is in reciprocity and without exertion of power by one over the other.

The terms of this good relationship and its manners of expression, however, change according to the context. Indeed, a good coaching relationship is not the same as a good relationship between friends; good relationships between care providers and patients are expressed differently and vary according to the disorder or disease, the setting in which it is treated, and the state of the patient *and* that of the health-care professional. All relationships, good or bad, regulate a system involving two or more people: one affects the other, and vice versa, in a circular manner. Everyone is affected by their partner in an interaction and has a unique response, which influences the interlocutor and so forth. As we all are very finely programmed and built to interact (skills without which we would not survive), we regulate our behavior toward that of our neighbor in its deepest subtleties. This allows us to communicate and empathize.[1]

DOI: 10.4324/9781003291831-4

A good relationship between the coach and client (or clients) is similar to a dance, it carries partners in stimulating creativity toward the goals chosen by the coachee(s). It can add an invaluable, lasting, and unforgettable quality to the process. *A good relationship is, indeed, along with the person of coaches, their most powerful tool.*

Specific aspects of coaching relationship

This relationship plays a fundamental role in all coaching processes and is the determining factor of its result.[2] To highlight the importance of coaching relationship, a North American study examined the impact of coaching on 100 leaders of various companies: 84% of them believed that the quality of the relationship they developed with the coach was a key factor in the success of their coaching.[3]

The coaching relationship has many similarities (the "common factors") with other forms of assistive relationships such as psychotherapy, mentoring, and counseling.[2] It includes all the exchanges between the coach and client (the coachee) because coaching is *established* on this connection. It is difficult to develop a *good* relationship without being deeply interested in the interlocutor and having great *respect* for the person that he/she is, namely, his/her identity. *Who they are*, ontologically, overrides *what they are* (e.g., socially, professionally, religiously, politically). The power of one individual over another has no place here; yet, in the coaches' interventions in the medical environment, they are confronted with power dynamics every day. These institutions are indeed based on a strong, deeply ingrained hierarchy. The external coach must, therefore, keep one foot in and one foot out and find his place without getting caught in the power play of domination.

The work of coaches starts with themselves. Before each coaching session, they take time to prepare themselves mentally and physically so that they remain calm, centered, open, and receptive in their sessions. In the first and following encounters, coaches primarily use their posture and nonverbal communication to maintain an equal position wherein they listen and do not impose themselves, leaving the dominant or equal position to coachees, according to their preferences and regardless of their hierarchical rank.

A summary of the characteristics necessary for a coach to develop a good coaching relationship with coachee(s) is as follows:

- Coaches truly listen without interrupting until their interlocutor stops speaking. They accept that coachees express *their* truth.

  ○ Coaches avoid judgment, ask open-ended questions[a] to allow clients to progress, and receive what clients present as aspects to understand them better. They use their creative resources and tools to help coachees define their objectives and continue their journey toward realizing those objectives.

- Coaches are clear, authentic, and transparent about their collaboration to prevent interference in the relationship.
- Coaches rely on their sensitivity to be neither intrusive (e.g., by asking questions that are too personal or useless for the set purpose or by proposing an extremely rigid agenda) nor distant (e.g., by hiding their empathy or spatially arranging chairs too far from each other).
- Finally, coaches take time to finish coaching by preparing a report for coachees and encouraging them to also examine the strengths and weaknesses of the work performed together, revealing the successes and, perhaps, developmental areas. Coaches avoid concluding with an unhappy coachee and are highly careful not to stop an open process that would leave clients dependent on their relationship.

Therefore, the coaches' *presence, inner strength*, and *self-confidence* allow them to find the appropriate distance and posture to be first accepted, then listened to, and, finally, heard in a shared work, wherein coachees set their path and follow it with the support of the coach. We expect the coach to be perfectly comfortable with these relational variables and their processes.

Comparing coaching and care relationships

In this section, we put into perspective coaching and caring relationships to better understand the similarities, differences, and possible interactions between these modes of relationship and exchange. In terms of similarity, both are part of the field of assisting others; they are outside the domain of sales or industry but in the domain of human services. However, when a coach and doctor work together, they convey two different approaches toward humans, the object of their activity. However, they must come to an agreement, which is not always easy. At this point, it is the coach's responsibility to use his relational skills for finding a way to interest, touch, and establish the relationship. In both areas, coach and care providers use tools, but—and this difference is important—those of the coach are limited, whereas in modern medicine, the means are many and part of every examination and treatment (e.g., technological, drug, nutrition). A good relationship is *the principal tool of the coach*. By contrast, in medicine, the more technology-based the specialty, the more is the relationship secondary to other means for the entire medical staff. Health-care professionals treat sick people, sometimes diligently once hospitalized, and their primary mission is to treat the disease (unfortunately not the *person*) to restore them to good health. By contrast, individuals or teams start coaching to improve their operation or accomplish concrete plans for change or development. Even if these healthcare providers suffer, they are not considered by the coach as "sick" but "coachees" who work to achieve their goals. Their "illnesses"—even burnout—are not considered by the management, and their suffering cannot be considered as such in the context of coaching in an institution of care. These people are encouraged to seek help from a professional in another setting, preferably external to the facility wherein they are working.

Typically, a failing leadership originates from bad relationships with the team. Or, put differently, a boss without respect and compassion for his colleagues will not be accepted and followed. Tensions will prevent the entire team from being effective. The same is true when two senior physicians or groups oppose each other chronically. The coach's job is then to bring to light the relational elements that are lacking, allowing teams or senior physicians or administrative executives to observe and address them to remedy the issues.

Coaches who pass through the door of health-care settings are confronted with various "cultures", depending on whether they are working with doctors, nurses, or other staff members and in which department they are involved, e.g., surgery, pediatrics, or psychiatry. The *types of professional and interprofessional relationships* the coach encounters reflect the types of tasks, duration of the treatment performed, level of technicality, condition of the patient undergoing treatment, and other characteristics of the team culture. For instance, a surgeon stated that if there is a problem in the operating room, "it's like being on a boat in a storm; the orders must be clear, precise, and obeyed to perfection according to the hierarchy." The surgeon is in charge, and patients are not in a position to be consulted, give their opinion, or participate in any of these mainly technical decisions. In some institutions, the surgeon only so much as shakes the patient's hand when the patient is already nearly asleep and does not always bother to greet him/her after the operation, instead sending someone else to do it. It is the technical gesture and not the relationship that interests the surgeon. This situation differs from that observed in chronic or long-term patients, or as is found in nephrology, diabetology, oncology, pediatrics, etc., for which the health-care team as a whole plays a considerable relational role. Treatment choices are discussed, explained, weighed, and considered with patients to make the best decisions with their consent.

The attitude of patients varies: some accept the proposals from the outset, and others seek second opinions or search the Internet for all available possibilities. In any case, *if patients oppose the prescribed treatment, they will not follow it.* Patients expect to be heard and that the care providers will make an effort to offer them the best possible treatment. The patient's *compliance* depends directly on his good relationship with his care team, as evidenced by the literature and clinical experience. A good doctor has a good bedside manner. There are excellent medical "technicians" (e.g., surgeons), but many of their patients suffer from not being treated as whole individuals, with their questions, emotions, fears, and hopes. Because a good relationship is two-way (or more), if one of the individuals does not feel it, the other will also not experience it. Additionally, similar to a clear mirror, when the relational skills are absent, the well-being and job satisfaction of medical care providers can decrease, *altering the quality of care.* However, remember that the purpose of any health-care institution, regardless of its size, is to ensure the treatment and care of patients to improve their health (except in cases of academic research, where the clinical purpose is sometimes far removed from the study's purpose). All efforts, at all levels, should ultimately aim for the well-being of patients, which, in a reciprocal manner, will also ensure the well-being of care providers.

Unfortunately, in some medical care settings, emotional, communicational, or organizational conditions are such that some care providers protect themselves from relationships. However, nurses, who are physically closer to patients than physicians, generally have better and deeper relationships with patients than physicians.

In psychiatry, the situation is different: care providers listen to, feel compassion for, and identify with the patient; their first objective is to make a connection with the patient. Furthermore, care providers and patients work *together* to improve their lives. Often, the therapists' search for connection includes family and close friends. The relationship style is highly similar to that of a coach. The coach can, therefore, feel at home in psychiatry and like a stranger in other parts of the hospital.

Wherever coaches go to work, they are responsible for adapting and speaking the language that allows them to create a relationship with clients. Coaches enter the setting with their values and relational skills as their compass. Moving forward to the coaching process, the coachee discovers and learns new ways of listening and collaborating by experiencing them. Coaches should use their nonjudgmental self, with glance, voice, posture, calm presence, dynamic energy, and relevant questions that make coachees think by surprising them. Thus, the coach stimulates the interest, curiosity, and motivation of the coachee to collaborate even when it has been requested by management. An alliance is gradually forged. Common ground is established wherein coachees feel that they have the right to refuse; that the coach will not impose anything on them; and that they may expect clear, transparent communication. A contract is established, written or otherwise, involving the commitment of both parties to the work and a reciprocal expectation. When coaching begins, the coachee, or the coached team, develops a plan of change and learning to reach a goal or objectives that require the assistance of the coach. Coachees hope to regain their well-being and sometimes suffer from dysfunctions—not physical—that they wish to be rid of through an active approach to coaching. The attitude of coaches, however, does not imitate that of a medical care provider in that they charge ahead in the direction of the objectives *defined by the coachee(s)*. Coaches do not put themselves in the position of someone who knows or prescribes but as someone who manages the process of providing assistance. In the process, coachees discover not only what they planned to learn but also how to listen, respect the other, and finally, feel compassion through the coach's behavior and *the experience of a good relationship*. This evolution is highly important in a health-care institution wherein everyone is expected to be considered.

Care providers, however, are often the most poorly cared for. How, indeed, can a nurse in a dysfunctional team show compassion for a patient when she does not feel respected and, perhaps, suffers from exhaustion? How can residents learn to make a diagnosis, i.e., listen to their patients, if their questions go unheard? How can an emergency surgical procedure be performed quickly and smoothly if the surgical team's rivalry with its counterparts in, for instance, radiology, laboratory, and logistical arrangements (Who decides? Who gives orders? Who takes precedence?) impedes its progress? How can a director expect good economic and medical results in his/her establishment if he/she promotes fear and violent behavior among the staff?

An excellent surgeon, without any consideration for his colleagues

Andy, an excellent surgeon, is the head of a division in a private hospital. Extremely upset by the behavior of one of his physicians and his team, he raises his voice to tell the coach that he will shut down this unit.

Coach: What is your vision of team management?
Andy: There is no team management possible with people so stupid.
Coach: I understand your frustration. What do you think are the obstacles to this closure?
Andy: … (he hesitates) … There are people of great value in there …
Coach: So, how could you respect them?
Andy: Maybe a team redesign or place them elsewhere; I have to think about it.

Up until this moment, the head of the division does not realize that he treats his colleagues as pawns on a chessboard, and it took time and some identification with the attitude of the coach for him to begin to perceive it. Later, he returned to his idea of possible closure and said, "I will meet with and listen to them."

In this dialogue, a gradual *identification* with the coach (listening) can raise the relational level of the coachee considerably. What this leader experienced was unconscious affective transmissions, always at work in human relationships, between two people or among a group. In situations of conflict, the transmissions increase manifold and manifest in different ways, for instance, somatic (various ailments, illnesses, accidents); emotional (anxiety, burnout, depression); or even in impulsive actions and reckless, sometimes dangerous, decisions. The most common consequences are job transfers, considerable absenteeism causing team instability, and increased costs for the institution.

What health-care professionals experience during coaching can be transmitted to their patients. Indeed, coachees integrate—if all goes well—the transparent, engaged, respectful, compassionate, tolerant, and active attitude of a coach who listens to their concerns, which leads them *in fine* to transmit this posture to others. If the objective of coachees is reached, their balance and mental and physical health as well as that of all those around them improves.

The coach, faced with broken relationships on several levels, must first *identify and understand them* to *then assist in resolving them*. His/her work, therefore, has indirect consequences at different levels of the *system*, from the individual, teams, divisions, and departments to, sometimes, the entire institution.

What, then, constitutes the chemistry of a good relationship? We describe four fundamental factors of the relationship: *trust, communication, empathy*, and *compassion* that enable true *listening*, the one that Carl Rogers[4] termed "active listening" or "benevolent listening." These factors are indispensable to the coach in his/her work. They are also needed by health-care workers in their teams and between teams.

The coach is perfectly aware of these four fundamental relationship ingredients and how to tackle them in coaching. He/she has to detect their presence and absence and work with coachees to enlarge their knowledge and vision as well as assist them in their trials and errors in learning. At a higher level, if the coach collaborates with the direction to implement a new organization, he/she should consider what follows.

Trust

Trust is as essential in relationships, between individuals or within teams, as oxygen is to the human body. It allows individuals to work efficiently, easily, and swiftly and to adapt quickly to new situations. Trust sets the foundation for productive relationships and a motivating, stimulating work environment, which is particularly important in the heavy, emotional, and stressful setting of illness, suffering, and death. Research conducted in companies is unanimous: without this element, the company is dysfunctional (at every level) and the outcomes are dire.

Development of trust usually takes time but can also be lost in an instant. Thus, the critical work of reestablishing trust is necessary.

How trust is built

We are born trusting, and this is a requirement for survival, given our state of immaturity and total dependence at birth as well as our very slow maturation. Moreover, we are social beings, constantly interacting with others, which presupposes trust. If our development does not proceed in an optimal manner, this fundamental assurance—in us and/or the other—is damaged and atrophies. How do we come to place our trust in others? Researchers from different disciplines suggest that we first and foremost trust individuals who resemble us the most,[5] i.e., the trust is based on, for instance, certain physical features of the face and body, age, sex, ethnicity, and clothing. Research also shows that we have more affinity for individuals who are friendly (sociable, smiling, making eye contact), part of our network, and demonstrate their reliability (e.g., they assure us of their good faith). This feature can also be a negative attribute because it becomes relatively easy for an abuser to take advantage of naive prey. Some people are too trusting and do not sufficiently verify the reliability of others; they are optimistic and underestimate the risks of making a commitment, but their character continues to be very open to relationships. By contrast, some persons are particularly suspicious, predict all types of dangerous scenarios, distill their trust gradually, and, thus, stay away from other people.

It proves useful for coaches to understand whether they tend to be suspicious or confident and to consider how they act as professionals when interacting with coachees. Understanding these aspects helps them recognize their preferences and adjust their attitude, if necessary. During interviews and in the course of coaching, they may have to address this subject.

How do you know when to trust "without risk"

We are always at risk of being disappointed, but without putting our trust in others, we will never know if they are reliable.

- As a leader, does your new subordinate have the necessary *skills* to earn your trust? If not, what can you do to ensure that he/she acquires them? What can you ask him/her to do considering his/her level of skills? Moreover, how can you make sure that he/she has received all the *information* necessary to carry out tasks and that he/she has the necessary *equipment* and *facilities* to carry out his/her work? Only then can he/she be *really* trusted. At this point, your colleague will still need you to check on his/her work sometimes but will feel more empowered if you wait until he/she has completed it. Additionally, observing *small signs* (e.g., arriving on time for an appointment and reporting not only positive endeavors but also difficulties) will provide good information on an individual's reliability, which will allow trust to be granted based on reactions and responses in stages. The effect of this type of progression is beneficial, and trust generally becomes reciprocal.
- As a subordinate, trust in a new leader usually starts with reputation, i.e., from what you have heard from third parties. When interacting with leaders, it is their personal behavior that encourages or discourages your trust: the way they listen, remember what they and you said, react to and

answer your questions and requests, respect you, ask you questions, and communicate clearly and quickly to provide the information needed. If leaders embody the values they advocate and fulfill their expectations of themselves and if their behavior motivates and encourages you, you find it easy to trust them.

It is useful to:

- Put on the table honestly the *consequences* of a possible breach of trust. This transparency allows for the other (or others) to be more engaged because they know all the facts.
- Establish a process of restoring trust if it has been broken to promote openness and redress for harm or injury. To accomplish this objective, trustworthy communication and transparency in words and actions is necessary.[6] Begin with the simplest strategies such as saying what you know, what you want, what you do, and so forth. Paradoxically, to restore trust, we must place our trust again, giving the ones who betrayed it the opportunity to start over and ensuring that they have the means to succeed. It is also essential to give yourself some time.
- Give clear and repeated signals that you are trustworthy (and do not think that it is obvious and that everyone can tell). Additionally, explain that the reaction to a breach of trust will be firm and consistent. In this way, those who can abuse your trust will keep their distance.
- Be empathetic and compassionate: put yourself in others' shoes and understand their viewpoints. The most trustworthy people are especially caring and compassionate. They know what behaviors and attitudes actively reassure and reduce the anxieties and worries of others.
- Check sometimes (not too often) if trust is still merited.

In a group, the complexity and fragility of trust increases exponentially with the size of the group: it is much easier to build trust between two individuals than between a coach and a team, let alone an institution. This phenomenon depends on many factors, including the motivation of coachees, such as who hired the coach (a very legitimate question, especially in a prescribed coaching); who signed the contract; who will pay the coach; how were the coachees, the team, and the institution informed of the coaching (method of communication); and who set the objective(s) (and with what respect for the participants). The fundamental questions here are as follows: How much freedom of expression do participants have? Is confidentiality guaranteed or will the superior (who is not present) be made aware of anything; if yes, of what? This question of confidentiality is particularly delicate and can completely destroy a coach's work if he/she does not regard it with seriousness (see chapter 7 and chapter 5).

In a group, the underlying feelings of coachees emerge, sometimes, in the form of overt hostility or passive or active resistance against the coach.

At other times, coaches are confronted with a division in the team between members who side with them against other mistrustful, or even opposing, colleagues. In this case, coaches could be tempted to favor their "supporters" but are most likely to contribute to reinforcing tension in the group or even encouraging a rift in the team. These emotional reactions are sometimes subtle and expressed in a roundabout manner, either verbally or through actions during or between sessions (e.g., arriving late, forgetting a session, losing the keys to the room, leaving the room a mess, organizing schedules so that a colleague cannot attend). The coach can pick up on these words and actions in a nonaggressive and non-accusatory manner to open a true discussion to resolve the underlying conflict with finesse without shutting down any possibility of dialogue. In this way, the coach earns the trust of the group.

What about the work of coaches on themselves? The surest means to update their strengths or weaknesses is to observe the level of trust in their relationships with coachees (i.e., How often is the coach's trust breached? What is the level of mistrust or, by contrast, the blind trust, of some coachees in their coach?). Based on what the coaches experience during coaching, they can gather considerable information on the underlying functioning of the team with which they are collaborating. Indeed, coaches are inevitably quickly incorporated into this system, whether they want it or not (chapter 3).

What hinders or prevents trust

Many factors are likely to alter trust between two individuals or within an entire medical or nursing team:

- False information, lies, things left unspoken (thus, a serious breakdown of communication)
- Inconsistent messages (broken promises, different information given to different units or people)
- Inconsistent relational standards (favoritism, different treatment of different colleagues, nepotism, cronyism, or sexual favors)
- Misplaced benevolence (not reacting to situations, e.g., flagrant or hidden incompetence, contagious negativity, or harmful behavior, such as someone who, by personal ambition, discredits colleagues)
- Insufficient transparency (talking behind the back of colleagues, not keeping them informed)
- Distrust of others (difficulty delegating, difficulty believing employees)
- Open secrets or the inability to name and discuss issues that everyone knows about
- Unfounded rumors (e.g., "The closure of the unit")
- Unsatisfactory results over time

The open secret

"A suicide in the psychiatric emergency room": it took no more than an hour for the entire staff to know about it, and soon, the news spread to other units. The tension rises, we murmur, we hint, we accuse, we whisper it in the ear of the next person, and we observe the reactions. Nothing happens. Days go by, and the division head does not talk about it in any team meeting until someone explodes with anger. However, at that point, the discussion is overdue, emotions are at their height, and no one can think clearly.

Unfounded rumors: Closure of the unit

The beloved boss died suddenly, too soon, too young. The team, disoriented and deeply affected, tries to keep working "as if nothing happened," but colleagues lose their bearings and anxiety creeps in. Rumors begin to circulate, assumptions increase, and imaginations become "reality" in their minds: their unit will be closed.

Only the intervention of the head of the division, who convenes a meeting and calmly explains the decisions, reorganization, and plans, can finally offer reassurance, put the team back on track, and silence false rumors.

Coaches must be trustworthy to ensure they can do their work properly. They may delve on how to demonstrate that they can be trusted and ensure that coachees genuinely trust them and feel, therefore, free to be as they are. By contrast, if coachees note the trust that the coach has on them, they must also be convinced that he/she is difficult to manipulate (Figure 2.1).

Research has identified different components of trust, of which two are fundamental: one is based on *competence* and the other on *benevolence*. The first component is inspired by what might be considered "objective reasons," for example, considerable experience, know how, making clear decisions, managing teams well, well trained, treating successfully patients with complex disorders, etc. The other component of trust is more subjective and based on perception, affinity, respect, reliability, empathy, and compassion. In the context of health–care professionals, two other categories are crucial: trust in the available *technology, methods, facilities,* and *equipment,* and trust in the *organization* of the team and the institution.

Most often, trust, once granted, quickly becomes mutual.

Figure 2.1 Four building blocks of trust.

Communication

We build experience, identity, relationship, knowledge, and culture through communication. How is communication established?

Nonverbal communication

In psychiatric studies conducted at the Affect and Communication Laboratory (LAC) in Geneva, we demonstrated that an unspoken, unintentional, and unconscious relationship *exists* between patients and therapists in a dual exchange and can even be highly intense. The relationship is the source of empathy and compassion and can even, if it becomes conscious, *allow the doctor to give a better diagnosis*. According to many researchers, this communication is based on a bodily echoïsation, namely, a type of imitation in echo that occurs sometimes overtly but mostly subliminally and thus unconsciously between partners. Brunel and Cosnier[1] described the "body-analyzer" as including all the "channels" of communication: speech, voice, facial expressions, posture, gestures, rhythm of speech, and movements and their range. This type of imitation elicits similar affects, allowing for identification. For example, accurately miming emotions (sadness, fear, anger, joy, contempt, and surprise) awakens the same affects in us. Ekman et al.[7] demonstrated that the corresponding brain zones are then activated, which is confirmed by the discovery of mirror neurons.[8] We can also experience this phenomenon by imitating someone else's posture or gait: we better understand what the other feels.

In conversation, we tend to adapt our facial expressions and the rhythm and tone of our voice to those of our interlocutor, and this occurs within a timeframe of approximately 30 seconds from the beginning of the interaction,[9] unless we have negative feelings about the partner (lack of empathy). In case of lack of empathy, expressions tend to remain different, even opposite (e.g., a smile in the face of anger). We also posit that empathizing with a physically dissimilar person is slightly more difficult than empathizing with a physically similar person.

In other words, we use our "body-analyzer" to connect with each other, regardless of whether we are a coach, coachee, care provider, or patient. The more the coach's eye is trained to observe behavior, the more valuable is the information he/she collects about coachees and what they experience at that moment. Indeed, *facial expressions* communicate emotions and contradictions because some muscles are difficult to control and betray us. By contrast, in-dividuals are also excellent at masking their true emotions, typically with a smile. These movements last less than 1 second and are sometimes of very low intensity. Therefore, the coach must be completely attentive during coaching and not take notes. Eyes lowered to documents or diverted to a screen would result in losing a treasure trove of information and severing the connection.

Even if individuals only observe *smiles and glances*, a host of clues are already conveyed by the style of communication and potential exchanges. For ex-ample, a coachee who constantly glances at the door while speaking conveys the sense that he/she either wishes to leave soon or is waiting for someone who could enter at any moment; these glances can put the coach on edge and make him/her feel that the coachee is not mentally present. At this point, it may be useful to tactfully point out the coachee's attention to the door.

A smile has many types: some smiles are for necessary politeness, others mask an emotion that is meant to stay hidden, and just one type demonstrates genuine joy. Shared smiles reinforce bonds and establish complicity. However, in case of a woman who smiles as she recounts the miseries she has endured, it is unclear if she is attempting to convince us that she is unaffected by these experiences or that the people who make her put up with it smile all the while? How should individuals react to her? If we smile with her, we either make her feel that we agree with her feeling that it does not matter or that we identify, like her, with those who treated her poorly. If we do not smile, we recognize the gravity of her speech and communicate that we do not take this event lightly. At this point, we do not aim for complicity but affirm that we support her in her suffering, which promotes a change in attitude.

The *voice*, the great vehicle of emotion, also gives away the attitude of an individual speaking to interlocutors.

Attending physician, really?

Valerie, an attending physician, has some concerns about authority. She is highly competent in her field and good natured. She uses a high-pitched, childish voice in the following conversation:

Valerie:	I do not understand, despite all my efforts, why I cannot seem to be taken seriously.
Coach:	What do you think you should do to make your team take you seriously?
Valerie hesitates:	Frankly, I do not know. I do not want to be an authoritarian.
Coach:	Let's start with your physical attitude: how would you like to introduce yourself? If you'd like, come in front of the mirror and show me ... (a dialogue about posture and gestures follows)
Coach:	And how do you think your voice should match these postures?
Valerie:	I never thought about it; I don't know.
Coach:	How does someone whose authority you admire speak?

Valerie imitates a former attending physician. The coach and she then modulate a series of tones, with slight embarrassment initially, but eventually laugh together. With her consent, the coach records her and makes her listen to her voice; Valerie is surprised by what she hears. She begins to understand that she can play with and vary her vocal expressions and that a deeper tone helps her come across as a more respectable leader.

Let's note that many aspects of communication can be improved or learned.

Silence is an extremely powerful element of interaction, and some people cannot stand it and fill the void with their chatter. Others find refuge in silence as in a fortress. The coach, by contrast, can use silence skillfully to let resonate what has been said, go down into the depths of coachees' spirit, and give time to sink in. From silence emerges new sensations, creative ideas, and repressed emotions.

The same could be said for *postures and gestures*, such as those that illustrate what we are talking about. It is not uncommon, for example, when speaking to a doctor, for patients to touch the part of their body where they feel illness or pain.

Nonverbal exchanges form a true body language, which is effective but largely unconscious.

When asked about the qualities of their care providers, patients consistently remark on the "warmth," a very physical quality. The importance of this quality persists across cultures and has been demonstrated by several studies.[10,b] This result partly explains why a face-to-face relationship cannot be experienced to the same degree via telephone or video conference. In a direct interaction between a coach and coachee, the relationship is so delicate and so tied to trust, which also depends on communication and empathy, that if we, coaches, want to use all our assets to our advantage, we must accord great importance to these nonverbal elements over verbal ones. This remark also applies to the doctor–patient relationship. Doctors and nurses in charge of a Swiss university hospital center spend more than half of their working time facing their computers[11,c]; it begs the question of whether they are able to devote sufficient time to their patients to know them and identify their needs.

Team communication

Today, medicine and care are team matters at all levels. No one heals alone. Health-care professional coachees are completely enmeshed and dependent on their professional network; they depend on others. Even in private practice, practitioners work closely with a pharmacy, laboratory, colleagues from different disciplines, and clinics and hospitals in the area with whom mutual trust should prevail. To this end, physicians should take time to communicate with their network—if they want to ensure that the situation meets their expectations.

In a medical institution, some organizational charts laying out the organization and cooperation between care providers promote efficiency, reliability, and quality of care. They are based on *communication* and *trust*. In response to the considerable complexity of a hospital, the distribution of information, responsibilities, decisions, and actions must be *clear* despite their *complexity* but should be neither oversimplified nor unnecessarily complicated. A vertical hierarchy is slow, cumbersome, and frustrating for all. If assistant nurse A observes signs of suffering in her patient and must inform her direct superior B, who must report to C, who himself must advise D, who will consult E, who finally decides the action to be taken and sends down the order along the same path, the patient's condition is bound to worsen.

By contrast, an inclusive, participative hierarchy wherein all members from A to E have direct relationships, frequent exchanges of information, and are vested with responsibility, including freedom to act in certain situations (see "Complex organization chart"), will have the opposite effect and enable staff involvement, true team cohesiveness, and a speed of intervention essential for ensuring optimal results. Teams that work in this manner have a particularly low turnover of their employees. Let us consider an example: Emily, who has worked as a nurse in the emergency room of the renowned Seattle University Hospital (USA) for 30 years was asked why she is loyal to her job. She said, "I'm involved in discussions, decisions, and research, and that makes all the difference."[d] She feels as if she belongs and is happy in her profession despite the enormous pressure she has endured for so long. Another example is a department head who termed his team "purple" to indicate the complete integration of the doctors (with the red badge) and the nurses (with the blue badge). His use of this word sends a signal to colleagues in other departments. Such positions of true leadership should be taken more often. This quality of work cannot be achieved without excellent communication coupled with complete trust.

A significant number of dangerous human errors occur in the intensive care unit (ICU), many of which could be attributed to problems of communication between physicians and nurses. Applying human factor engineering concepts to the study of the weak points of a specific ICU may help reduce the number of errors. Errors should not be considered unresolvable but rather preventable phenomena.[12] By comparison, the High-Performance Teams and the Hospital of the Future project found that "hospitals with high teamwork ratings experience higher patient satisfaction, higher nurse retention, and lower hospital costs."[13]

The optimum size to ensure the smooth functioning of a hospital team ranges from 16 to 20 or, depending on the task, from 15 to 25 people.[14] These teams are spontaneously divided into subunits of work (e.g., a group of nurses is assigned to one division and subdivided into groups of two or three to care for each patient). Beyond this scope, new groups should be created and intergroup communication established to encourage cooperation and avoid rivalry between them. Indeed, if each group achieves adaptability, flexibility, efficiency, and an ideal speed on its own but remains compartmentalized and closed to intergroup communication, performance is reduced. Just as no one care provider works alone, no one team works alone. Inter-team communication must be considered, organized, and applied. Training to this end could be instituted by wise management so that connections can be made between colleagues in the same profession as well as between employees of different specialties. Such connections enable, for example, fast problem-solving, finding new alternatives, and becoming more creative, and would allow more people of all levels to know each other. Thus, to promote inter-professionalization, a technician from the department of gynecology would be encouraged to exchange with his/her radiology counterpart and a neurology nurse would be asked to converse with an internal medicine laboratory assistant to open up new prospects and help improve techniques or methods. Communication such as this, in addition to the direct supervision of the department head, can only raise the levels of teams, without overloading managers, to enable them to devote themselves to their duties.

McChrystal Group[15] is a company that consults with companies and institutions through personnel restructuring (e.g., health-care institutions). It uses a communication-based model to improve accountability, efficiency, and employee well-being. McChrystal Group has developed the following diagrams to illustrate its model (Figure 2.2):

- The first organization chart (Command) illustrates a traditional approach: everyone knows their place and the level of hierarchy they are located at,

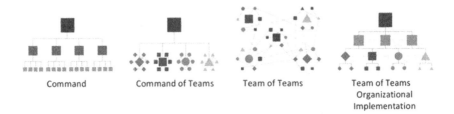

| Command | Command of Teams | Team of Teams | Team of Teams Organizational Implementation |

Figure 2.2 Command; Command of Teams; Team of Teams; Team of Teams Organizational Implementation.

who depends on whom, and who gives orders to whom. When they encounter a problem with a colleague at the same level, they know who will make the decision. However, research has demonstrated that this finding is incorrect because there are zones of influence; moreover, some people possess more power without being at the top of the chain of command.

- Command of Teams: Employees prefer working in small teams, which reach high performance after working together for 2 years. If teams become hyper performing, rivalry and competition begin to creep in and information becomes siloed.
- Team of Teams ("Complex Organization Chart"): The company preserves small teams (where people perform at their best and acquire an identity) but develops connections between teams to encourage a more efficient exchange of information. A sense of openness must exist beyond the immediate team identity for teams to benefit from useful information and *share* theirs readily.
- Implementation of the Model ("Team of Teams Organizational Implementation"): The hospital restructures the role of attending physicians and fellows (not the hierarchical order but according to their specific competence and experience, how they work, how they communicate, and their procedures) to disseminate information in a manner such that the staff can understand the context and make connections while leaving senior physicians to take on the tasks that only they can accomplish.

Communication within teams and between teams is essentially involved in everyone's successful functioning and well-being. The elements of this communication are as follows:

- Clearly define who is responsible for what and under which circumstances, including a clarification of roles and tasks
- Assign responsibility to everyone, even the most junior staff, who will be motivated and will enhance their skillset

- Facilitate direct communication; indeed, information passed through a chain of communication (the game of "telephone") loses all precision and messages become distorted
- Receive constructive feedback on the actions taken and if they are performed successfully. Head physicians with significant experience sometimes overestimate their residents and assign them a treatment plan that they are unprepared for. An important aspect is that the individual who gives the order directly ensures that the order is understood and that the resident can execute it
- Provide feedback and allow colleagues to receive feedback on their actions (e.g., treatment results, follow-ups). The manner of giving feedback should be constructive. First, space should be allowed for colleagues to explain their approach. Second, questions should be asked that help them reflect. Finally, recommendations may be made on how to improve
- Respect and listen to all members of the team

These graphics are thought-provoking when considering a communicative flow of this nature. Indeed, a rigid vertical hierarchy does not adequately facilitate a rapid, direct exchange of information. Subordinates hesitate before reaching out to their supervisors. They also do not dare to disagree, and even more so, if they do not know their boss well. Moreover, subordinates dare not admit any uncertainty, much less a mistake. This situation can have disastrous consequences. For example, a chief surgeon was only informed of the death of his patient overnight upon meeting the family in the morning. Similarly, in such a structure, information only rarely descends the hierarchical rungs, depriving subordinates of insight and understanding.

In a properly functioning team, all involved care providers make bedside visits, regardless of their rank. They then discuss the case as a team in a manner that can be ideally summarized as follows: (1) This is what I believe we are dealing with here. What do you think? (2) This is what I think we should do; (3) What are your thoughts about it? (4) This is what we must look out for; (5) Is there something you do not understand or cannot do that I have not noticed? This model satisfies the need for face-to-face communication, and provides a framework to ask questions and assure understanding. Verbal and nonverbal (emotional) exchanges occur at the team level.

Who works most closely with patients? In a hospital setting, mostly nursing aides do, those who carry out menial tasks. They observe signs, but may not know which ones are important and urgent. Nursing aides do not have the correct language, and in any case, would they even be heard?

- The "Team of Teams" or "Complex" structure is meant primarily to promote this type of communication. However, to communicate in this way, *the entire staff must possess the knowledge, capacity, and competence necessary to participate.* Time devoted to this training is crucial and provides an excellent "return on investment," as economists would say, because responsibility motivates value creation and stabilizes the team. That is where coaches can bring huge improvements.

When a Team Lacks Stability

Anita requests for coaching as she is discouraged, extremely tired, has become increasingly tense and anxious at work, cannot sleep, and is afraid to make mistakes. When she makes mistakes, she tells herself that "it's burnout." Notably, Anita is a "temporary" employee recruited by the hospital from an employment agency. In recent months, she has been successively assigned to three teams. She cannot adapt quickly, hardly knows anybody, and does not understand some of the tasks assigned to her.

Coach: What do you really want?
Anita: I want to have a secure position and to get out of this agency and this institution.
Coach: How is your work important to you?
Anita: I loved what I did when I was good at it. That's what I want to find again and exit this terrible situation.

Indeed, this nurse cannot be efficient, happy, and satisfy her colleagues and patients when having to repeatedly adapt to a new environment. She has the feeling of being used as if she were a robot.

From this perspective, the decision for a large hospital to limit its staff at all levels and rely on agencies to provide temporary employees to "reduce its budget" is difficult to understand and appears to refute the requirements of high-quality care, staff competence, communication, and team stability. Medium- and long-term financial benefits also appear unlikely.

Peter: Teams that collaborate effectively

Paramedics arrived in a few minutes, three of them at first, and evaluated the situation instantly: No, Peter passed out on the bed and was not drunk. Next, two more paramedics entered with an ECG device, and while it was being set up, the doctor asked Mary about treatments, Peter's age, and what had occurred that day. Watching the ECG run, a paramedic says, "He is having a heart attack," and they leave for the hospital. There, a rear garage door is wide open and the lights are on: they are expecting Peter. The stretcher is immediately wheeled up to a room where medical staff attends to him while a nurse takes charge of Mary and answers everything she wants to know. Mary feels involved in the process.

In intensive care, the other bed in the room is unoccupied and the compassionate nurse suggests that Mary lie down there and get a little sleep amid the sounds of beeps in tones of various lengths, such as alarms sounded by different organs. Later, during the procedure, Peter is awake and can follow the progress on a screen and discuss the procedure; after it is completed, Mary is informed of everything that has been done. A few days are spent in a pretty room. The case is followed up, and doctors and nurses are updated and competent, available to give any necessary information Peter asks for.

Two days after Peter's arrival, Mary receives a note from the administration asking her to fill out some forms. She remembers a friend from another country who had to put up a large sum before being admitted to their local university hospital. This is not the case with this humane clinic. Peter and Mary are grateful to the teams and the hospital.

The various teams considered the patient, respected him, and gave him the right to speak and refuse treatment. The perfect *information sharing system* contributed immensely to the good outcome. The patient felt considered, and the staff's ability to listen (the *good relationship*) was especially critical.

Gabrielle: Communication between physicians and the family

Ashen and thin in a hospital bed, Gabrielle, at 95 years, is drifting between two worlds, in a fog. The young surgeon in charge suggests, says the nurse, operating on the bones in her face that were broken in a fall. Her son notes that Gabrielle has signed advanced directives (end of life instructions) that do not allow invasive intervention.

Nurse: But this paper is only considered in case of an inability to discern, but right now, she can answer herself.

> *Son:* In fact, she agrees to what is said to her. She agrees with me when I tell her that this operation is serious, invasive, and that at her age, recovery will take a long time.
>
> *Nurse:* But the surgeon explained to her that she will be better after the operation, and so Gabrielle approved.
>
> *Son:* May I speak with the surgeon directly?
>
> *Nurse:* No, unfortunately, she is too busy. She can't talk to the families.

This lack of communication between the doctor and patient can only cause misunderstandings and dissatisfaction on both sides. The patient and her family feel like "objects" and tend to react emotionally to draw attention to their presence. The doctor, chronically overloaded, is sometimes ill-prepared to consider patients as people with their own issues (slow, with difficulty understanding medical jargon, overwhelmed by pain). The doctor quickly considers the necessary treatment measures, applies them, and, then, is frustrated by the oppositional attitudes of the patient and her family.

It is helpful for the coach to consider the different time frames of the health-care provider and recipient.

Empathy and compassion

"Comparing a lower-tech New Zealand ICU with its American counterparts, I remarked to a New Zealand physician that the United States was technologically intensive, and he responded, 'It's not technology that makes intensive care work, its people who intensively care.'"[16]

Working with joy

Nathalie is a happy, strong adolescent, surrounded by friends. With her high school diploma completed, she thinks of becoming a nurse. Before enrolling in nursing school, she enters an internship program for several months. There, she encounters suffering, decrepitude, and death but also the immense contribution of care providers to the well-being of patients. Toward the end of her internship, she changes her mind because, she says, "I cannot commit to being in a good mood every day."

She is correct. Nurses and aides determine the atmosphere in a hospital room, just as much as in private practices or outpatient clinics; nurses build trust and hope and encourage a patient to accept and then adhere to treatments.

Health-care professionals in direct contact with patients are most likely to feel empathy and compassion. Our "body-analyzer" enables us to "feel what others feel" (emotionally), which helps us put ourselves in others' place (on the cognitive level) to a greater extent.

Empathy and compassion: where do they come from?

We are born with a growing capacity for emotional connections with others. Even in the nursery, one newborn's crying triggers distress in succession, as if *contagious*. As adults, we retain this ability, for example, when we seize the hysterical laughter of our neighbor, or their yawning, or even their tears. We develop an increasingly sophisticated system for the detection of intent, and by 2 years, we are able to attribute thoughts to others (and to oneself), the "Theory of Mind." Thus, we understand that another person has intentions, beliefs, cultures, and perspectives different from ours. Finally, we acquire the capacity to *feel with the other*, be it suffering or joy, and this is *empathy*.

Indeed, positive emotions and feelings, such as joy and happiness, can resonate as much as negative ones such as pain, sadness, anger, and fear. However, unlike a contagious emotion, in empathy there is less blending of oneself with others. The subject perceives the distinction while experiencing the emotion of the other. Much research has been devoted to empathy and has found that it is modulated by several factors according to the relationship between subjects, gender, and personality. Singer et al.[17] observed and measured the reactions of people who witnessed a partner experience pain (a sting on the hand) after playing cards together; women have slightly more empathy for their partner, even if the partner won by cheating just before. Despite self-differentiation, empathic reactions can take opposite directions: we respond with either real empathic distress (sometimes caused by prolonged exposure to the suffering of others or physical fatigue) or compassion. "Empathic distress can provoke a strong aversion and a self-centered response accompanied by a desire to withdraw from the situation to protect oneself from excessive negative feelings."[18] If the situation becomes chronic, it can lead to all manner of physical and psychological disorders, particularly among medical professionals because they are constantly confronted with pain. Burnout is common in these professions, even to the point of suicide, whose incidence is higher in medical professions than in the general population (chapter 10).

Compassion, by contrast, is the subject of interest, promising new psycho-neurobiological research conducted in some of the world's most famous universities (e.g., Stanford, Chicago, Harvard, Max Planck). Researchers have demonstrated that empathy can be overridden by compassion. Compassion allows a person not only to feel what the other feels but also to distance themselves because of an instinct to help. This phenomenon is defined as "the emotional response when perceiving suffering and involves an authentic desire to help."[19] In a compassionate state, we do not share others' pain but have an impression of warmth and concern for them and a genuine desire to ease their pain. Notably, the neural networks of empathy and compassion are not the same and do not overlap.[20,21]

This innate capacity can be detected even in rats, chimpanzees, and young children, also when barriers have to be overcome.[22] This natural, pre-programmed pattern of help without the expectation of returns is a survival mechanism for the human race wherein an individual is unable to be self-sufficient in the many years of childhood and, thus, must rely on the group to survive. For children, the instinct to help seems to be rewarded simply by the sole pleasure of seeing another's suffering diminish. This tendency persists in adulthood but can be mitigated for many reasons, particularly by fear of the judgment of others and education that does not encourage it.

Compassion can, however, be encouraged, stimulated, and taught, especially through meditation. Indeed, several studies, including some involving medical professionals, show strengthening of compassion through meditation practices inspired by Buddhism. Notably, it is less the technique of meditation than its altruistic purpose that appears to provide positive results. As you might expect, veteran meditators exhibit a level of compassion far above average and appear happier. For care providers with busy schedules, however, the duration of meditation training and practice were significantly shortened in these experiments without sacrificing all the anticipated benefits. We posit that even a daily practice of seven and a half minutes is likely to increase the feelings of closeness and connection. Moreover, because of the sense of well-being that it brings, compassion protects practitioners from the harmful effects of stress and diseases such as cancer.[23] The motivation to help rather than hedonistic pleasure encourages greater longevity because the experience of joy associated with compassion protects the individual from diseases more than self-centered pleasure does.

When compassion inspires ideas

One gloomy November night in oncology: The smiling nurse on the night shift stands by the bedside of a musician in the grip of severe pain. The nurse turns on the light and begins to sing and dance *Swan Lake* in her white blouse and her clogs, making her patient laugh heartily, and the pain subsides.

This story illustrates the creativity that compassion can inspire. Indeed, the vast majority of health-care providers love their profession. They are motivated and stimulated even under considerable stress when they manage to maintain a sense of compassion because unlike empathy, it does not lead to fatigue. This type of compassionate relationship brings great satisfaction as well as good health. "In a longitudinal study at a health-care facility, a culture of compassionate love was associated with reduced employee emotional exhaustion and absenteeism, and increased work engagement (i.e., teamwork and satisfaction)."[24] Additionally, patients heal better when they are brought into a compassionate environment rather than a cold, distant setting.

"Active" or "benevolent" listening

Flowing very naturally from this genuine consideration, empathy, and compassion for another person, listening develops in the majority of the care providers, regardless of whether they are coaches or health-care professionals. They know that the other person has something to say, and in any situation, they put themselves on the same wavelength and are open to receiving information through all five senses (their body-analyzer). Thus, they can put into words the emotions of another person if he/she is unable to do so. These listeners do not miss an opportunity to speak, even on serious subjects, including taboos such as mistakes, illness, and death, or if they perceive in their interlocutor the shadow of a question on the subject. Sometimes, just listening encourages the other person to think and speak, and he/she is motivated to continue the search for solutions and well-being. When two people are in tune with each other, a dynamic, inspiring, and harmonious relationship, even amid conflict, encourages endeavors, which then succeed beyond all expectations. Not everyone possesses this essential relational skill to the same degree; it is personal. However, as we have observed, this positive relational quality can be increased, cultivated, broadened, and refined for the benefit of coaches and coachees through learning (we have conducted many workshops on this theme).

Rogers[4] presented his extensive listening experience, which he described as "benevolent" or "active listening," in his book *The Development of the Person* (1961). He provided verbal and nonverbal parameters for paying attention to another person:

- Ignore preconceived ideas and any attempt at interpretation
- Adopt a posture of availability
- Let others speak without interruption
- Ask open-ended questions
- Encourage others to clarify their thought process when it is perceived as imprecise or too general
- Demonstrate many visual and verbal signs of interest
- Repeat others' remarks in own words and then rephrase them

- Practice silence
- Show empathy and affirm understanding
- Remain neutral and caring

When these relational factors are in place and partners are in harmony with each other, a creative pas-de-deux occurs where the coach and coachee lead together. They do not need to love each other, only to agree to move toward the goals chosen by the coachee.

Conclusion

A good relationship between coach and health-care providers is essential for the continuation and success of the contract and is the coach's most powerful tool. Coaches need to be aware not only of its importance but of the details of its ingredients such as trust, communication (verbal and nonverbal), empathy, and compassion (which are different); active listening naturally follows to use them adequately. Coaches are sought in for situations that mostly require some improvement in relationships, be it on an individual level or with teams. Coaches need to then detect failures and assist in finding better ways to exchange, collaborate, respect, and listen to others because there are many ways to learn and improve relationships.

The enhancement of relationships within the staff significantly influences the well-being of care providers and may, thereby, positively influence the healing processes of patients. The improvement follows as if in a cascade, from coach to coachee(s) to patients.

Coaches develop and become more effective when they remain attentive to their own feelings because they serve as compasses and indicators of underlying issues for coachees. If coaches are attentive to these signals, they can use them to clarify situations and encourage conflicts to resolve, attitudes to change, difficulties to iron out, and peace to be reinstated. It is helpful for coaches to pay careful attention to expressing with finesse their trust, emotions, ideas, and compassion. These interpersonal skills allow them to effectively assist coachees in demonstrating their stability and strength. Moreover, after experiencing this type of relationship, their clients may learn how to address colleagues and adopt similar styles in their relationships.

Notes

a An expectation of an "open-ended" question is that the answer will be other than "yes" or "no."
b "Lack of warmth in the doctor–patient relation and failure to receive an explanation of diagnosis and cause of the child's illness were key factors for the noncompliance."
c This is also the case in innumerable other hospitals worldwide.
d Personal communication.

Bibliography

1 Brunel ML, Cosnier JL. *'Empathie. Un sixième sens*. PUF, Paris; 2012. Or see in English: Cosnier J. Empathy and Communication, *Humanities*, no. 68, 24–26, 1997.

2 O'Broin A. Where we have been, where we are now, and where we might be heading: where next for the coaching relationship? *Dan J Coach Psychol* (special issue) 2016;5: 57–72.

3 McGovern J, Lindemann M, Vergara M. Maximizing the impact of executive coaching. *The Manchester Review* 2001;6:1–9.

4 Rogers CR. *On Becoming a Person*. Houghton Mifflin: Boston, MA;1961.

5 DeBruine LM, Jones BC, Little AC, Perrett DI. Social perception of facial resemblance in humans. *Arch Sex Behav* 2008;37(1):64–77.

6 Kramer RM. Rethinking trust. *Harv Bus Rev* 2009; June Issue. https://hbr.org/2009/06/rethinking-trust

7 Ekman P, Davidson RJ, Friesen WV. The Duchenne smile: emotional expression and brain physiology II. *J Pers Soc Psychol* 1990;58:342–353.

8 Rizzolatti G, Craighero L. The mirror-neuron system. *Annu Rev Neurosci* 2004;27: 169–192.

9 Steimer-Krause E, Krause R, Wagner G. Interaction regulations used by schizophrenic and psychosomatic patients: studies on facial behavior in dyadic interactions. *Psychiatry* 1990;August:209–228.

10 Francis V, Korsch BM, Morris MJ. Gaps in doctor-patient communication: patients' response to medical advice. *N Engl J Med* 1969; 280:535–540.

11 Rosier F. www.letemps.ch/sciences/chuv-medecins-passent-trois-plus-temps-devant-ecran-quavec-leurs-patients [February 3, 2017].

12 O'Leary KJ, Sehgal NL, Terrell G, Williams MV. Interdisciplinary teamwork in hospitals: a review and practical recommendations for improvement. *J Hosp Med* 2012;7(1): 48–54.

13 Donchin Y, Gopher D, Olin M, Badihi Y, Biesky M, Sprung CL, Pizov R, Cotev S. A look into the nature and causes of human errors in the intensive care unit. *Crit Care Med* 1995;23(2):294–300.

14 Karlgaard R, Malone MS. *Team Genius. The New Science of High-Performing Organizations*. HarperCollins, New York; 2015.

15 Fussell C. *One Mission. How Leaders Build a Team of Teams*. Portfolio/Penguin, New York; 2017.

16 Cassel J, Buchman TG, Streat S, Stewart RM. Surgeons, intensivists, and the covenant of care: administrative models and values affecting care at the end of life. *Crit Care Med* 2003;31(5):1551–1557

17 Singer T, Seymour B, O'Doherty J, Kaube H, Dolan RJ, Frith CD. Empathy for pain involves the affective but not sensory components of pain. *Science* 2004;303(5661): 1157–1162.

18 Singer T, Klimecki O. Empathy and compassion. *Curr Biol* 2014;24(18):R875–R878.

19 Seppala E. The compassionate mind: science shows why it's healthy and how it spreads. *Observer* 2013;26(5).

20 Ricard M. *Altruism: The Power of Compassion to Change Yourself and the World*. Little Brown, New York; 2015.

21 Klimecki OM, Leiberg S, Ricard M, Singer T. Differential pattern of functional brain plasticity after compassion and empathy training. *Soc Cogn Affect Neurosci* 2014; 9: 873–879.

22 Warneken F, Tomasello M. Altruistic helping in human infants and young chimpanzees. *Science* 2006;311:1301–1303.

23 Brown SL, Nesse RM, Vinokur AD, Smith DM. Providing social support may be more beneficial than receiving it: results from a prospective study of mortality. *Psychol Sci* 2003;14:320–327.

24 Barsade SG, O'Neill OA. What's love got to do with it? A longitudinal study of the culture of companionate love and employee and client outcomes in the long-term care setting. *Adm Sci Q* 2014;1:1–48.

Further readings

Covey S. *The Speed of Trust*. Free Press, New York; 2006.

Oliver C. Reflexive coaching: linking meaning and action in the leadership system. *In*: Palmer S, McDowall A (eds.). *The Coaching Relationship. Putting People First*. Routledge, New York; 2010.

Seppala EM, Hutcherson CA, Nguyen DTH, Doty JR, Gross JJ. Loving-kindness meditation: a tool to improve healthcare provider compassion, resilience, and patient care. *J Compassionate Health Care* 2014;1:5.

Tang CJ, Chan SW, Zhou WT, Liaw SY. Collaboration between hospital physicians and nurses: an integrated literature review. *Int Nurs Rev* 2013;60(3):291–302.

3 Supervision, a Necessity!

Véronique Haynal

Introduction

Regardless of the skills, experience, and talent possessed by coaches, they benefit immensely from the assistance of a supervisor. The best professional coaches know this and practice it for life, such as my colleague who has 40 years of experience and asks for help when he is caught in a complicated interaction. We, as authors, regularly request supervision for our greatest benefit. The goals are multiple. First, supervision provides better assurance of customer protection and improves the coach's skills in the sense of developing his professional identity, which is inseparable from his personal identity. Second, supervision is a privileged place to learn and, if necessary, self-assess the skills of the coach. Coaches are offered the possibility to see themselves from the outside with a critical acuity close to that of their colleagues or clients.

In groups or individually, when we work together and learn from each other, we broaden our perspectives and knowledge.

What is supervision?

Supervision is the protected place where coaches can, in complete confidentiality, share their experiences, impressions of success, doubts, reflections, questions, emotions, feelings, and discomfort. Everything can be said, even the untold. Coaches can share their tension and frustrations and express their emotions, even negative ones. This is the privileged space where they can learn about themselves (this may be the most important aspect), for example, explore their relationship with money or understand their emotions. This enables them to discover how they situate themselves amid personal, interpersonal, and institutional unconscious phenomena with which they are confronted and in which they are absorbed (and sometimes swallowed). In this way, coaches can reflect together, and, finally, take some distance.

Supervision entails the pursuit of learning and opening up to innovative techniques, unexpected tools, and unexplored aspects of the job. It provides

DOI: 10.4324/9781003291831-5

individuals maturity that is useful professionally and personally. No other training better prepares individuals for professional meetings.

A retired psychotherapist was asked whether he missed his patients. He answered that he missed them deeply. However, he also missed supervisions, because "there you experience your work with different supervisees, each having another personality, and then, you make up your own individual style, like no one else!"[a]

Coach sometimes thinks "What a mess I got into!" when faced with a problematic health-care team. Indeed, they may be "outsiders" but are inevitably caught up in subtle games of alliance, power, antagonism, and various complicities. They may also be involved in unconscious[a] processes such as resonance and countertransference,[b] which may complicate the coaching dynamics. Being fully aware of these phenomena is almost impossible. Coaches usually wish to remain neutral; however, *neutrality* does not exist. This notion is widely used in psychoanalysis, but many psychoanalysts who advocated it after Freud, who, by the way, never used this word, are re-thinking their stance. Coaches feel differently for all the people they coach. While some clients are kinder than others and some manage to upset coaches, some cause coaches to worry and others are attractive. In coaching teams, we are often drawn to one side of a group, which can be divided by "contagious" antagonisms. In addition, on a deeper personal level, some clients impact or hurt us, while some make us adopt deep-rooted attitudes characteristic of old relationships; they awaken reactions well anchored in us. Coaches do not show it but these reactions are apparent, especially if overlooked or disregarded. This situation causes the coaches to divide internally, with their nonverbal and even verbal expressions betraying them. In this case, coaches are perceived as an uncomfortable, inauthentic, and not highly credible person. This attitude serves (even unconsciously) as an unfortunate model for coachees, regardless of whether they are part of a team or on a one-on-one process. In addition, the physical and mental health of coaches may well be affected by this split in the short or long term.

By contrast, if coaches focus on all their senses, emotions, feelings, associations of ideas, and imagination, they are bound to make great strides in their understanding of the situation and active phenomena in coaching people. The authenticity of coaches (similar to that of psychotherapists) is manifested in their communication and is a key vector in transforming the relationship. Their "alignment" i.e., consistency between nonverbal and verbal languages and between actions and words will help resolve the issues.

This objective can be achieved through endless work on oneself. Supervision is a prime situation in advancing on the path of true personal development.

In general, supervision is the space to explore and express feelings to identify parallel processes, "blind spots," and isomorphisms, i.e., the factors that are not highly conscious but rather active in interactions between the coach and coachee(s). A parallel process is an intrapsychic phenomenon close to the concept of "transference" in psychoanalysis. It is the act of unconsciously re-enacting when an individual is affectively touched, certain patterns of relationships, roles, ways of being, and behavior experienced in other situations. These unconscious attitudes can then be repeated in coaching and again in supervision when the supervisee presents a case to the supervisor.[c] Other coaches use the terms "thinking process," "mirror effect," or "parallel re-enactment,"[1,2] which are less precise, less defined, and above all, less studied. These phenomena hamper the coaching process and can often be highlighted in this particularly privileged learning situation.

An insecure coach

A coach, Alex, finds himself in a new situation of coaching a highly qualified team with extremely smart people divided by many antagonisms. He is impressed. In supervision, Alex presents his work to his supervisor, Paul, with a certain slowness and hesitation in his remarks, which is confirmed by the audio recording of the session. Paul thinks of a parallel process and asks Alex to comment on his pace and confidence in the supervision session. The latter, already accustomed to making a return on himself, notes the similarity of behavior in the two situations. This awareness allows him to get some insights. He notes that this mandate causes him high anxiety, he does not feel confident, and he is impressed by the status of his clients. Paul then asks Alex how he feels when interacting with him. Alex concedes that he is also impressed by Paul (and his higher status) and that because he is dissatisfied with himself and his performance, he is afraid of appearing mediocre. Paul then encourages Alex to tell him above all about his issue of insecurity. This would then benefit Alex's coaching of the team.

These phenomena of reproducing attitudes from one situation to another are particularly notable through nonverbal expression. For example, they can be detected when the supervisee unconsciously reproduces certain expressions of a coachee, such as voice, gestures, and attitude. The coaches, thus, express their identification to the client. Next, they transmit unconsciously and nonverbally to the supervisor what the client makes them go through, and then, the supervisor experiences what the supervisee experienced during the coaching. Because of the supervisor's acknowledgment of these complex feelings, coach and supervisor can now verbalize them and deepen their understanding of the situation.

These events are significant, and we observe them in most relationships. The supervision situation, however, is a type of laboratory where the events can be particularly highlighted because of focus on communication. "… the unconscious replication of the therapeutic relationship in the supervisory situation is familiar to most supervisors. It is an intriguing, often enigmatic or uncanny phenomenon."[1]

To allow the coach to feel better armed, more confident, and more imaginative, certain qualities of the supervisor are particularly useful and appreciated:

1   Supervisors must be aware of their own patterns and attitudes to differentiate what comes from themselves from what emerges from their supervisees. They must have worked on themselves.
2   They create an atmosphere of trust, security, and nonjudgment. This confidence reduces the anxiety inherent in the situation and thus addresses the issues that deeply affect the supervisee.
3   They ensure confidentiality in a group as well as individually.
4   Their contribution will be most appreciated if they are open, encouraging, and supportive.
5   They feed on their experience. One can imagine the unfortunate situation where the supervisor is a beginner and feels anxious and insecure. If we continue with our aforementioned example, Paul would then experience the same feelings as Alex, and they would therefore have considerable difficulty in resolving this issue, which they share and which is, therefore, likely to be perpetuated.

When the supervisors recognize a parallel process, they are faced with the delicate task of making the supervisees aware of it. They then tactfully endeavor to assess *when* and *how* to intervene and allow the supervisees to introspect and observe their inner processes and relationship with others. When real confidence is established, the supervisors ensure that the anxiety level is low; the supervisees are sufficiently available at this moment to accept personal, emotional questioning; verbal and nonverbal means are used to pass the message on. This makes it a powerful intervention.

It is necessary to maintain a balance between the investigation of parallel processes and other elements of supervision such as the techniques and tools to be used. The same is true of the information that the supervisor can offer on, for example, the functioning of a specific institution, culture of a particular medical field or financial system. However, supervising coaches should be sufficiently attentive to the request of their coachees-supervisees to not fall into the trap of "teaching," "leading," or dragging them into questions that they do not want to approach. The coach's supervision is based on most *principles of coaching*, and the practice is similar to coaching.

For the supervisee, it is an effective learning process to start looking inward regarding a given situation. Literature also indicates[3] that the supervisee sometimes reproduces the supervisor's attitude during coaching. The causes of this phenomenon vary. For example, supervisee might be unsure of themselves and imitate their supervisors; in this case, the supervisee is not yet authentic and continues to transmit his/her insecurity. In another example, the supervisee integrates the supervisor's attitude (e.g., openness, security, nonjudgmental) so well that this new way of being results in real progress in coaching and, in general, the life of the coach.

Supervision of a group of care providers—a model for a group of coaches' supervision

"Don't describe ... play!"[4]

A supervisor works with a group of care providers from a closed crisis unit in psychiatry (a demanding job) every week. The adopted format for the sessions has three parts: time to focus on the case of a patient in practicing role-playing; time for discussion; and time for experimenting new techniques, relaxing and preventing burnout.

1   The first part processes as follows: the group is seated and a nurse, Juliette, provides brief information on Marie, a patient for whom she is a referent. Marie reports the patient's problematic behavior that she has been unable to manage. Next, the group stages a one-to-one session, either in the past or—as Juliette plans it—in the future. She takes on the role of the patient, Marie, and puts herself "in Marie's skin" by adopting her bodily attitude, gaze, rhythm, gestures, and facial expressions. (As it is often difficult to identify with someone who is feeling emotionally very disturbed, it is necessary to take time to prepare.) Another participant of the group, Claire, plays the care provider's role. If during the "one-to-one session," Claire is caught off guard, she can be replaced in her role by another participant. The improvisation during the session is based on what Juliette perceives as Marie, and Claire responds spontaneously according to what she perceives and how she understands the situation.

At the end of the role play, the team usually takes a moment to "get out" of their roles.

2   A discussion is held. The floor is given first to the person who played the patient, then to the one who played the care provider, and, finally, to the spectators. Plenty of time is devoted to discussing the feelings and emotions felt during the play, everyone's observations, and confrontation of opinions. Finally, everyone draws conclusions about the patient, her disorders, her needs, and the relationships she has with her care provider and other people around her.

3   The third part is devoted to experimenting with new approaches, for example, the use of silence, touch (e.g., hand, shoulder), physical distances (and their effects), furniture placement, relaxation techniques, relaxing movements and postures, burnout prevention techniques (necessary for any health professional).

It is critical to play the role of the patient, including every imaginary detail. "The participation of the body in any endeavor to question oneself is essential: there is no disembodied individual truth, and a human word is only true by its weight of flesh."[5] Doctors and nurses have the opportunity, often painful, to identify more deeply with what the patients experience. They, thus, participate in patients' sensory, emotional, and imaginary experience, which allows them to adopt a more adequate constructive attitude when they resume their care providers' duties. We observed that most often, the supervisees play patients who induce in them either significant emotional reactions or a feeling of helplessness. When they slip into the patient's role, they manage to understand her even better, which sometimes triggers introspective processes. In addition, in her role as "care provider," Claire provides a new viewpoint on the relationship with this patient. Her attitude may differ from that of Juliette, in which case Juliette can come to understand that Marie affects her personally (her "transfer" or "parallel process"). Thus, if Juliette wishes, she will speak in front of the group and explain how she feels and how Marie affects her. These explanations will help her disentangle what belongs to her from what is of the patient. By contrast, if Claire feels the same emotions and helplessness that Juliette experienced in the real situation, we learn something more about Marie and the reactions she provokes in her interlocutor. One might think that if the two care providers have the same feelings, other people certainly experience their relationships with this patient in the same manner. This information helps the group understand and find treatment and communication strategies.

In this form of supervision, the supervisee is completely immersed in the situation. By playing the role of and fully identifying with the client, she uses the best means to understand her and, thus, avoid intellectualization or rationalizations that would hide her emotions, making them perceptible only through parallel processes in supervision. These clarifications make it possible to find new answers, strategies, or attitudes for further meetings with the client. Notably, the sessions following the supervisions usually confirmed what was discovered during staging. In addition, the care providers' awareness of their unconscious processes and what patients experience generates changes in the patients.

This method of supervision is a very good tool when applied to coaching of teams: one of the supervisees plays the coach, and the remaining people in the group play the coached team; there is at least one observer to maintain a third and often enlightening perspective. "Balintian psychodramas," a training in the patient–care provider relationship for health staff and, particularly, for doctors is practiced in a comparable manner. We note the implication of the whole person, i.e., a "multichannel experience." Undoubtedly, the authenticity of its body language is why it is so efficient. More than other purely verbal methods, this technique allows a truer approach to a doctor–patient or nurse–patient relationship, which is never limited to a purely spoken exchange.

Conclusion

Supervision is a crucial method of learning and development after graduation and allows coaches to continue to develop emotionally and cognitively. We can only encourage practitioners to use it as much as possible. Supervision is the place to distance yourself and better understand and manage complex relationships wherein the coach is often caught unwillingly, especially in situations involving several people (e.g., teams, client prescribers, coachees). Supervision is also the place to learn appropriate techniques and information about the specific environment in which coaching takes place.

Regardless of the supervision technique used, it is inspired by coaching and can be a space for creativity and authentic meetings that benefit all partners: coachee(s), coach, and supervisor.

Notes

a Personal communication.
b A term mostly used in psychoanalysis: the influence of the patient (or coachee) on the coach's unconscious feelings.
c Some authors term this level "isomorphism," distinguishing this interpersonal dimension from the intrapsychic phenomenon to which they reserve the term "parallel process." However, as it is often very difficult to distinguish these notions, we only focus on parallel processes.

Bibliography

1 Morrissey J, Tribe R. Parallel process in supervision. *Couns Psychol Q* 2001;14(2): 103–110.
2 Crowe TP, Oades LG, Deane FP, Ciarrochi J, Williams VC. Parallel processes in clinical supervision: implications for coaching mental health practitioners. *Int J Evid Based Coach Ment Health Pract* 2011;9(2):56–66.
3 Tracey TJG, Bludworth J, Glidden-Tracey CE. Are there parallel processes in psychotherapy supervision? An empirical examination. *Psychotherapy (Chic)* 2012;49(3): 330–343.
4 Caïn A. Introduction du psychodrame-balint dans la formation psychologique des médecins. *Psychothérapies* 1993;13(1):7–10 (our translation).
5 Anzieu D. *The Group and the Unconscious.* Routledge & Kegan Paul, London, Boston; 1984.

Further readings

Bachkirova T, Jackson P, Clutterbuck D. *Coaching and Mentoring Supervision*. McGraw Hill, Maidenhead, England; 2011.

Bernard J, Goodyear R. *Fundamentals of Clinical Supervision*. 4th ed. Pearson Education, Boston; 2009.

Koltz RL, Odegard MA, Feit SS, Provost K, Smith T. Parallel process and isomorphism: a model for decision making in the supervisory triad. *Fam J Counsel Ther Couples Fam* 2012;20(3):233–238.

Part II

Practice of hospital coaching

4 Healthcare providers and their professional culture

René Chioléro

Introduction

The professional culture of healthcare providers has been built from the high antiquity of a holistic vision of health, illness, suffering, and death. It is highly specific and cannot be inferred from that of other professions. Today, it is made of tenacious residues of this past and progressively associated with new paradigms that have gradually built the culture of healthcare professionals over the previous century.

This chapter aims to describe the basic aspects of the socio-professional culture of the medical and nursing professions, which significantly influence the implementation of coaching. Understanding this culture will facilitate the coach activities within the highly specific environment of the hospital.

Culture of care providers: basic aspects

According to UNESCO, culture in the broadest sense pertains to a set of distinctive spiritual, material, intellectual, and emotional features of a society or social group. In addition to arts and literature, it encompasses lifestyles, ways of living, value systems, traditions, and beliefs. It conditions language, communication systems, manners, and institutions and represents the social heritage of a community.

The culture of healthcare professionals profoundly influences their way of being, language (jargon), way of thinking, communication, of beliefs and values, as well as certain behaviors. Such an assertion may be initially surprising because it is derived from the contemporary image of modern scientific medicine in continuous development with practice based on evidence and high technology. However, the professional culture is built of other elements related to representations of illness and care, as well as of ancestral beliefs and values (the "virtues" of ancient physicians), such as honesty, empathy, altruism, compassion, and respect for the patient and his life, as inscribed in medical thinking since antiquity.

DOI: 10.4324/9781003291831-7

Care for the sick and dying patients has traditionally been provided by women. It was only in the nineteenth century that the medical profession developed as such during the industrial revolution. At that time, medicine was an exclusively a male career, in contrast with the exclusively female nursing practice. From then onward, nurses were auxiliaries of doctors without being assigned a specific area. The specific and autonomous domains of the nursing body were acknowledged only in the second half of the twentieth century, and a university-level training was conceded to them in Anglo-Saxon countries and later in continental Europe. This movement explains to a large extent the relations of the domination of the physicians facing the nursing staff, which often persists today. Although the hospital medical profession has gradually become feminized over the last three decades, a large part of the executive positions is still held by men in most European countries. In 2016, at the Faculty of Biology and Medicine in Lausanne, only 10% of tenured professors and department chairs were awarded to women. Such inequality was even more marked among the surgical specialties. This reality is reflected in the professional culture, which remains masculine and often "macho."

Even today, the nursing professional culture differs noticeably from that of doctors, beginning with training. Although doctors are immersed very early in a competitive and individualistic academic environment (i.e., entry exams, encyclopedic learning with huge amounts of knowledge to master, and marked rivalry), nursing students soon become accustomed to working in teams and setting up effective communication systems. The result is a different "cognitive map," which leads physicians and nurses to construct different representations and ways of thinking about health, illness, work, and relationships, as well as their profession.[1]

In a schematic manner, the design of nursing care is centered on three types of knowledge, namely, case, patient, and personal knowledge.[2]

- The *case knowledge* is notably concerned about biomedical aspects, such as physiology, laboratory, radiological examinations, and diseases. This type of knowledge is scientific in nature, objective, generalizable to groups of patients, and independent of a given patient.
- *Patient knowledge* mainly covers experience of the disease and response to treatment: such an analysis requires proximity to the patient as provided by physical care (i.e., physical and intimate contact like skin touching).
- *Personal knowledge* includes an evaluation of a person's life story, activities, explanatory model of illness and health, beliefs, fears, and wishes.

Alternatively, we observe that physicians are mainly interested in the analysis of the case and less in the knowledge of the patient or its history, except in certain specialties, such as psychiatry and family medicine.

Difficult decisions

A multidisciplinary symposium is organized in a university hospital center. The main theme focuses on therapeutic futility in the clinical field. A clinical vignette is presented and is analyzed by stakeholders from different medical and non-medical professions. Care providers expose the case of an elderly patient suffering from a progressive neurodegenerative disease complicated by pneumonia and other diseases. After three weeks of treatment, two opposed clinical scenarios are discussed, namely, transferring the patient to the intensive care unit (i.e., prolonging acute and specialized care) or implementing palliative care.

The neurologist presents his view concerning the "case" as he considers: description of the disease, presentation of MRI images, and a differential diagnosis. He concludes that an active treatment remains possible and, therefore, should be undertaken in his opinion.

A nurse describes the patient as observed by the nursing team: altered state of consciousness, lack of verbal communication with the nurses and family, nocturnal agitation, and signs of pain during care. The family is very present and worried about the evolution, questions the nursing team, and largely misunderstands the explanations given by the doctors. For the nursing team, the time is right to consider palliative care.

A palliative care specialist notes that his colleagues have yet to be consulted and he disapproves. He shows the various elements that should be taken into consideration when deciding on active or non-active therapy, in particular, the stage of the disease and its prognosis, as well as the preferences of the patient and his relatives. He insists on the importance of information delivered to the patient's wife, who is the patient's surrogate decision-maker. He highlights the need for effective analgesia and sedation.

Furthermore, the intensive care specialist explains the shortage of intensive care beds and the criteria for admission of patients. He is not against proposing a short stay in the unit given that the therapeutic limits are defined.

The chaplain finally declares that he has met several times with the family and sees that they are suffering. He explains the importance of maintaining an empathic and compassionate practice of medicine.

Notably, the analysis made by the chaplain appears to be shared by all, but the discussion is not pursued further.

Doctors learn early to assume responsibilities and leadership, especially to make decisions under any circumstances. However, they find often that sharing this leadership in interdisciplinary conditions is difficult due to fear of loss of power. Culture, in their learning, is mainly focused on knowledge, science, and action instead of on relational aspects. This case is particularly true in medical–technical specialties, such as radiology, anesthesiology, and surgery.

The attitudes of physicians in training (second-year residents of internal medicine and family medicine), advanced practice nurses, and social workers at the master's level on the value and effectiveness of work in interdisciplinary team, as well as the role of physicians in the team were compared in eight American university centers.[3] The majority of participants agreed that interdisciplinarity is beneficial for patient management and can save time. However, the approval rate of physicians was less than that of nurses and social workers. The biggest difference lay on the role of physicians. Although 73% of physicians believed that the role of nurses and social workers is to assist physicians, the latter only supported this proposal at 44% and 47%. Eighty percent of doctors declared they have the right to independently change the therapeutic plan, which is a proposition supported by only 35% and 40% of other professionals. The study shows that the education of physicians should be modified to prepare them for the numerous interdisciplinary activities of contemporary medical practice.[4] This aspect has been gradually improved in recent years with the emergence of common courses for medical and nursing students, where they are given the opportunity to share interdisciplinary activities.

Constructing a project of care for a transplant patient

A 58-year-old patient was treated for severe heart failure and received a heart transplant. The post-operative period was complicated as the patient suffered from severe bronchopneumonia followed by progressive failure of vital organs. Cardiac surgeons and transplant specialists claimed for maximal therapy "because the patient has received an organ, which is a rare and precious resource." The intensive care medical team was divided, whereas the nursing team felt that excessive measures have been taken and that the suffering of the patient was unnecessarily prolonged. The family was very affected by the catastrophic evolution of their loved one and developed a passive attitude. They waited for the doctors to make the necessary decisions. Five days later, the situation remained the same. The nursing team was mobilized to be heard. The head nurse warned the medical officer in charge of the patient that "soon no one in the team will agree to take care of this patient." A multidisciplinary discussion was organized with the nursing team. This meeting allowed each professional group to express opinions and make proposals. The discussion highlighted the significant difference between the views of the surgeons and the nursing team. Finally, the teams decided to continue the actual treatments without therapeutic escalation and organize a daily meeting of the leaders of the three groups of care professionals to agree, decide together, and set up the continuation of therapy.

In this vignette, we find typical differences in the expression of the professional cultures of physicians and nurses. The nursing team, who takes care of the patient by the clock, is more sensitive to the issues of futile therapy and associated suffering than surgeons and transplant specialists. Nurses are more open to accepting a fatal outcome, which is frequently considered as "the best" issue because it will alleviate the suffering of the patient and his family. This option is in contrast with that of the medical teams, who are more focused on action and on the refusal of death, which is considered a therapeutic failure and indicative of a culture of life preservation called "diehard." Finally, we note that the patient's consideration as a person is stronger in the nursing culture than in the medical culture, which is more focused on results.

Appropriate professional cultures have developed during the previous decades in all health professions in an independent manner without worry of creating common elements. This process certainly complicates communication and interdisciplinary work at hospitals. In addition, this background is passed on to new members during training and through socialization processes related to practice. Surprisingly, it remains less known to other health professions.[5] This process has fostered the emergence of a system of "silo cultures," in which each profession has developed its training curriculum, specific language, and approach to the health problems it encounters. This promotes the acquisition of a specific professional identity in healthcare students during their training course in addition to professional knowledge and skills.[1,6]

Rituals and symbols of the medical profession

The incorporation of the professional culture is implemented from the beginning of health professional training. In physicians, it represents a true "hidden curriculum," which includes the senior physicians as role models.[6]

The *white coat* is a universal symbol of the medical profession. Traditionally, it represents not only medical science and authority, healing, and sterility but also the hospital environment.[6] Notably, many doctors wear it in all circumstances even when unnecessary, such as during administrative and working group activities. For a hospital physician, the white coat corresponds to a real uniform, which is enhanced by the color of the badge and differentiates him from other health professionals. Many medical schools (and other healthcare professions) in North America begin on the first year with the *white coat ceremony*, which marks entry into the medical profession and highlights the importance of rituals in medical practice. Studies have found that wearing the white coat reinforces the patient's confidence in the doctor, although it can also be associated with anxiety, as evidenced by the coining of the term *white coat syndrome*, in which the patient expresses his fear of the doctor by an increase in blood pressure.[6]

The *language of physicians* is a characteristic feature of their culture: medicine has developed its dialect, which is also known as a real "jargon" that has departed from that of other professional circles. This language is composed of expressions, turns, specialized words, and shortcuts, which other professionals, patients, and relatives find difficult to understand. Frequently, the coach himself experiences such a difficulty during meetings with medical teams. Diversities in the jargon of different medical specialties may be observed. In other words, a surgeon, a pediatrician, and a psychiatrist may express themselves in various means. The division of medicine into multiple specialties has further accentuated such differences. However, nowadays, they are mitigated by the requirements of interdisciplinary practice, which is necessary to care for the most complex cases. This prerogative in turn broadens the links and sharing between medical disciplines.

Depersonalization of the patient as soon as a doctor leaves the patient's bed to switch to a dialogue between colleagues is another typical element. The patient then becomes a case, an object, or a "thing," whose history is reported with clinical elements and imagery external to any sensitive and existential elements. Personal information is frequently reduced to biological and medical data, thus excluding the dimension of the person. Similarly, the patient's complaints, observations, and expectations are little considered in establishing a diagnosis. Surveys of patients and their families indicate not only poor understanding of the doctor's explanations especially if the doctor uses specialized terminology but also difficulty in being heard and in asking questions.

Liver transplantation in a patient with psychosis?

The choice of patients to be placed on the waiting list for an organ transplant is made by an interdisciplinary group of health care providers who represent the main partners involved in the therapy, such as transplant surgeons and specialists, intensive care specialists, anesthesiologists, psychiatrists, as well as representatives of the nursing staff.

A patient with terminal liver failure is presented. In addition to liver failure, he suffers from chronic psychiatric pathology, which turns out to be "paranoid psychosis." How to appreciate his quality of life and ability to follow treatment after the transplant? The discussion between the specialists is animated.

Hepatologist:	This patient meets all the criteria for a transplant. He is young and in good somatic health, except for liver failure. I met him several times and did not have trouble getting in touch with him. I am therefore in favor of listing him.
Anesthetist:	What is the long-term perspective related to his paranoid psychosis?
Psychiatrist:	No need to use the word "psychosis." It is a label that does not correspond to anything outside psychiatry and penalizes the patient.
Anesthetist:	Although we are not psychiatrists, we still have an idea of what psychosis is. I repeat my question: what is the long-term perspective?
Surgeon:	I would also like to know the direction we are taking to prevent this patient from taking the place of other patients on the waiting list. This question is very serious given the lack of organs.
Hepatologist:	I also point out that he has other medical problems that could influence immunosuppression.
Intensive care specialist:	And the patient, what does he say? Does he understand his situation? Is he a plaintiff?
Nurse:	I join in this question. We must remember to consider the patient as a person. Does he understand all the issues, in particular, that listing is a very tight selection?

For the coach in the middle of a group of doctors, mastery of spoken language is part of the obstacles to overcome to grasp the communication and facilitate the interactions with his interlocutors. How does one intervene effectively if one lacks understanding of the meaning of part of the exchanges? This situation applies particularly to meetings of senior physicians, which are often enmeshed with medical questions or issues concerning the organization of care.

A half day of training with a group of specialists: not always easy to follow!

Coaching is undertaken with a group of medical attendings in a large regional hospital. In addition to the regular sessions with the coach during meetings with the senior medical physicians, an afternoon of coaching is planned to carry out in-depth work on tension and conflicts that frequently disturb the functioning of the group. A second coach, with experience limited only to the non-hospital environment is invited to this session, which was prepared by the two coaches. The first hour of work is devoted to the synthesis of all development and research projects of the department in the presence of the medical director. Many priorities are defined, and one of the projects is identified as important for the entire department. During the break, the second coach admits his poor understanding of the presentations and discussions due to medical jargon.

Significant differences among medical specialties

The micro-culture specific to each medical specialty goes beyond the framework of language. As previously mentioned, we can speak of a "cognitive map" specific to a given specialty.[1] The latter is expressed in representations of health, illness, medical practice, interactions between physicians and nurses, interdisciplinary relationships, and many other things. Thus, the daily relationships between physicians and nurses can be relatively different in a surgical, internal medicine, or psychiatry department.

The representation of the "invincible" physician is another characteristic element of the medical culture specific to certain specialties, although most often unconscious. The doctor named "brave knight invincible" attacks diseases and can even face death. Until recently, this trait has helped to unbalance the doctor–patient relationship, which was often expressed in a paternalistic manner. This representation has weakened over the last two decades in parallel with the increase in patients', rights, who must be informed about and participate in all medical decisions. However, in certain specialties, such as surgery, interventionist specialties (i.e., cardiology and radiology), and oncology, a paternalistic approach of the patients often remains. This aspect also concerns end of life and the relationship to death as illustrated in the following vignette.

An anthropologist immersed in three intensive care units

An American anthropologist conducted an ethnographic study by performing long-term immersion in three American and New Zealand intensive care units.[7] The first unit was led by surgeons, the second by intensive care specialists, and the third by surgeons and intensivists together. Over a two-year period, the author observed the interactions of approximately 600 persons: doctors, nurses, family members, where 80 patients died. End-of-life processes, as well as interactions with nurses and families and relatives, were influenced by the medical specialty of the physicians in charge of the unit.

When surgeons were responsible for decisions, the anthropologist observed that they struggled to the extreme in all cases. Their goal was to fight death at all costs, the "enemy," to defend their patients. This objective contrasted with the more pragmatic attitude observed among intensive care specialists, who considered death as a natural and inevitable process.

In the case where decisions were made by surgeons and intensivists, conflicts were frequent, thus reflecting the clash of different cultures based on unshared beliefs and values. Families were frequently held hostage, receiving conflicting messages from one another about the therapeutic project and the evolution of their parent. A source of recurring conflict was transplanted patients, whose surgeons struggled to abandon heroic care, as opposed to intensivist. We also have lived such conflicts concerning transplant patients in our hospital center.

In the third unit, New Zealand, bed resources were limited. This situation led the senior intensivists to develop a pragmatic and equitable approach to the use of resources to provide intensive care to as many patients as possible. Again, the author observed tension between intensivists and surgeons for the use of intensive care beds related to the lack of consensus and shared culture on the fair distribution of beds, a rare resource.

Another study in the United States reported considerable differences in the duration of survival in end-of-life patients treated by surgeons or oncologists. Medical orders of non-cardiopulmonary resuscitation (DNR) were given 63 days before death in surgical patients and only 22 days before death in patients treated by oncologists.[8] This rate underlines the marked difference between these specialists regarding the appropriate time for their patients to undergo palliative and end-of-life care. A French study showed that decision-making processes aimed at limiting end-of-life treatments were considered satisfactory by 73% of doctors, but only 33% of nurses. This finding again illustrates the cultural differences between the two professional corporations.[9] Many other European and American studies have provided evidence of such differences.

The issue of death

A real question then arises: "How do physicians and nurses experience the death of their patients?" Of course, this question is one of the fundamental ones that affect all human beings. However, care providers opt to relieve pain and fight death as a profession. How then do they live death for themselves? What are their thoughts about it? The difference between death and suffering is that the first is irreversible, whereas the second can be reversed. For many, death is a failure of medicine, and many care providers may feel a degree of culpability. During my 35 years of practice in intensive care medicine, I have repeatedly observed the difficulty of several care providers to accept the reality of death in their patients. On some days, I myself have doubted my ability to serenely approach the execution of end-of-life projects in my patients. I realize today how the practice of medicine and care refers us to our human condition and our finiteness.

The "ETHICUS study" evaluated medical practices at the end of life[10] and conducted in 37 intensive care units in 17 European countries, which included 31,417 patients. In this population, a total of 4,248 patients died or had therapeutic limitations. The authors noted significant differences in the types of treatment applied at end of life, depending on the region (northern, central, or southern Europe) and the religion of physicians: a therapeutic withdrawal was more often advocated by doctors of Catholic or Protestant religion (41 and 44%, respectively) than by Greek Orthodox (13%), Muslim (9%), or Jewish (16%) doctors. Acceleration of the end-of-life process was actively practiced (opiate and sedative administration) in only seven countries.

In 2005 in France, the General Inspectorate of Social Affairs (*Inspection Générale des Affaires Sociales*) conducted an investigation focused on hospital deaths. It covered 527,516 deaths, of which 42% were in a public hospital.[11] The results are rather surprising. It is stated that

> "in the hospital, as elsewhere, death is a taboo and its evocation is uncomfortable, with the exception of the intensive care and palliative care departments, which deal with it every day and have forged adapted behaviors. Hospital staff often sees it as a failure, especially physicians".

From these data, the study concludes that one method of protecting oneself from contact with death is to evacuate the dying patients as far as possible. In departments where this is not possible, care providers learn to manage it at best, but may suffer consequences, such as exhaustion and burnout.

Eventually, many of them adapt to this reality and develop a form of resilience in this field.

We nearly never had the opportunity to address the issue of death in our hospital coaching practice, but only in life coaching (chapter 7).

Professional identity

Professional identity is forged over the years, first during the lengthy medical studies, then in the training of the young physician to strengthen thereafter as a clinical fellow and finally as a senior physician. North American studies have assessed professional identity in family physicians (GPs). It is formed around three main fields, namely, (a) as an Ethos: a universal philosophical ideal; a holistic and integrative attitude toward life and care; and in this area, family medicine is based on the bio-psychosocial model of health and illness. (b) As a set of typical professional behavior traits corresponding to a given role and associated with personal preferences in practice: "as a general practitioner, here is what I offer to my patients ...." Lastly, (c) as a guardian of the health system (Gatekeeper).[12] This model focuses on the importance of family medicine in the health system and leads generalists to consider themselves a different group of specialist physicians. This feeling is further reinforced by the progressive exclusion of an entire series of areas of practice that are currently reserved for specialists, such as pediatrics, medical gynecology, obstetrics, and trauma care. In addition, the fees awarded to GPs are typically low in comparison with their colleague specialists, which reinforces interdisciplinary barriers.

Among physicians in academic hospitals, differences can be observed between the behavior of those active in the academic field and the pure clinicians. These cultural differences have increased during the last decades in parallel with the rapid development of academic medicine. Career prospects are different in both streams. The academic path enjoys more prestige and more recognition in exchange for low salary, which contrasts with clinicians, who feel more pleasure in treating patients and benefit more from living and meaningful interactions with them.

Choosing a specialty does not happen by chance. Studies conducted show that the choice of surgery, internal medicine, or psychiatry as a specialty is linked to concrete motivations. In a survey of approximately 5,000 Swiss doctors in training, the most frequently cited reasons for their choice were work intensity and schedules, career aspects, and interest in training for the relationship with patients.[13] For surgeons, intensity and work schedules were considered the least important factors, whereas the opposite was true for physicians who select psychiatry or radiology. However, these factors were more significant for women than men. Career aspects are considered the most important criteria for future surgeons, but not for psychiatrists or general practitioners. For physicians training in anesthesiology and orthopedics, the relationship with patients plays little role, whereas it is considered a major criterion for physicians specializing in psychiatry, internal medicine, pediatrics, and general medicine. These preferences remain stable along their careers.

Another study compared 52 health care professionals from different backgrounds working in the operation room, such as surgeons, anesthesiologists, nurses, surgeons, and anesthesiologists-in-training. The mental constructs elaborated by each group about the roles, values, and motivations of other professional groups were largely different from those expected by the others.[14]

The "explanatory model"

Another aspect of culture is the vision of illness and health. The socio-anthropologists of medicine call it the "explanatory model," which is constructed not only by the patient but also by the doctor who cares for him.[15] It shows that sick people conceive their illness through social and personal experiences and associate it with representations that constitute their explanatory model of this disease and its meaning, prognosis, and possible treatments. Although the patient's explanatory model mainly reflects his or her origins and social background, the doctor's model is more influenced by his training and professional environment. It influences the doctor–patient relationship, as well as the behavior of the physician in clinical practice. Physicians nevertheless retain representations derived from their basic culture, as shown by the marked influence of religion on their medical practices at end of life.[10] Several North American studies show that racial, ethnic, or language differences significantly influence the doctor–patient relationship.[16] Patients from minority populations, particularly of African American origin, were less likely to be positively and empathically perceived by a white physician than white patients. Other evidence of racial prejudice was reported, for example, when treating patients in the emergency department for fractures. Studies observed that pain was better managed in patients of Caucasian origin than in those of Hispanic or African American origin.[16]

Significant differences between the patient and physician's explanatory models complicate the doctor–patient relationship, particularly when dealing with serious and protracted illnesses, such as cancer. This case is true when establishing effective interdisciplinary collaboration between physicians from different backgrounds. For example, the sharing of the medical practice of physicians trained in conventional (scientific) medicine with their colleagues in alternative medicine (i.e., traditional Chinese, Ayurvedic medicine, and homeopathy) is often difficult. Where the former refers to science and is evidence-based, the latter has a broader and personalized approach to medicine based on other non–exclusively scientific thinking systems. This opposition disrupts communication and may even block it, which complicates collaboration, and is frequently a source of tension.

Coaching a group of complementary and alternative medicine practitioners

Integrative medicine aims to broaden the practice of conventional scientific medicine and offer the patients a wide range of therapies that combine biomedicine with complementary and alternative medicines. Currently, a marked demand is observed for integrative medicine, particularly from patients with cancer with proven benefits.

Coaching is initiated in a group of doctors who practice various complementary and alternative medicines. One of the doctors, a traditional Chinese practitioner, is the project leader. His practice in cancer patients has convinced him of the value of integrative medicine and of patients' expectations about it. He asks for coaching to facilitate the implementation of the project.

A group of colleagues is formed around this practitioner to implement the project named "integrative medicine at our hospital," which was joined by an oncologist and two internal medicine specialists interested in the project. The coach participates in the group sessions with the role of a facilitator of the cooperation process. He notes that if the dialogue is courteous, open-mindedness is weak. That is, complementary and alternative practitioners are reluctant to take a step toward biomedicine and its scientific approach, thus, considering collaboration with biomedicine specialists is difficult for them. A year later, the arrival of new practitioners who are open to integrative medicine gradually changes the state of mind of the group, thus allowing the project to advance step by step.

Common myths and beliefs

Care providers share many myths and beliefs, which are passed on to them gradually throughout training and reinforced during clinical work. We present a few examples.

- "The care providers who knows, the ignorant patient." When one is a doctor or a nurse, one knows what is good and the answers and solutions to health problems. The patient does not understand medicine and fails to see what is good for him. This perspective is an ancient and founding myth, which is still observed by many practitioners despite the advancements of patient rights.

- "The savior lifeguard." The other (patient) is weak and made vulnerable by his illness. He needs help even if he does not ask for it, thus, I have to help him.
- "Invincible doctor." When one is a doctor, one does not need help because the doctor is invincible. This belief is particularly developed in surgeons and in many leading medical specialists.
- "Medical omnipotence." Medicine is all-powerful, whereas death pertains to failure. As such, the doctor must fight with all his weapons against it. This belief is particularly marked among surgeons and physicians involved in transplantation medicine.
- "Science is all-powerful." It gives appropriate responses to all the needs of patients. This belief is deeply held among many leading experts. The opposite belief is often present in many practitioners of complementary medicine, such as "science should be considered dangerous and bad" because it can aggravate diseases and disrupt health, such as vaccines.
- Using plain and clear language reduces the power of the doctor, whereas an obscure language maintains it. "Speech is a tool of power," which must be controlled by the doctor.
- "To heal is a sacred mission," which sometimes requires the sacrifice of oneself. This belief, which is common among older-generation physicians, seems to be reinforced among care providers suffering from burnout. It may explain why doctors frequently experience difficulty in managing their health and illnesses.

The high and dominant position of the doctor

The use of the *high position* in relationships and interactions with others is part of the intimate culture of many physicians, who are often unaware of this attitude. It is a posture acquired early in the learning of medicine and expressed in multiple contexts: relationship with patients, relatives, and nurses, the interdisciplinary exchanges, communication with colleagues practicing complementary and alternative medicines, and interactions within the hospital medical hierarchies. This case can also be true in terms of relations with the coach, mainly at the initial stage of coaching.

A training physician in a dominant position

I receive a coaching request from a young doctor-in-training in an orthopedic department. Amy received a catastrophic assessment at the end of a 12-month training period, thus making further training very uncertain. She experienced similar difficulties during her training: she was refused in an academic hospital after two years of general training, with the mention that she did not have the profile and character to become a good surgeon. She says she is very touched by the current events in her life. For this reason, she wants to start coaching.

During his last assessment interview, her evaluator, a professor senior trainer, deviated from the usual evaluation process. He immediately gave her an unpleasant list of supposed defects:

Professor: You know, Doctor X, I do not appreciate you. In the current team, I noticed that you are little educated, you often cut the floor to your colleagues and give your opinion regardless of right or wrong. I do not like working with you. I do not like to practice surgical operations with you. I will therefore give up on training you. However, I am willing to make an effort if you demonstrate the ability to change ...

Amy: I was deeply touched by this interaction. I was not really expecting such a speech, it was a real shock to me.

After a few days of reflection and discussion with the senior physician in charge of training, she concluded that continuing training under these conditions is impossible, and the time was right for her to do something to change.

Amy: I am aware of my imperfection, but I want to improve my relationship with my boss, which is the reason that leads me to coaching. After reflection, I realize that I am extremely spontaneous at times, less tolerant, and feel a little "atypical," in comparison with colleagues. In fact, I think I'm scared of my boss.

The coaching begins smoothly, and the development of the objectives is carried out without problem. After a few sessions, two of her colleagues notice positive changes in her behavior.

This vignette illustrates the tendency of many physicians to place themselves in a high and dominant position in the relationship with other people. This attitude has long been described by patients in opinion polls. Many patients appreciate this kind of relationship when they want to have a doctor who decides everything in their place, whereas others appear not to appreciate or even disapprove such positioning.

This attitude is also reflected in interprofessional relationships, medical groups, and hierarchies, as described in the aforementioned vignette. Training and pursuing a career in the medical world can be difficult, especially for those who lack self-confidence or behave atypically. In academia, this attitude is particularly marked and can lead to situations of true abuse. This tendency for the high positioning of physicians must be acknowledged to hospital coaches because the initial stages of coaching require a positioning that is rather withdrawn to avoid resistance or confrontation.

Medical studies emphasize the mastery of scientific knowledge that is currently considered the "Rosetta Stone" to address and understand the functioning of the human body and diseases. The selection of medical students is largely based on scientific knowledge to the detriment of learning of humanism, traditional virtues of physicians, and emotional and symbolic dimensions of human beings.[17] Many medical students complain of the harshness of the hospital medical world as well as its lack of compassion (chapter 11).

The very strong belief of many physicians in a scientific truth, which surpasses all subjective and experiential aspects of medicine, such as clinical experience, doctor–patient relationship, value of patients' speech, and listening, led several medical sociologists to describe medical knowledge as primarily a real and objective knowledge. In this perspective, Janelle Taylor describes medicine as perceiving itself as a "culture of no culture."[18] This perception is clearly noticeable in medical education where students must blend into the mold of the dominant culture from the beginning. A simple illustration of this process is the notes in medical records, which translate the patient's narrative language into medical–scientific jargon. The result is a translation of verbatim into a strictly biomedical mode, but outside the reality of the patient.

The rapid development of integrative medicine, which aims to integrate the practices of alternative and complementary medicines with those of biomedicine pushes doctors to open up this reality. It focuses on moving from a static view of culture, which is anchored in fixed values and beliefs (i.e., the truth of scientific knowledge) to a more dynamic vision of culture conceived as a process in which scientific and practices are dynamically affected by social transformations, conflicts, and power relations.[19] This necessary evolution also applies to the teaching of cultural competence during medical studies and postgraduate training, which are associated with significant resistance. Anthropologist Anne Fadiman reports the impossibility of an American medical team to effectively treat a child of emigrants Hmong, suffering from severe epilepsy:[20] "The spirit catches you and you fall down: Hmong child, American doctors, and the collision of two cultures." For the parents of the child who is unable to speak and understand English, epilepsy is caused by a spirit that grabs their child's brain and causes it to fall. In this cosmology, drugs alone can do nothing, and they must be associated with certain measures to neutralize the evil spirit, that is, the intervention of a shaman. The inability of doctors to understand and respect this manner of thinking led to the inevitable aggravation of the disease and death of the child. As Fadiman writes:

"For better or worse, Western medicine is univocal (one-sided). Doctors endure extended medical training to gain knowledge that their patients do not have. As long as the medical culture does not change, it is illusory to consider that our view of reality is only an appreciation, but not the reality itself".[20]

Interdisciplinary relationships: doctors and nurses

The relationship between doctors and nurses has considerably changed in the last 20 years. From a position of absolute domination of doctors until the middle of the twentieth century characterized by the complete subordination of the nursing staff, the development of this profession, accession to a curriculum of university studies, development of academic activities (particularly research), and need to work in teams in many areas of hospital medicine (i.e., intensive care, emergencies, psychiatry, and oncology) has gradually imposed changes to this relationship. At the beginning of the twentieth century, an American doctor, McGregor Robertson, wrote: "A nurse must begin her work with the idea firmly implanted in her mind that she is only the instrument by which the doctor sees his instructions executed."[a] In 1917, Sarah Dock, an Australian nurse, seems to adhere to such work relationship model "at any level, the nurse will never become a reliable professional, as long as she is not able to obey without asking questions!"[b]

However, the quality of the relationship between physicians and nurses is one of the major determinants of patient outcome. In intensive care, several studies showed a reduction not only in mortality but also in readmission rates, length of stay, and costs when collaboration between doctors and nurses was positive.[21] Interdisciplinarity, that is, the ability of different professionals to work and collaborate effectively, is therefore an important issue in current hospital practice.

Six American studies performed over the period of 2001–2007 evaluated the nurse–physician relationships among more than 20,000 hospital staff nurses and published a synthesis paper in 2009.[22] Five types of nurse–physician relationship were identified, namely, (1) collegial: equal trust, power, and respect; based on equality, (2) collaborative: mutual trust, power, and respect; based on mutuality, (3) student–teacher: either the physician or nurse (e.g., with residents) can be the teacher; (4) friendly–stranger: a formal exchange of information with a neutral feeling tone; and (5) hostile–adversarial relationships: verbal abuse, aggression, anger, real or implied threats, or resignation. In the 2007 study,[22] staff nurses reported the dominant unit climate as collegial 81%, collaborative (85%), friendly–stranger (59%), and adversarial (17%), taking into account that the five types of relationships can and do exist simultaneously.

Several studies observed contrasting assessments between doctors and nurses on the quality of collaboration in intensive care units. Thomas et al. observed that 73% of doctors considered working in a collaborative atmosphere compared with only 33% of nurses[23] in a US unit of critical care medicine. Ferrand found similar results in France (50% and 27%).[9] These studies urged the medical and nursing association leaders to set up projects to promote interdisciplinarity work at the hospital. The training of medical and nursing leaders in a collaborative interdisciplinary approach has positive and long-term effects in intensive care, thus demonstrating the feasibility of such a change. The same is true of medical and nursing education in colleges and universities, where joint courses between nursing and medical students are organized throughout the course of studies. In 2014, the Swiss Academy of Medical Sciences drew up a charter on collaboration between healthcare professionals.[4] It emphasized that different tasks in the care process are performed according to the needs of patients and their relatives, respecting the professional skills required. The division of tasks does not meet the hierarchical criteria. However, interdisciplinary groups should be prepared to delegate tasks or take on new responsibilities depending on the situation. Such an approach indicates that healthcare professionals intervene according to their specific skills and abilities. It corresponds to the new concept of the nursing profession with its own activities apart from any medical delegation.

Messages for the coach

Understanding the basis of the professional culture of healthcare providers is a necessity for the coach that aims to exert activities within the hospital. The enhanced outlook will facilitate individual and team coaching, as well as promote the efficiency of the assistance, particularly at the initial stages. Many physicians are reluctant to accept the usefulness of coaching prescribed by the hierarchy. For them, such an offer is difficult to accept because it can be experienced as a weakness, a risk of stepping down from the pedestal, and expose a possible fragility. This tendency can be expressed by the refusal of coaching or a difficult start, which is hindered by resistance, as shown in the thumbnail later (chapter 5).

Refusal of coaching

I received a request from the medical director of a regional hospital for the coaching of a chief physician. I noted many indications of serious dysfunctions in his department, such as disagreements, tension, and conflicts between senior physicians, repeated complaints from residents about supervision, complaints from nurses about relations with the head physician and a few of the senior medical attendings, and delays in administrative tasks. The director informed me that he had repeatedly offered coaching to the chief who initially refused. The threat of sanctions led him to finally agree to meet the coach. The meeting was difficult because the doctor was not open to any change, denied most of the criticisms against him, and quickly stated a lack of time or interest in engaging in coaching. At the end of the interview, his view remained the same, and he repeated his refusal to undertake a personal development process. Six months later, the situation continues.

However, once initial resistance is lifted, the physician often proves to be a motivated client and able to benefit from coaching, as will be illustrated in subsequent chapters. Based on the authors' experience, a premature termination of coaching and failure to progress to the main objectives are rarely experienced in the hospital setting. In addition, a faultless, unhurried start-up and the coach's ability to establish a working relationship based on trust are key elements that promote a positive dynamics in the advancement of coaching.

Conclusion

The professional culture of care providers has been forged over the centuries. It continues to evolve rapidly today but remains largely different from those of many other professional categories. It is non-homogeneous and varies according to medical specialties and hospital environment. It is also different in many aspects from the nursing culture, which is more homogeneous and focused on the needs of patients. Many symbols and rituals characterize medical culture, such as wearing of the white coat, language, and functioning of hierarchies. These sociocultural elements influence professional identity, which is identifiable among care providers of all types and forged as early as during medical school and reinforced over the years. In a similar manner, the relationship between the medical profession and nursing staff has evolved in recent years. Nevertheless, a tendency for physicians to adopt a dominant position in the face of nurses and many other persons remains. Such positioning undermines the interdisciplinarity necessary for the practice of hospital care.

Notes

a McGregor-Robertson, J. 1902. *The Physician*. London, Gresham Publishing.
b Dock S. The relation of the nurse to the doctor and thew doctor to the nurse. Am J Nursing 1917; 17: 394-396.

Bibliography

1 Hall P. Interprofessional teamwork: professional cultures as barriers. *J Interprof Care* 2005;19(Suppl 1):188–196.

2 Stein-Parbury J, Liaschenko J. Understanding collaboration between nurses and physicians as knowledge at work. *Am J Crit Care Off Publ Am Assoc Crit-Care Nurses* 2007;16(5):470–477; quiz 478.

3 Leipzig RM, Hyer K, Ek K, *et al.* Attitudes toward working on interdisciplinary healthcare teams: a comparison by discipline. *J Am Geriatr Soc* 2002;50(6):1141–1148.

4 Académie Suisse des Sciences Médicales. Collaboration entre les professionnels de la santé. *Charte.* 2014. https://www.samw.ch/fr/Publications/Recommandations.html

5 Schroeder RE, Morrison EE, Cavanaugh C, West MP, Montgomery J. Improving communication among health professionals through education: a pilot study. *J Health Adm Educ* 1999;17(3):175–198.

6 Boutin-Foster C, Foster JC, Konopasek L. Viewpoint: physician, know thyself: the professional culture of medicine as a framework for teaching cultural competence. *Acad Med J Assoc Am Med Coll* 2008;83(1):106–111.

7 Cassell J, Buchman TG, Streat S, Stewart RM, Buchman TG. Surgeons, intensivists, and the covenant of care: administrative models and values affecting care at the end of life. *Crit Care Med* 2003;31(4):1263–1270.

8 Connors AF, Dawson NV, Desbiens NA, *et al.* A controlled trial to improve care for seriously ill hospitalized patients: the study to understand prognoses and preferences for outcomes and risks of treatments (SUPPORT). *JAMA* 1995;274(20): 1591–1598.

9 Ferrand E, Lemaire F, Regnier B, *et al.* Discrepancies between perceptions by physicians and nursing staff of intensive care unit end-of-life decisions. *Am J Respir Crit Care Med* 2003;167(10):1310–1315.

10 Sprung CL, Cohen SL, Sjokvist P, *et al.* End-of-life practices in European intensive care units: the Ethicus Study. *JAMA* 2003;290(6):790–797.

11 Lalande F, Veber O. *La Mort à l'hôpital*; 2009. Available from www.ladocumentation francaise.fr/var/storage/rapports-publics/104000037.pdf

12 Stein HF. Family medicine's identity: being generalists in a specialist culture? *Ann Fam Med* 2006;4(5):455–459.

13 Van Der Horst K, Siegrist M, Orlow P, Giger M. Residents' reasons for specialty choice: influence of gender, time, patient and career: residents' reasons for specialty choice. *Med Educ* 2010;44(6):595–602.

14 Lingard L, Reznick R, DeVito I, Espin S. Forming professional identities on the health care team: discursive constructions of the "other" in the operating room. *Med Educ* 2002;36(8):728–734.

15 Kleinman A. Culture, illness, and care: clinical lessons from anthropologic and cross-cultural research. *Ann Intern Med* 1978;88(2):251.

16 Ferguson WJ, Candib LM. Culture, language, and the doctor-patient relationship. *Fam Med* 2002;34(5):353–361.

17 Coulehan J, Williams PC. Vanquishing virtue: the impact of medical education. *Acad Med J Assoc Am Med Coll* 2001;76(6):598–605.

18 Taylor JS. Confronting "culture" in medicine's "culture of no culture". *Acad Med* 2003;78(6):5.

19 Guarnaccia PJ, Rodriguez O. Concepts of culture and their role in the development of culturally competent mental health services. *Hisp J Behav Sci* 1996;18(4):419–443.

20 Fadiman A. *The Spirit Catches You and You Fall Down. A Hmong Child, Her American Doctors, and the Collision of Two Cultures*, Paperback edition. Farrar, Straus and Giroux, New York; 2012.

21 Knaus WA, Draper EA, Wagner DP, Zimmerman JE. An evaluation of outcome from intensive care in major medical centers. *Ann Intern Med* 1986;104:410–418.

22 Schmalenberg C, Kramer M. Nurse-physician relationships in hospitals: 20 000 nurses tell their story. *Crit Care Nurse* 2009;29(1):74–83.

23 Thomas EJ, Sexton JB, Helmreich RL. Discrepant attitudes about teamwork among critical care nurses and physicians. *Crit Care Med* 2003;31(3):956–959.

5   Coaching: from request to contract

René Chioléro

Introduction

The contemporary hospital is a distinct business because it is not directly economic; its purpose is centered on all aspects of patient care and medical practice, but not on profit. The development and complexification of management processes influenced care providers to abandon these areas they did not master. They have been replaced by professional managers in all areas (e.g., management, finance, human resources [HR]). As a result, a gradual shift in management concepts has forced care providers and managers to adapt and develop effective communication and collaboration systems. Despite consistent efforts, substantial differences between these two professions in their culture, business vision, and management of priorities persist. Furthermore, the hospital environment differs markedly from other types of businesses because of the specific aspects of care and health care provider organizations. We may easily observe this reality as coaches, during the accompaniment of executives and hospital teams.

This chapter aims to describe the basic knowledge of hospital organization necessary to perform coaching in this setting, as well as the description of coaching implementation.

Basics of hospital organization

The public hospital is a company that differs from all commercial enterprises because its "raison d'être" are care, health, and illness and not profit (except for private clinics). Over the last 30 years, hospitals have undergone spectacular development related to the rapid progress of medicine, the emergence of new medical specialties, the large increase in the number of care providers, and the contingencies of management and cost control.[1] Hospital management has evolved in parallel, starting from nonprofessional managing performed mainly by the heads of care providers, to a complex organization, with multifunction management performed by high-level professionals, comparable to that of a large company. The coach who starts a mission in a care institution must have basic knowledge of the operation of the hospital, the departments'

DOI: 10.4324/9781003291831-8

organization, the relations between the many categories of health care providers, and the functioning of hierarchies to effectively support the individuals and teams requiring coaching.

Missions

Hospitals have three main missions:

- *Patient care and therapy*
- *Teaching, education, and training* (e.g., physicians, nurses)
- *Research and innovation*

To this list, we can add *hospital management*, as a fourth mission, indispensable to ensure the permanence of all structures and systems necessary to perform day and night hospital care. Hospital management concerns two categories of professionals: the managers and the medical and nursing heads responsible for organizing and running their departments. In a modern system of medical organization, controlling the enormous expenditure of medicine has become a priority of increasing importance, which significantly influences the organization of care (health economics).

The *clinical mission* covers many types of activities, for example, nursing care, medical diagnosis and therapy, and services performed by other care providers. These activities cover all fields of medicine performed in the hospital. They require multiple medical and care providers. Table 5.1 summarizes the list of the main medical specialties of a large university hospital (e.g., Lausanne University Hospital Center). Coordinating all these care professionals distributed into multiple medical specialties, whose interactions must be effectively regulated, is difficult. For example, the initial management of a patient after a liver transplant requires considerable teamwork, putting in phase many transplant specialists, such as hepatologists; surgical, anesthesia, and operating room teams; transfusion teams, and intensive care physicians and nurses; as well as other specialists when a patient has complications.

The *teaching mission* concerns not only physicians and nurses but potentially other care providers of the hospital (e.g., physiotherapists, radiology technicians) and the administration. It can represent a highly complex organization in a university hospital, requiring many education professionals.

The research mission concerns mainly university and large hospitals and covers many fields, for example, medical research, nursing, clinical research, fundamental research, innovation, and developmental research. In the modern medicine, research is a high priority activity, which is the primary source of advancements in therapy and care.

Organizing and managing the medical departments and divisions (hospital units) is part of the mission of the leaders of the medical and nursing teams. This high-priority role is a key element in the proper functioning of the medical and nurse teams and thus of all hospital departments.

Table 5.1 Departments, services, and divisions of an academic hospital (Lausanne CHUV, simplified)

Management, three departments:
- Hospital direction: general; medical; nursing care; center of training; communication; HR; projects and strategic organization
- Administration and finances direction
- Hospital logistics direction

Department of Research and Training

Department of Medicine: preventive medicine; dermatology; endocrinology, metabolism, and diabetology; genetic medicine; geriatrics; gastroenterology; immunology and allergology; internal medicine; infectious diseases; nephrology; pneumonology

Department of Surgery and Anesthesiology: anesthesiology, visceral surgery, thoracic surgery, surgical research, ENT (otorhinolaryngology), urology, septic surgery

Department of Community Health: addictology, forensic medicine, social and preventive medicine

Department of Musculoskeletal System: plastic and reconstructive surgery, physical medicine and rehabilitation, orthopedics and traumatology, rheumatology

Department of Clinical Neurosciences: neuroscience research, memory, neurosurgery, neurology, neuropsychology and neurorehabilitation, spinal surgery

Department of Psychiatry: adult psychiatry, psychiatry of the child and adolescent, psychiatry and penitentiary medicine, psychiatry of advanced age, community psychiatry, liaison psychiatry, psychiatric neuroscience center

Department of Oncology: hematology, immuno-oncology, oncological research, analytical oncology, medical oncology, experimental therapy, radiation oncology

Department of Medical Radiology: radio physics, nuclear medicine and molecular imaging, radio diagnostics and interventional radiology

Department of Heart and Vessels: angiology, cardiology, cardiac surgery, vascular surgery

Department Mother and Child department: pediatric surgery, obstetrics & gynecology, childhood hospital, neonatology, adolescent health, pediatrics, intensive care pediatric

Department of Interdisciplinary Centers and Medical Logistics: endoscopy, sterilization and disinfection, adult intensive care medicine, center of operating theaters, emergency medicine

North Psychiatric Sector

South Psychiatric Sector

Department of Ambulatory Medicine & Clinical and Community Prevention: cardiology, gastroenterology and hepatology, hematology, genetic, immunology, dental polyclinic, tropical travel medicine, pneumology, podiatry, socio-medical consultations, pharmacy

The hospital is managed by administrative teams, trained for this task, who should provide optimal working conditions for the care teams; unfortunately, this is not always the case. Regulating the interactions between all categories of care provider and non-care provider leaders who run the hospital is challenging in large hospitals and university hospitals. Physicians often report their misunderstanding of the administrative hierarchy and vice versa.

Types of hospitals

Several categories of hospitals can be distinguished according to their main characteristics: size; type of activity (general hospital; hospital with specialized medical activities, pediatric or adult hospital; teaching hospitals, university hospital); for-profit versus not-for-profit hospitals; community, non-community federal hospitals, etc. For each category, specific organization and management is required.

Such differences may influence the course of coaching, particularly its initiation. When a coach receives a request to intervene in a hospital, he therefore must inquire about the type of institution to understand its characteristics and organization. This understanding facilitates the coach's contacts with the different stakeholders; it also clarifies the coaching mandate. Working in a small, regional hospital of 80–120 beds to support a department head is a different work setting (and usually simpler) from performing the same mission in a 1200-bed university hospital. In a regional hospital, the coach manages a simple organization headed by a general manager that oversees small health care teams led by a limited hierarchy. Conversely, a large size university hospital is often a complex structure with hierarchical lines with multiple floors, and these characteristics frequently complicate coaching at all stages. In such an environment, communication and interactions are generally difficult to control, as are management and control systems that vary by institution.

Medical and nurse organization

The medical–nursing organization varies according to the type of institution. In public hospitals, patients are grouped into departments and divisions (or units) that usually correspond to the medical specialties, for example, medical specialties (e.g., internal medicine, cardiology, pneumology), surgical specialties, gynecology, obstetrics, and pediatrics. In university and large hospitals, these specialties are grouped into departments created according to a purely medical logic (e.g., surgery and surgical specialties, medicine and medical specialties, pediatrics and pediatric surgery) or in pathways or poles to promote interdisciplinary collaborations (e.g., brain department, cardiovascular department, locomotor department). The nursing organization is usually more centralized than the medical organization. Tables 5.1 and 5.2 summarize the deployment of clinical departments and divisions in a Swiss regional hospital and a Swiss university hospital. They illustrate the complexity of the multiple specialties and sub-specialties of hospital medicine and underline the necessity to establish effective systems of communication and cooperation to avoid excessive fragmentation of the medical practice.

Medical hierarchies are multiple and layered. Physicians occupy residents' positions during the first years of their training. Subsequently, they can be promoted to the position of chief resident, in which they may acquire specific skills in specialized fields. Attending physicians (i.e., executive physicians) occupy a permanent position and represent the team of professionals necessary to perform the activities of the medical specialties and to supervise the in-training physicians. In university hospitals, medical hierarchies include several levels, according to the medical organization: chiefs

Table 5.2. Example of a Swiss regional hospital

Number of beds	500
In patients	40,700
Number of consultations and ambulatory cares	472,000
Ambulance interventions	2514
Patients admitted to the Emergency Department	71,500
Number of births	2425
Radiology: mean number of SCANS per day	76
Laboratory exams	3,600,000
24/24 hours medical specialties	16
Hospital staff (total)	5200
Senior physicians (heads of departments/divisions, attendings)	75
Physicians in training: residents & chief residents	350
Medical departments and divisions recognized by the Swiss Medical Association for medical training	50
Nursing staff (total)	1530
Paramedical staff	392
Nursing and paramedical staff in training	800
Medico-technical units	13
Hospital turnover	CHF 692,000,000 = $762,300,000

of departments, divisions or units, and attending physicians. The hierarchies in regional hospitals are simpler, whereas in private clinics, there is usually little or no medical hierarchy.

The *small hospitals* usually operate with less than 150 beds and provide general medical and nursing services, excluding highly specialized practices. They are characterized by a simple structure and little hierarchy. The relations between the administration and the medical and nursing hierarchies are direct; the general director knows all the medical and nursing chiefs. She is often personally involved in the prescribing of coaching: when coaching is initiated, she is usually aware of the process, meets the coach, and must be considered by the coach as a major stakeholder. This role contrasts with that the medical director, who in small hospitals generally occupies the functions of coordinator and spokesperson of the medical profession, rather than a hierarchical role.

In such an environment, the coach quickly becomes familiar with the general operation of the hospital and clinical departments. He can therefore rapidly begin his mission. This proximity of the administrative and care provider heads usually facilitates the start of coaching; however, it could also complicate the coaching if the hospital management has different views from those of the medical hierarchies on the objectives of the coaching and the final result to be achieved. Another point of interest concerns the hierarchical organization, which can be almost horizontal (hierarchy of low weight) or more vertical when the leadership of the department head is of the authoritarian style.

Medium-sized regional hospitals usually have 150–400 beds and provide services in conventional medical branches (e.g., medicine, surgery, pediatrics, gynecology-obstetrics) and in certain specialties that require complex structures and equipment (e.g., specialized cardiology, cardiac surgery, neurology, intensive care medicine). Compared with small hospitals, its organization is more complex, depending on the types of departments and number of care providers, and its hierarchies are more extensive. In addition to a general manager, there is usually a medical director, a director of nursing care, and an HR department who interact with the coach.

Clinical departments (or divisions) can be large, with multilevel medical and nursing hierarchies, and can coexist with smaller divisions (Table 5.2. In such a structure, the coach should inquire from the beginning of his mandate about the overall functioning of the hospital structure, which varies by institution. In particular, he should know the respective roles of the general, medical, and HR directors in the organization and in the follow-up of coaching. In such a complex structure, the influence of the medical director is usually strong. For the coach, the medical director is a priority interlocutor, often knowledgeable of the functioning of departments and departments, who plays a significant role in many decisions concerning the medical profession.

Holding a meeting with all stakeholders to conduct group work in small- and medium-sized institutions is often difficult because their medical endowments are extensive and heavy.

University hospitals, compared with the other aforementioned types, have the largest size (usually 500–over 1000 beds), a broader mission, and require an even more complex structure (Tables 5.1 and 5.3). At university hospitals, the training and research and development missions are prioritized, resulting in a complexification of the medical and nursing hierarchies. On the medical level, in addition to the clinical hierarchy (e.g., department head, attendings, and chiefs of residents [non-permanent]), there is a parallel hierarchy in the academic field. The coexistence of clinical physicians and researchers in the same department is sometimes difficult. The increasing professionalization of researchers and their distance from clinical settings requires a specific organization of medical teams, to reconcile different modes of work and statuses, e.g., day and night work, care requirements for clinicians, and salaries (often reduced for researchers). Malfunctions or tensions in the medical team have been observed.

Administrative staff and care providers: different cultures

The basic elements of the cultures of medicine and nursing are described in detail in chapter 4. In this section, we summarize a few key points by highlighting the differences between health care professionals and managers.

• For *care providers*, the organization should focus on the areas of patient care, diagnosis, treatment, and all medico-therapeutic services and

Table 5.3 Organization of a university hospital: Lausanne CHUV (2016 annual report)

Number of beds: total/somatic diseases/psychiatry	1420/1080/340
In patients	40,496
Patients admitted to the Emergency Department	74,093
Number of births	3220
Hospital staff (total)	11,039/8971
Hospital staff: number of nationalities	100
Physicians (total)	1572
Senior physicians (e.g., attendings, hospital physicians)	345
Physicians, heads of departments and divisions	64
Physicians: full professors	70
Physicians in training: residents and chief residents	1218
Medical departments and divisions recognized by the Swiss Medical Association for medical training	50
Nursing staff (total)	3398
Paramedical staff	392
Nursing and paramedical staff in training	800
Medico-technical staff	1034
Administrative and logistic staff	2703
Hospital turnover, CHF (or USD, with the 2020 change rate)	CHF 1,700,000 = $1,877,600

facilitate all these processes. Economic reality is secondary, as are planning and management problems. When a patient needs a specific therapy or care, every effort is made to deliver it; otherwise, there is a risk of "care system failure." The diversification of medicine into multiple specialties has aggravated this sectoral vision of care providers and therefore fragmented their vision of the care; today, most hospital specialists are unaware of the duties and needs of their colleagues in other specialties. Thus, it is difficult to explain to a group of pediatricians that their requests for equipment are refused, when those of another surgical division are considered a priority—in a given year. In general, medical organization is more flexible than nursing organization, for example, the management of work schedules and overtime was much more rigid for nurses.

Many hospital doctors have a manifest, sometimes exaggerated, mistrust of the administrative body, which may include management and the medical director. "The people in the administration do not understand us, they complicate our lives," is the type of message often reported by medical leaders to the coach.

• The culture of care providers contrasts with that of *managers and administrative staff,* who have a traditional corporate culture and are focused on the rigor of management, the need to respect budgets, and the organization of the company. Staff management is a good example of the considerable difference between the views of a senior physician and an HR staff member: how to explain to the head of a department that the institutional procedures and rules that she must follow to dismiss a collaborator becomes a relevant question? Overtime management is another example of the importance of different viewpoints, and this is particularly the case in the surgical specialties. Thus, another relevant question is how to explain to the HR supervisor that non-compliance with work hours is not caused by bad will but by the difficulty of predicting the duration of a surgery or working with a patient whose condition has worsened.

How to close an intensive care bed?

The arrival of a new head in the anesthesiology department in a university hospital causes a vast operation to transfer resources. To pay for new positions in the anesthesia department, she has convinced the general manager to close an intensive care bed. The head of the intensive care unit (ICU) is in a hierarchical dependence under the anesthesiology department head and unsuccessfully attempted to curb this unrealistic project because of the very high occupancy of the ICU. He meets the hospital general manager.

Head of the ICU:	This closure is unrealistic; it could block the flow of patients in the divisions of the department of surgery, particularly those patients operated on urgently.
Director:	You, the doctors, are all the same in managing your resources without caring for others. I made my decision, and it is final.

Closing is performed. Three months later, more than 15 overnight readmissions have been required, and several department divisions report increasing difficulties in managing patient flows in the ICU. After 12 months, the analysis of the figures shows alarming data, in particular, an increase in readmissions linked to too early transfers and associated with serious complications. The management then increased the number of ICU beds by two units to restore balance in the management of patient flow.

This vignette illustrates the difficulty of communication between the highly competent manager and the head physician of the ICU who is anxious to respond to requests from colleagues to admit more patients. However, how can it be explained to the manager that bed management, complicated by emergencies, organ transplants, and the unplanned evolution of some patients, cannot be managed as a mathematical model? These complications and the misunderstandings on both sides could have been avoided. Thus, how can the communication between medical and administrative leaders be improved?

The coach who receives a management mandate to work in a department must be aware of these cultural differences to adapt, feel comfortable, and effectively interact with the hospital management and his medical or nursing clients. In large hospitals, similar cultural differences exist within the administration: the views of, for example, the general manager, medical director, director of care, and HR director can differ greatly on the aspects of coaching. Therefore, it is necessary to specify the expectations of all parties involved for the implementation of the coaching mandate (e.g., management, medical director, coachee) and to develop a work contract achievable by the coach.

Coaching request

Working with the medical director

In large hospitals, the medical director occupies an important position, usually with considerable power. There are two ways to perform this function: a full-time or part-time activity. A full-time director devotes all his time to his management activity, he abandons all clinical activity. In this mode, the medical director generally behaves as if a medical manager, often far removed from the clinical reality and rather distant from his colleagues and close to the management. This mode contrasts with a part-time medical director, who maintains clinical activity and close relationships with department heads and thus has a better understanding of the clinical setting. In this situation, the proximity of the medical director to management is less, which goes hand in hand with improving the image projected to the clinicians.

In all cases, being an ally of the medical director is an asset, to facilitate the start and conduct of coaching. He is a valuable source of information at the beginning of the support because he usually understands the problems posed by the beneficiaries of the coaching; however, he sometimes embarrasses the coach when he transmits information that the coachee ignores. This leads the coach to explain to the medical director that this department head must receive from the management all the information that concerns him, as well as all complaints about the operation of his department.

When starting the coaching of a disputed leader, the coach must also receive all the information related to the situation of his client. In particular, an important point to clarify concerns a possible dismissal ("last chance coaching"). Supporting a coachee to manage a difficult dismissal is different from supporting the same person to progress in her leadership. We recently had this experience: the coaching imposed by the hospital director on a young head physician was parallel to a project of dismissal.

Strengthen the leadership of a new division head or another agenda

The general director of a hospital contacts a coach to propose coaching to reinforce the leadership of a new head of a medical division with little management experience. During the first meeting with the coach, the director assures the coach that it is important to support this leader to "reinforce his authority and the quality of his management." This assurance is repeated during the quadripartite meeting with the general and medical directors, the division head and the coach: "We want to help you improve your leadership and management, to consolidate your leadership role. These goals are specified in the coaching contract."

The coaching is successful and the head physician is eager to improve to maintain his position. Coaching goals are approved by management. Despite an improvement in the quality of leadership and management, it is impossible for the coach to meet with the general director, as planned, to present the work accomplished. The relationship between the medical director and the head physician is deteriorating inexorably. The coach attempts several times to schedule an appointment with the director but is unsuccessful. Finally, the division head is demoted because of multiple deficiencies, according to the direction. This pushes this head into a serious personal crisis and to resign.

This vignette highlights many aspects of coaching prescribed by the hierarchy and demonstrates the importance of obtaining all the information before starting coaching. Notably, once the dismissal was announced, the general director explained to the coach that this change did not correspond to the original project. The vignette also demonstrates the need to remain in contact with the management, provide feedback on the evolution of coaching, and stay abreast of any new data. Another aspect concerns power relations, which are common in medical hierarchies. The attitude normally expected from the medical director in such a situation is that she conforms to her initial position, namely, that she strives to support her young collaborator in his difficulty. The vignette, however, demonstrates the opposite, and the care provider is demoted.

This vignette finally underlines one of the essential aspects of the dynamics of implementation of the prescribed coaching: the coach interacts with the medical director, the prescriber, and the beneficiary of the coaching. This relationship is *triangular*, with all its ambiguities and potential for psychological games and manipulation. In the aforementioned case, the director takes the role of the "persecutor", the client the role of the "victim", and the coach (despite himself) the position of the "saviour" (see the dramatic triangle in chapter 8). When there is a hidden conflict between the medical director and the coachee, the coach may be in an uncomfortable position and may be trapped by one or both of the parties, depending on the circumstances. Unintentionally driving the medical director places the coach in a risky situation, which may lead to the cessation of coaching. The only solution for the coach in this case was to efficiently support his client to manage this disguised launch.

The opposite situation may occur: the management unconditionally supports a chief physician who should improve her leadership, management, or behavior. Such unconditional support will probably prevent this leader from questioning herself, becoming aware of her problems, encouraging her to minimize these problems and not to put herself in a position to remedy them.

You are doing well, continue your mission, but change your behavior!

Susan is a young head of a division who has been in her job for two years. The beginning of her activity as a chief was difficult due to her predecessor's failing management: an ineffective organization of the division and a team of inefficient senior physicians, mainly composed of self-centered individualistic persons, who are not much inclined to participate in the reorganization.

Shortly after Susan's arrival, she began the reform of the division organization, with the support of the hospital management. She undertakes this mission with energy and enthusiasm, but with little consultation with her partners involved in organization (e.g., head nurse and nursing team, medical team, heads of departments). This reorganization results in the rapid development of the structure and services (e.g., number of patients treated, types of services, training, quality assurance). Tensions and blockages are observed within the medical and nursing teams, as well as with certain other departments and divisions of the institution. These problems lead the management to propose external coaching for Susan to bring the various stakeholders into phase and pacify the conduct of the development project.

In the initial meeting with the management (general director, HR director [HRD], medical director), the coach is struck by the complimentary manner of presenting the problem: "This head of division is really dynamic, I appreciate him a lot" (GD); "She is a nice colleague whose energy I appreciate, even if she sometimes puts the system under tension by conducting radical reforms" (medical director); "My collaborators like to work with her, she is open and attentive" (HRD).

Coach:	You are thinking of offering a coaching course, whereas it seems to me that you appreciate and support unanimously this division head. What do you expect from this coaching?
General Director:	That's right, but still, I think this young chief would be better off being less impatient and learning to manage change less aggressively.
Medical Director:	I think we need to help this young colleague to better manage stress and to involve the teams in the change process.
HRD:	I also think she could become more mature.
Coach:	Are you waiting for her to improve?
General Director:	That's it, that's what we want.

The meeting with the division head quickly confirms the description of the three directors. She is dynamic, very performance-oriented, but admits being impatient and sometimes putting pressure on her staff. She wholeheartedly accepts the management's proposal to start a coaching.

This vignette shows the negative role that can be played by too much support from the management on the motivation to change a valued head physician. As we often observe, doctors with executive responsibilities need to feel recognized and supported by the hospital management. However, such support does not eliminate the need for an evaluation of the performance and behavior of this collaborator, to correct if necessary, her management and how she leads her projects.

As in other companies, the HRD is frequently involved in initiating coaching in the hospital setting. She is an important player in the strategies to help and support employees with problems. However, she generally has less knowledge of the professional culture of care providers than her colleague the medical director, who is an irreplaceable source of information.

Demand analysis

The demand analysis begins with the person who prescribes the coaching, often part of the hierarchy, to define her analysis of the problem, goals, and expectations. The initial meeting brings together the first elements of the situation: the context, stakes, problems as perceived by the prescriber. This meeting allows the coach to inform the prescriber regarding how he works and possibly highlight aspects of his ethics and deontology, particularly confidentiality. Information is generally incomplete at the first meeting; it is subsequently completed with the beneficiary and sometimes with medical and nursing staffs. Then, it is necessary to integrate this information in the departmental and hospital context.

You have to put order in your division!

The HRD of a large hospital contacts the coach to initiate coaching in a key medical division of the hospital. The first meeting takes place in the presence of the medical director who leads the discussion. She relates the many problems posed by the poor functioning of this division and by its leader. He is a recognized specialist in his clinical field and medical training. Notably, he is described as a mediocre leader of the medical team whose management is described as sometimes "chaotic." Several department heads have reported difficulties with collaborating with this division. In addition, the medical director reports delays in the overall administrative management—closing medical records and statements of medical services—causing financial losses for the hospital and complaints from doctors in the region. The HRD adds that she has met several times with the department head, who would be willing to accept support from a coach.

Meeting the stakeholders of the coaching

The beneficiary of coaching

Once the management request has been registered, it is necessary to contact the beneficiary of coaching to listen to her point of view and assess whether she agrees to engage in such support. This meeting is crucial because it marks the first stage in the construction of the privileged relationship between the coach and the coachee. In hospital settings, this reunion is often mistrustful, especially with a medical staff unaccustomed to accepting outside help. The purpose of this opportunity is to furnish the beneficiary with essential information on coaching, how it works, and the possible benefits. Notably, the medical profession's insufficient knowledge of the coaching approach (at least in Europe), which is often confused with other methods of support.

During this first meeting, the coach has the opportunity to supplement the information received by the management and hear the point of view of the department head and her specific concerns, which often differ significantly from the statements of management.

In a large hospital, the situation may be complex, involving nursing teams and their chiefs, or other medical departments or divisions. Notably, the points of view and the expectations expressed by the various stakeholders (e.g., general director, HRD, medical director, department head, head nurses, etc.) may diverge, especially during a crisis.

A variously appreciated division head

The medical director of a large regional hospital is requesting coaching to improve the functioning of a medical division. For her, the main problem is the weakness of the leadership of the department head.

According to the medical director: "This division includes a team of excellent specialists, but they are unable to work together and collaborate effectively. We are witnessing multiple dysfunctions such as repeated conflicts, complaints from the nursing team, and poor coordination of the work of attendings. For me, the main problem is the division head, who lacks authority. I am rather pessimistic about his future as a chief."

By contrast, according to general manager: "This division is one of the most efficient in the house, particularly if one considers the results of clinical activity, economic management, and teaching activity. Of course, the head of the department has trouble managing his staff, but for the rest, he can be congratulated and must be supported."

The department head complains mainly of medical under-staffing. He recognizes his "lack of grip" wants to improve the functioning of the team and resolve conflicts that disrupt relations between some executives.

This vignette illustrates a common reality in today's hospital: There are parallel systems between the administration, the medical director, and the medical divisions, who often have deficient communication and no shared culture. This reality should lead the coach to start by carefully analyzing all aspects of the situation, to search for unspoken and hidden differences of opinion, to start coaching in good conditions.

The first session with the recipient plays a key role in creating the first link and establishing a climate of partnership based on listening, trust, and interest. Information on the purpose of coaching must be provided in an open fashion. The coach presents himself and describes the fundamental processes of coaching, the respective roles of the coach and the coachee, and the differences between coaching and other forms of help relationships, especially psychotherapy. Discovering the active role of the coachee, particularly in the development of goals and decision-making probably reassures many doctors, worried about revealing themselves in front of the coach and losing power. Coaching an individual who is disinterested or resistant to the process is very difficult to impossible: this scenario is particularly relevant in the medical setting. Thus, a proposal to start with three or four sessions to experiment with coaching in practice will probably make it easier to get started.

The first interview with the beneficiary makes it possible to gather the maximum amount of information on the situation. During this session, the coach has the opportunity to discover her reading of the reality and the problem, her possible difficulties, and if she dares to discuss it, her analysis of the situation, which can vary greatly from that of the hierarchy. This discussion also provides her the opportunity to express requests that have often not been heard by management. This exchange helps outline the general purpose and some objectives of coaching and identifies any fears the beneficiary may have about her bosses or management. The first interview should be planned to meet the coachee for about 60 minutes without interruption, which is not guaranteed with a hospital physician.

First chaotic session

Joy is head physician in the emergency department. In addition to her day-to-day duties, she is responsible for the medical training, the continuing education program for physicians, and several hospital commissions. Her schedule is primarily governed by her clinical activities, which she considers to be priorities, and which she prefers not to delegate. On the days with low activity, she is available for the remainder of her functions; on days of high activity, she runs throughout the day. Her relationships with the senior physician team are sometimes difficult: they blame her for her lack of participation in the management of the department and her remote manner of leading the medical team, which they report causes tensions and multiple conflicts. Coaching is proposed by the medical director, which is reluctantly accepted by Joy.

The coach has an appointment with Joy for the first interview on a busy day. The session is interrupted by many calls on the beeper. After 50 minutes, she leaves the meeting in a rush to treat a patient in cardiac arrest. For the second session, the coach takes the lead by asking her to leave her beeper with her secretary, which he hopes will ensure a quiet session that allows him to finish this part of the coaching process.

This vignette describes the reality of coaching work in the most acute departments of the hospital. In such a context, a working period without disruption is not always possible, like in other work environments. This reality implies minimal adaptation for the coach who learns to operate effectively in such an environment.

Prescribed or requested coaching

The initiation of coaching in the medical setting is the most difficult phase. A key question sets the tone for coaching: is the coaching *prescribed by the management or medical hierarchy* or is it *a request from the beneficiary*? This difference is important to analyze because prescribed coaching is often poorly accepted by the medical profession, as described in chapters 1 and 4. When coaching is requested directly by the head physician for himself, without intervention from the hospital management, the situation is different: in this context, the physician is the applicant, he is motivated and pays for the coach, and he expects a beneficial effect.

Prescribed coaching is difficult to undertake for many reasons:

- In general, a physician with executive functions has difficulty recognizing his problems and weaknesses and thus accepting the help of a third party outside his hierarchy. He sees a coaching proposal as a disavowal, or even a threat, as a result of poor performance. His first reaction is often the resistance or complete rejection of the proposed coaching. This provokes a climate of mistrust and tension in a difficult professional context, for example, leadership failure, personal crises or crises in the department, and conflicts within the teams. For the head physician, he can carry the meaning of failure, non-recognition of his merits, loss of confidence, and autonomy in the direction of the hospital. In addition, the prescribed coaching represents for the beneficiary a true *double bind,*[a] namely, it poses a choice that is not a true choice because it means that "I prescribe you the want to change." Although the beneficiary of the coaching can in principle refuse it, as anyone can who considers this type of support, in reality, he cannot do so without suffering negative consequences, which can include dismissal. When the prescription is binding, the coach should begin with metacommunication work to analyze and disassemble the injunction to the sponsor and the potential recipient, to reach a freely agreed decision (see the following vignettes).
- The poor knowledge of hospital doctors about coaching and its possible benefits in the European area, unlike North America.
- The difficulty of integrating a coaching into the already overbooked schedule of a hospital doctor.
- The sometimes-tense relations between the institutional management and the heads of departments who often feel the measures of improvement by the management as a means of control and a loss of freedom.

The coach must be particularly attentive to these obstacles to take them into account and overcome them, from the first meeting with the beneficiary, before the effective start of coaching. In practice, it is therefore a question of choosing appropriate strategies, and in particular, to follow rigorously the initial steps of coaching, i.e., an analysis of the request; separate meetings with each of the interested parties, the management, and the "beneficiary" of coaching; a subsequent tripartite meeting with all parties; the development of initial work objectives; and preparation of the contract. The coach also needs to mobilize his skills to rapidly establish a relationship of trust with the beneficiary, a key element in the success of the process.

A study conducted in Canada at the University of Toronto in the Departments of Surgery highlights the reluctance of university surgeons to consider the usefulness of coaching as part of their professional development.[2] Fourteen surgeons from several surgical specialties were interviewed several times to determine their attitudes regarding a *performance coaching proposal* aimed at improving their operative abilities. Most participants were ambivalent about the value of coaching as part of continuous surgical training. Three types of reservations were observed: (1) the fear of being considered incompetent by accepting coaching; (2) the fear of a loss of autonomy; and (3) the reluctance to consider improving technical performance on an individual basis. The authors concluded that proposing a coaching to surgeons is a challenge in this professional culture that values competence and autonomy.

Julian accepts a coaching prescribed by the medical director

Julian is a senior physician in a large regional hospital. His boss, who has been in conflict for a long time with the hospital management, is abruptly dismissed. The medical director proposes to Julian that he become the acting department head for 12–15 months, pending the job competition. He conditions this promotion on coaching, which Julian unsuccessfully attempts to refuse, because the medical director indicates that without the coaching there will be no promotion. Thus, Julian accepts this condition reluctantly and without conviction.

The initial meeting with the coach is at first remote: Julian explains from the outset that he is not the applicant for coaching and that this approach was imposed by the medical director and that he is disinterested.

Julian: This department has not been effectively directed by my predecessor. There is a lot of catch-up work to do, especially reviewing the medical organization, relations with the nurses, and supervision of the residents. I do not have time to start a coaching on top of that.

Coach: Before determining if there is any interest in working together, I have a question for you. What do you know about coaching, how it unfolds, and its benefit in the hospital setting?

Julian: I'll be honest, not much. Explain to me what we could do together.

Coach: Okay.

The coach briefly explains some fundamentals of coaching, particularly the roles of the coach and the client.

Julian: I think I am beginning to understand why the medical director insisted on the benefits of coaching.

The atmosphere gradually relaxes, and finally, Julian is interested trying some coaching sessions. He quickly describes his career: high-level training in his specialty, and appointment as a medical attending at 34 years old. Julian has neither participated in the meetings of the management group of the department nor received training in management or team management. Notably, Julian is motivated to become a department head while recognizing that his skills and experience are insufficient for this new position.

The tripartite meeting goes smoothly. Julian and the medical director agree on the general objectives of coaching: developing Julian's leadership and reviewing the management and operation of the department.

This vignette illustrates the initial reluctance of Julian, a young executive who performs well in clinical practice but is inexperienced in management, to accept coaching at the beginning of his term as a department head. Julian embraces the common tendency of senior doctors to position themselves as reference persons, who know better than the others all about the exercise of this profession, including the management of a big department. The explanations of the coach allow the opening of the dialogue and promote the acceptance of the support. The vignette also shows the coach's care in establishing trust with his client at the start of their relationship. Notably, much of coaching work is based on the coach's ability to be the driver of the relational process and interactions with the client. We want to emphasize that the *person of the coach* is his instrument of work. The quality of the coaching relationship is one of the major determinants of the progress and outcome of coaching; a chapter of this book is devoted to this theme (chapter 2).

Notably, the attitude of the nursing staff and non-care providers often contrasts with that of the medical corps because of a different, more open professional culture, which more easily accepts external help. Of these two groups, the nurse professionals have a better knowledge of a coaching's value and accept more easily the proposal from the hierarchy to begin this type of support.

Tripartite (or quadripartite) meeting

The tripartite meeting brings together the prescriber(s) of coaching, the beneficiary, and the coach; it allows the prescriber to describe her reasons for proposing a coaching and her expectations regarding the beneficiary and the coach; express her version of the general purpose of coaching; and where appropriate, set the terms of the coaching (e.g., number of sessions, duration, intermediate steps, evaluations). This meeting enables the beneficiary to express his point of view, expectations, and perception of the proposed support and provides him the opportunity to express his disagreement about coaching and its modalities. The coach presents a short summary of his contacts with the management and the beneficiary and then presents the most important information he has gathered during the interviews with management and the beneficiary. The coach then briefly introduces his proposal on the modalities of coaching; he may add some information on the methods he uses.

The ensuing discussion provides a unique opportunity to align and clarify the stakeholder views in the context of the rationale and goals of coaching, to review opinions and minimize misunderstandings. Ideally, this process involves discussing all the elements of departure: the observations, expectations, divergences of each. This is unfortunately not always possible. For the beneficiary, for example, a department head who often does not benefit from periodic evaluations, this discussion offers an opportunity to receive important information that he may not yet know: complaints from colleagues, reproaches, and expectations of management. Of course, the confidentiality of the exchanges between the coach and the coachee must be guaranteed from the outset. It must be specified and differentiated from the concrete elements of coaching, in relation to the request, which are not confidential and will be transmitted to the prescriber, such as objectives, intermediate assessments, and problems encountered in the hospital.

Everything must be discussed!

Daniel was appointed head of unit in a large hospital to lead a new sector. He was chosen by the nominating committee because of his particularly thorough medical training (two specialist titles and his assertive, enthusiastic personality and interest in management). During the first year of his mandate, he set up the main elements of the organization and operation of the new sector and developed specific training for doctors. However, many collaborators complained about his style of management, a combination of efficiency and pressure. After several complaints, management acted to remedy this situation. A coaching is proposed to Daniel, who accepts it reluctantly. During the initial meeting of the coach with the management, the general director cites numerous examples of recriminations from Daniel's unit personnel and stakeholders from other divisions, complaints confirmed by the medical director. At the end of the meeting, the coach insists on the importance of Daniel receiving all the information that concerns him.

The tripartite meeting takes place without any problem at first: Daniel and the management agree to initiate a coaching. However, the coach must insist that all the grievances collected by the management be transmitted to Daniel, who seems astonished by the importance of the complaints about his leadership but agrees that he wants to remedy these as soon as possible. At the beginning of the first coaching meeting, he returns to the tripartite meeting and receives the following message:

Daniel: You know, I must tell you that I was unpleasantly surprised, to say the least shocked, by what the general manager said about me. I have met him several times this year, and I have never received such messages.

Coach: I understand that you're touched, it's difficult to hear such things. What do you want to do with that, what do you need to move forward in this situation?

Daniel: In fact, I admit that I was touched, that it touched me to hear such things, because I devote a lot of time and energy to this reorganization project. I am a little disappointed, but I have no choice, I think we have to do something.

Coach: That's fine. What could be the first step in initiating this change?

Daniel: In my opinion, the first step is complete because I am now aware of my situation and the necessity to improve my management of and relationships with my colleagues.

Coach: Well done, that's good, even if it's not easy. Do you agree to prepare goals for change?

Daniel: Yes, absolutely, it is necessary, and I feel ready.

This tripartite meeting allowed Daniel to realize the extent of his leadership problems with the colleagues of his unit and with colleagues from other departments. Because of the frankness of the two directors, he received essential information that enabled him to better assess his situation, which prompted him to engage in productive coaching work.

This meeting is particularly important during a prescribed coaching because it allows the coach to start with a framework and objectives shared by all parties and if possible, without unspoken or hidden agendas. It provides the coach the opportunity to show how much he considers *transparency* as an indispensable condition at all stages of his activity. Such clearness is particularly crucial in the context of a prescribed coaching, in which the hierarchical relationships between the management (the prescriber), beneficiary, and coach inevitably disrupt the beginning of coaching. Working transparently will probably induce beneficial changes between the coach and his client from the beginning of the work, especially a relationship of trust.

Last chance coaching

Lauren is head nurse in charge of the surgery department in a small hospital. The hospital director of nursing proposes a coaching to this head nurse who clearly does not give satisfaction for an extended period. The director describes among other things a weak leadership, multiple conflicts in the nursing team, and problems in the quality of care. Several evaluations have highlighted these shortcomings, but Lauren has not responded by adjusting her behavior. The coach first meets the head nurse and then some of the team members. He attends a team meeting and notes Lauren's difficulties in managing her team; tensions are perceptible between several senior nurses.

After the tripartite meeting with the hospital nursing director, Lauren, and the coach, the shared work objectives are set: strengthen her leadership and improve her team leadership and conflict management, with indicators to assess the progress. A contract is established. Three months later, after eight individual coaching sessions, the coach and Lauren are summoned before the management committee for the first assessment. Despite a slight increase in the coaching indicators, the management committee interrupts the coaching and removes Lauren from her position. Notably, this eventuality had been evoked by the coach during the initial interview but excluded by the prescribers.

Table 5.4 Assessment grid before starting a coaching

- Is the coachee likely to benefit from coaching based on the initial assessment of the coach (and the hierarchy)? How is coaching the best answer to the problem? Could another approach be indicated, for example, psychological or psychiatric support for a leader in crisis or suffering from serious burnout?
- Is the coachee free to refuse the support, and did he understand the proposal of the management and the information given by the coach? What is the level of approval of the management proposal?
- Are management expectations realistic and achievable? Is it necessary to clarify the description of the situation of the coachee and her relations with the management before starting the coaching?
- Is this coaching accompanying an undeclared dismissal (Chapter 6)?
- Did the beneficiary receive all the information at the source of the management proposal, for example, leadership failure, complaints from within or outside the department, and breaches?
- Does the coach have all the skills and experience necessary to provide this support? Does he have sufficient knowledge of the hospital environment to intervene? Is the coach ready to ask for supervision by another sufficiently experienced coach if necessary?
- Is the coach motivated, and does he want to lead this support?
- Does the coach have any conflicts of interest? If so, is this an obstacle to his approach?

This vignette illustrates the difficulty of having all the information at the beginning of coaching, especially about the finality of coaching. The possibility of being fired at the end of coaching ("last chance coaching") was hidden in Lauren's situation, a consequence unacceptable for both the coach and the beneficiary. Notably, the coach, responsible for the conduct of coaching (e.g., process management), can never guarantee the results of the coaching (i.e., the achievement of goals).

The tripartite meeting allows the prescriber, beneficiary, and coach to decide whether to conduct a coaching and to define the first steps of implementation. For the coach, multiple elements must be assessed before agreeing to start a coaching. An evaluation grid can be used for this purpose (Table 5.4).

I'm hiding the truth!

The medical director of a hospital proposes that the coach lead an intervention in a key department of the hospital. According to the medical director, this department has multiple dysfunctions—conflicts in the medical team, repeated complaints from the nursing team, difficulty collaborating with other departments—mainly due to the failure of the leadership of the chief. The department head has held this position for five years, after the departure of her predecessor who was appointed to a university hospital center. The director thinks that a prescribed coaching for this department head would improve the situation. The HRD thinks that this department head is not effectively leading the medical team and should be replaced by her substitute, a senior physician with an authoritarian leadership style.

The department head reports that the insufficient staffing of senior physicians exhausts the medical team; she then mentions her difficulty in managing the conflicts and problems of this team: "I probably lack authority, I do not like fighting; What can I do to encourage my colleagues to behave like adults? In addition, I do not get along with my substitute, often opposed to my views and who complicates the conduct of the team."

The coach insists that the hospital management provides the department head with all her observations and expectations, which is accepted. The tripartite interview allows the department head to discover that she has not been informed of all the complaints made against her and her team. She is surprised to realize that her stepping aside to be replaced by her more authoritarian substitute was mentioned. This situation is difficult for her, and she partly challenges the allegations against her but maintains her decision to accept a coaching. "I thought it out, I feel that I need to be accompanied to change the way the medical team works; today I feel that it's time to change direction style."

Finally, the management and department head agree on the general goals of coaching and decide that a first evaluation of the work will be conducted after four months.

This vignette illustrates the importance of starting coaching in a clear framework, recognized by all parties. It emphasizes the attention that the coach must bring to the observable elements and the possible hidden or unrevealed expectations from the outset, for example, a project of setting in step, dismissal, or mutation.

Goals and objectives

The goals and objectives of coaching are usually developed by the beneficiary and the coach when setting up the process. In a situation of prescribed coaching, the situation is more complicated than in non-prescribed coaching because it is necessary to determine general goals that are acceptable to both the management (the prescriber) and the coachee. In the case of expressed or unexpressed disagreement, common in the hospital context, the simplest procedure is to negotiate a list of two or three general goals acceptable to both parties, starting with the demands of management (e.g., improve the functioning of the senior physicians' team, review the medical organization of the service) and of the coachee (e.g., resolve conflicts within the medical team, review the delegation of tasks, and so on). Operational objectives will then be developed with the coachee and addressed to the management for approval or discussion.

Let me prove myself!

A young division head without management experience is prescribed a coaching by the medical director at the beginning of her activity. The goal of the director is simple, to provide "an external coaching to begin the mission of the head of division, especially to lead the medical team, composed of physicians older than the new leader." The division head is opposed to this proposal but does not dare to challenge it. He attempts to drown the fish and delay coaching for at least six months, to discover the new division herself and establish the first steps of her management. The medical director agrees to postpone the start of coaching for two months.

The division head sits reluctantly; she proposes a review of all the specifications of the senior physicians as the initial goal of coaching. A subsequent discussion makes it possible to agree to and retain two main work goals: review the specifications of senior doctors and chief residents, including the tasks delegated by the division head, have the coach accompany and support her in the meetings of the medical team, to work on the process of delegation of tasks. An assessment will be made at the end of this period to evaluate her satisfaction about the support. In the second step, the department head, supported by the coach, develops a division project with the senior physicians and head nurses that describe the roles and tasks of each executive.

In this case, the tripartite meeting resulted in common ground between the medical director and division head. The remainder of the coaching was easy.

Steps to the contract

When the coach receives a request for coaching, his initial work, in the hospital as in other business, comprises following a general process that leads from the initial request to the decision to provide support, evidenced by a contract of employment. In our experience in the hospital setting the bene-ficiary(ies) is usually a manager or group of executives with the following aims:

- remedy failing leadership;
- accompany a manager in crisis or suffering from undetected burnout;
- improve the functioning of a team;
- remedy a crisis of a team
- end repeated conflicts in a team or between teams;
- improve the organization of a department or division (management coaching); and
- provide support in a major transition (e.g., merger, major reorganization).

This request is usually from the HRD or the medical director, more rarely from the direct hierarchy (department head, head of division), and even more rarely from the person concerned. The demands of life coaching are generally discussed with the coach outside the hospital context.

Once the initial discussions are complete and the decision on coaching is made, a contract must be established. This step is usually negotiated with the HRD and does not differ from that in other types of businesses.

In special situations, where the beginning of coaching takes place in a difficult context (e.g., poor leadership, repeated conflicts, threatened department head), it is useful to provide, from the outset, repeated intermediate reports that follow the evolution of the coaching. This allows an exchange of information with the management, where the coach and coachee report the work completed and inform the prescriber(s) of the perspective of the problem.

Conclusion

At the hospital, the request for coaching is usually from the senior management (general director, medical or nursing director) or HR and more rarely from the beneficiary (the department or division head). Collaborating with the medical director, often the prescriber of the coaching, implies adapted strategies to avoid insufficient transparency or decline of the coaching. In addition, confidentiality must be guaranteed to the coachee because the work is within a triangular relationship between the beneficiary, medical director (the applicant), and coach. Although prescribed coaching ("imposed") is common, private coaching, directly requested by the recipient, is less frequent. Differences in work culture and hospital environment have significant consequences for coaching. Basic knowledge of the operation of the hospital and the organization of the health care providers is necessary to efficiently lead the coaching process.

Note

a A *double bind* is a dilemma in communication in which two or more conflicting messages are given to a person or a group, with one negating the other. Such a dilemma induces misunderstanding and stress.

Bibliography

1 Taylor N, Clay-Williams R, Hogden E, Braithwaite J, Groene O. High performing hospitals: a qualitative systematic review of associated factors and practical strategies for improvement. *BMC Health Serv Res* 2015;15:244.

2 Mutabdzic D, Mylopoulos M, Murnaghan ML, *et al.* Coaching surgeons: is culture limiting our ability to improve? *Ann Surg* 2015;262(2):213–216.

6 Executive coaching for leadership

René Chioléro

Introduction

Many images are attached to a leader, who is thus described as, for example, a fantastic organizer, a visionary leader who always dreams of an inaccessible future; an authoritarian but effective leader; Jupiterian; weak; non-existent; charismatic or manipulator. The same representations are expressed in the hospital, both in the medical and nursing hierarchies.

The topic of leadership is particularly sensitive in the context of health care provider teams. Nurses receive targeted training at each stage of advancement in their careers, but this is often not the case for physicians. In public hospitals, the focus is primarily on clinical medical skills, and in university hospitals, the focus is on academic performance. By contrast, managerial skills are often neglected because they are considered a low priority. The outstanding qualities of hospital leaders are therefore mainly linked to their direct professional competences (e.g., clinical, teaching and research skills, radiance, personal qualities) and not on their performance as managers and team leaders. This results in difficulty to organize their department or to lead their team; the latter impairs team cohesion and slows the sharing of tasks and development of a common culture. The consequences are serious: no shared vision, unequal distribution of tasks, inadequate evaluation system for physicians, inefficient management of conflicts, altered quality of care and medical activities. The weakness of leadership leads the hospital management to take measures, such as soliciting coaching.

The purpose of this chapter is to present important aspects of executive coaching at a hospital, especially leadership coaching. Different forms of leadership failure are analyzed.

Fundamental processes and models

Leadership refers to the ability of the manager to ensure the functioning of the company, adaptation to changes in the environment, achievement of objectives, team management, and motivation of employees. Notably, the executive and leadership requirements have been increasing progressively in the last

DOI: 10.4324/9781003291831-9

three decades, in parallel with the progressive development of hospital systems. The constant evolution of the economy, organization of businesses, rapid changes in the environment, complexity, volatility, and uncertainty of today's world require particularly broad skills and capacities to lead. The same is true in the medical enterprise, where numerous competences and abilities are expected from the executive physician.[1]

A distinction between management and leadership has gradually occurred. Kotter stresses the need for all large companies to cover both management and leadership roles.[2]

Different models and theories of leadership have been developed for over 50 years, depending on the strategies used by leaders for governance and employee leadership, for example, authoritarian or autocratic, situational, charismatic, shared, transactional, transformational and spiritual, and "laissez-faire" (hands-off) leadership. For the hospital coach, it is preferable not to be attached too much to these models and to adopt an open approach to assist the leader in his progression toward effective leadership, which satisfies himself and his collaborators. Shared leadership is indeed the preferred model in medicine, whereas authoritarian leadership is often poorly endured by health care teams.[3]

To develop shared leadership

Thomas has been running a medical division in a regional hospital for over 15 years. During this time, he creates a state-of-the-art modern division, with the help of a small team of motivated colleagues, recognized throughout the region. Although he demonstrates high capabilities in the field of medical development, this is less the case in team management. The attendings and chief residents complain of tensions that prevail in the medical team, which suffers from a permanent power struggle between some senior doctors. Following repeated complaints from the nurse chief and other medical division heads, a coaching is proposed by the medical director; this is accepted by Thomas, who seems reassured by this offer.

He complains bitterly of the absence of shared values and selfishness of some of his executives:

Thomas: How can I continue the development of the division while some executives are dragging their feet and put energy into fighting rather than helping me build the unit?

Coach: How did you establish the governance of the division with them, especially the definition of the roles of the division

	head and executive, the development of a common vision, and the shared values and priorities in development?
Thomas:	No, this remained unclear; I must admit that I did not have the time to manage it and that it will be a day to do it.
Coach:	Can you specify your expectations of this coaching? What do you want to achieve in our work?
Thomas:	I would like to be able to successfully lead the team of senior physicians to promote the development of the division.
Coach:	Ideally, if we had a magic wand, what changes would you see occurring in your executives?
Thomas:	I'm just waiting for them to become more mature, stop fighting, and develop a little bit of goodwill for their colleagues. Second, I would like to see them all actively interested in their work, as our projects progress.
Coach:	Have you ever talked about these concerns with them?
Thomas:	Yes, but always in a fragmented, superficial way.
Coach:	I interviewed your attendings; they appreciate you and emphasize your great commitment.
Thomas:	Yes, but that is insufficient to bring order and lead them to share a common vision.
Coach:	Would you agree to work in a coaching with them in a second time, once the individual coaching is over?
Thomas:	Certainly, for me, this is an essential step, and I would be happy to finally be able to lead a team with strong cohesion.

This vignette shows the aspiration of this department manager to share his vision with his team and who suffers from the misunderstanding of his executives. He realized the weakness of his leadership, which he wants to strengthen.

In the executive coaching work, we often use a bipolar model, which offers the choice between two opposing points of view, which are expressed within the six fields of leadership. This sensitizes the leader and questions his management strategies by focusing on the following topics:

- *Tasks* or *people*
- *Flexibility* versus *dogmatism*
- *Centralization* of leadership versus *sharing and delegation*
- *Incentives and rewards* versus *criticism and punishment*
- Importance of the *objective* in relation to *available resources*
- *Structured leadership* where processes are fixed, versus *organic leadership*, in which processes are adaptable (not fixed).[4]

This model offers the chief a tool for a critical analysis of leadership style and to broaden the leader's consciousness, in order to open his mind to the main aspects of leadership, for example, to develop a task without neglecting the needs of others, eliminate an unproductive dogmatism, and realize the demotivating role of punishment.

Many companies continue to operate in the context of traditional leadership, namely, directive or transactional, which involves little to no sharing of leadership. In the directive mode, the leader makes all the important decisions, without any real consultation. He provides his vision to his collaborators and indicates most of the actions to take. The transactional style is characterized by the use of incentives (e.g., compliments, positive feedback, rewards) and means of correction (e.g., remarks, negative feedback, evaluation, punishment) to modify the behavior of the collaborators. This case is observed in many hospital departments in which employees report receiving negative remarks often and compliments or congratulations rarely. These traditional driving systems are associated with a tendency of employees to exhibit passivity and a low level of satisfaction.[3]

I am the boss!

In this university hospital, the surgical operating program is finalized by an attending of anesthesiology and the head instrumentalist nurse. That day, it was impossible to open an additional operating room because of a lack of staff, despite the insistence of a professor of surgery. Three attendings of anesthesiology were summoned by the head of department, a professor of orthopedics.

Head of Department: I have learned that you have refused to open an additional operating room today for my colleague Professor X. I find that unacceptable!

Attending 1: It was impossible to do otherwise, considering the surgical emergencies of that day: we had to organize an urgent organ procurement for a patient from neurosurgery.

Head of Department: This is not an excuse; you are paid to find solutions.

Attending 2: Some days, this is not possible. Today, my colleague could not help but refuse this request ...

Head of Department: I do not want to know; do it better next time!

This vignette reflects a true story, which occurred approximately 15 years ago. In this case, the three attendings were disappointed and demotivated because of the actions of the office of the department head. Since then, the style of management in medical departments has evolved, but some authoritarian-type leaders remain, ready to impose their views in all circumstances.

The more actual *models of leadership* are the *shared or participative* type. This is the case of the *transformational system*, which aims to strengthen the links between a leader and her collaborators, to develop a shared vision and motivate them to improve their performance. This type promotes intellectual stimulation and professional and personal development of employees, and enhances cooperation and synergy within teams. In hospitals, the satisfaction, motivation, and performance of health care teams and the satisfaction of physicians in training are improved by this type of leadership.[4]

Team-leading is one of the major challenges that must be overcome by health care executives. It includes a complex set of processes and tasks that condition the work in groups, namely communication, cooperation, trust, learning, and sharing. This conduct represents a difficult task for many department heads, more interested in their medical practice than in the difficulties of team management.

To lead my colleagues is not easy!

Harry, a department head at a regional hospital, is struggling to manage his medical team. The nursing team complains of the lack of communication between some of the senior physicians who disrupt nursing work and prevent the development of care plans; the secretaries report their difficulties in organizing the consultation schedule. Harry is nevertheless ambitious: he wants to develop his department, extend the services, improve the quality, and develop the research. However, this does not occur as he would like: he cannot obtain the support of some senior doctors for his vision and management system. The team is divided into two opposing clans, which complicates the management of the department and the organization of care. The distribution of tasks and the organization of the medical call plan often pose difficult problems related to the lack of will to cooperate. After several discussions with the medical director, he offers Harry a coaching. Harry is initially reluctant to agree to coaching. He says he is afraid of wasting time on unproductive activities and questionable efficiency. The determination of the medical director prevails, and finally, Harry accepts the offer.

Subsequently, Harry is motivated and involved with conviction in the process.

After six individual coaching sessions, which allow the coach to readjust the attitude and positioning of Harry and the conduct of some fundamental team processes (e.g., communication, distribution and follow-up of tasks, team meetings), a team coaching is started. The general goals are to promote participatory leadership, improve communication and conflict management, and revise the organization of work and distribution of tasks.

This manager is a hard worker, whose clinical excellence is recognized by hospital management. Leading his team is another matter he does not control. His lack of self-confidence and his fleeting attitude in conflict management led to serious dysfunctions. Long-term coaching (more than 12 months) was required to improve leadership, manage conflict, and establish a participatory management system accepted by the senior physicians.

Competences and abilities

Some of the most import necessary competencies and abilities for leadership activities are the following:

- self-confidence and self-esteem and the ability to be unpopular and tolerate loneliness;
- ability to communicate and build relationships with others;
- ability to trust;
- ability to delegate and ask for help;
- ability to manage conflicts;
- ability to show empathy and, in a holistic vision of management, compassion;
- ability to acknowledge the value of collaborators, and their work;
- humility, the ability to challenge oneself, to recognize one's difficulties and mistakes; and
- self-knowledge, the ability to self-criticize, and the ability to take care of oneself.

This non-exhaustive list constitutes a real personal challenge and generally requires prolonged learning. As department head, it took me years of learning to gradually broaden my managerial and human experiences, based on my successes and mistakes. Support from a colleague who is more qualified may help an inexperienced head physician improve her leadership skills, but this is rather uncommon in the medical field. Support from a coach is justified if the ability of the leader is insufficient to ensure the operation of the department and manage crises, but this is usually a late decision. If she does not correct this disability, a prolonged failure of leadership can lead her to lose her position, especially if she oversees a key service in the hospital (e.g., intensive care unit, emergency department, operating room).

Self-confidence and self-esteem are essential qualities of leaders. When a manager at the beginning of his career is chosen to lead his former colleagues, he sometimes has to impose measures against their will and make unpopular decisions. If he lacks self-confidence, this is quickly perceived by staff and colleagues and may prevent the establishment of effective shared leadership and induce team dysfunction.

I would like to become a recognized chef

Max has been a senior doctor for several years at an institution for elderly patients. A new CEO is appointed with whom he quickly develops difficult relationships. His contacts with the head nurse and particularly authoritarian and result in conflicts. He is summoned several times to the management of the hospital, who repeatedly criticizes him for his sometimes bad communication with the nursing team and patients' families, his lack of a clear line of treatment and consultation with his colleagues, and delays in closing the files and billing.

Max asks for a coaching whose general aim is to improve his interactions with the management and the nurse head. His initial goal is to strengthen his self-confidence and authority at the hospital.

Coach: What's bothering you most about your professional work?

Max: I lack confidence in my professional life and everyday life.

Coach: Can you clarify what you mean by lack of confidence and give examples so that I can better understand what you mean by that?

Max: For example, I am afraid of my director. I am particularly afraid of face-to-face sessions with him, during which I feel dominated, sometimes even crushed, and the desire to flee. I also fear the remonstrances of the nurse head, a determined, authoritarian woman.

Coach: And in your family life?

Max: (silence) ... hum, It's not satisfactory either. I did not get along with my wife anymore, and we separated a year ago. When I meet my three sons, it's complicated because they do not like my new girlfriend.

> *Coach:* I understand better now your project to strengthen your self-confidence.
>
> *Max:* That's exactly it. I would love to learn confidence, especially in my professional life, but not only.

This vignette illustrates the difficult situation of a chief physician, whose leadership is weak and who suffers from markedly insufficient self-esteem. This prevents him from taking his place as a leader, positioning himself in front of the director and the nurse head, and solving his family problems. The coaching initially focused on leadership and then evolved into extended life coaching. The goals were focused on three areas: (1) reinforce his self-confidence so that he becomes able to lead at work and at home. This first area required in-depth work on resources, skills, abilities, and personal successes (2) to learn to develop trust in others at work and at home, including the practical aspects. These first two goals should allow Max to consider finding a substitute physician to replace him and to be able to choose him and (3) develop the ability to take care of himself, for example, work–life–private-life balance, lifestyle, sports practice, and nutrition. The duration of the first coaching period was approximately two years. This was complemented by two short periods of support to achieve new objectives that subsequently emerged.

Conversely, *overconfidence*, including an invading narcissistic personality, is common in the academic medical world, which values success, visibility, and rivalry, often to the detriment of social relationships and humanism. Such a management style promotes a dysfunctional medical staff and conflicts with the nursing team, chiefs of other departments, and sometimes patients and their families. For the executive (and his coach), finding a good balance, with optimum self-confidence and a just humility allowing the necessary adaptations, is one of the most important challenges of leadership coaching.

It's up to the others to follow me!

Henry runs a surgical department in a university hospital. He is a self-confident surgeon, internationally known leader in his field of excellence, often invited to give lectures in medical congresses, and the president of a European medical society. He has established a reputed research laboratory of 18 people with many international honors. Notably, his interactions with his team are difficult: his authoritarian leadership style is little appreciated by his attendings, whom he belittles regularly. Many of them reported his authoritarian and harsh behavior and insensitivity to the medical director. Henry's chief residents and doctors in training fear him and report that he disrespects regulations, particularly the limitation of working hours.

A situation occurs where surgery leads to complications, the family asks for explanations, and the relationships are tense. A complaint is reported to the medical director, who intervenes to reassure and calm the family. Once the crisis is over, the medical director proposes a coaching to Henry, to improve his leadership and professional interactions and reduce his collaborators' reports of his inappropriate behavior.

During the tripartite interview, the medical director explains some recent elements that relate to Henry's inadequate method of communicating and repeats his proposal to offer him a coaching. Henry, from the outset, says, "I do not see the interest in this approach. I consider it a waste of time, even devaluing. I think that a department head must be able to manage it without the help of a nanny ..."

At the insistence of the medical director, he finally accepted a meeting with the coach.

The session is rather cordial, but Henry remains inflexible in his refusal to undertake a coaching.

Henry: My division functions more or less because I impose my management system and they all have to obey.

Coach: Do you see opportunities to improve its functioning?

Henry: Maybe with the nursing team, but I do not have time to manage it now.

Coach: What satisfaction do you get from your job as a boss?

Henry: It depends on the moments: I like to lead; I always wanted to do that. But I must admit that I often feel that no one really supports me.

Coach: Do you want to work on this aspect of your business? The medical director thinks that could be productive.

Henry: The academic medical world is a daily struggle where the best wins while the others become subordinates and must align. I do not see the point of starting a coaching, it's not the moment; I do not have the time. My presidency of European society takes a lot of time. But later, maybe ...

Coach: So, it's not the right moment?

Henry: Absolutely, it's no, despite the insistence of the medical director.

Difficult decisions

Some difficult decisions present a daunting challenge for a little-affirmed leader: how to decide on priorities, to follow the advice of some of his executives but not others, to finalize the appointment of senior physicians and academic promotions, and so forth. The chief must constantly maintain his ability to reason at a high level and consider many factors in a changing and sometimes hectic environment. It is important to emphasize the emotional and sensitive dimension of some decisions; working exclusively in a logical and Cartesian system does not enable a team to adhere to a shared vision or establish a participative system worthy of its name. Sharing inevitably involves exchanges that include emotional factors of all types. Shared pleasure amplifies energy and motivates team members. Namely, coaching provides an opportunity for the leader to explore and expand decision-making processes in his team while being aware of his emotional responses and ability to share.

I have adopted a participative leadership

Natalie, head of department at a university hospital, accepts a coaching proposed by the medical director to improve the functioning of her team. It was agreed to start with individual coaching. Natalie's complaints are mainly focused on her difficulty in delegating tasks to certain attendings, obtaining compliance with patient care protocols, and sometimes providing medical supervision of in-training physicians during on-call hours. Natalie says she wants to establish a system of participatory medical governance, but the analysis of the reality shows something else.

Coach: I suggest that we explore your way of doing things, particularly how you circulate the information among your collaborators, make decisions, and regulate the "incivilities" with respect to the delegation and the protocols. Let's start with the flow of information, how are you doing on the ground?

Natalie: I provide the main information during the weekly meeting of executives. I must admit that very often I first inform the two attendings that I feel closest to.

Coach: And how do others react?

Natalie: They often complain about being informed late.

Coach: And for incivilities?

Natalie: I gave up discussing them directly with those responsible because I'm wasting my time. I send them an e-mail with a

> copy to all their colleagues, so that everyone knows who does not respect the rules of operation.
>
> *Coach:*   And for decisions or rather the decision-making process: how do you practice decision-making?
>
> *Natalie:*   I make the decisions after informing the attendings and explaining my position.
>
> *Coach:*   Do you think it's a shared decision-making system?
>
> *Natalie:*   Maybe not completely, but I'm their boss?
>
> Natalie decides to include the following elements in her work objectives: how to inform, how to enforce the rules of operation, and how to make shared decisions with her team. She says she wants to establish a participatory system. She begins to realize that achieving this goal is about working with colleagues and integrating their points of view.

This leader believes that she is practicing participative leadership; however, she does the opposite. It should be noted that the coach seems also drawn into a more directive attitude, mirroring the coachee. This typical parallel process occurs unconsciously in the dyad of coach and coachee. One month later, during a supervision session, the coach realizes this phenomenon, which helps him in the subsequent sessions. Many department heads claim to be in favor of a participatory system, but the examination of the practice sometimes shows the opposite: the theory (the speech of the head of department) is different from reality (that the coach can observe on the ground). During the initial phases of coaching, the coach begins to observe the system in place and type of leadership; this allows him to support the head of department to implement any changes (with or without the participation of attendings).

Leading a department

Appropriate leadership is one of the key elements that determine the effectiveness of the management and operation of a department. This directly affects the quality of care, dynamics of medical teams, care provider satisfaction, interdisciplinary relationships, and quality of training.[3] To exercise effective leadership, which motivates the health care teams, implies the acquisition of a broad pallet of specific competences.

The organization of medical and nursing systems must consider the basic characteristics of medical activity, care, training, and research in large hospitals. In practice, an effective system must be developed for the management of the unit in all its aspects, which mainly include the following:

- Clinical activities to ensure the quality of services and patient care; the operation of the department 24 hours a day; quality assurance management.
- Education of doctors to ensure good training conditions and the quality and safety of clinical work.
- Leading medical teams and the appointment of doctors.
- Interactions with medical teams of the other specialties: a growing activity due to the interdisciplinary nature of current medical practice.
- Provide effective interactions with nursing teams.
- Academic activities in the fields of education, training, and research, a large workload in university hospitals.
- Management of relations with patients and families.
- Strengthening of patients' rights, with its parallel increase of lawsuits.
- Manage the administrative tasks and ever-increasing weight of the hospital administration.

This list is a summary of the many tasks that chiefs and their executives must perform to succeed in their mission. Thus, we are not surprised that the coaching activity in the domain of leadership is constantly increasing in the contemporary hospital.

A new department head

The medical director calls Danny, the newly appointed ad interim head of the Internal Medicine department, after the prolonged illness and resignation of his predecessor. Danny, 41 years old, has been a senior physician for two years. Until now, he was responsible for supervising doctors in training and handling reports from dissatisfied patients and their families. He has never managed a department or a medical division and admits that he has received no training in management, having preferred to train in current fields of his specialty. To assess his experience in management, the medical director asks him to prepare a draft of his specifications and a short draft of the department project, which he is asked to finalize with his colleagues. Danny is quickly overwhelmed: in addition to his clinical work, his teaching, and his activities in the national society, he must now devote a large part of his time to management, billing private patients, and participation in the meetings of the Department and College of Physicians, as well as many other time-consuming thinks. He relies on his secretary, who knows some essential elements of the administrative management of the department. Two months after taking up his new duties, he reports to the medical director that he is overwhelmed by his management tasks. The director then offers coaching to improve the organization of work, the establishment of priorities, and the preparation of the department project.

Until recently, many hospital's medical heads were selected principally on their medical and academic competences and received no training in management and team-leading. However, strong evidence has emerged that the acquisition of purely medical skills up to the level of expert is no longer sufficient to effectively lead a medical unit. This problem is particularly acute in European university hospitals, where the tradition of a single leader, responsible for clinical practice, teaching, and research, has been preserved. In Switzerland, in the last ten years, the inability to run a hospital unit has led several heads of departments and professors to be fired. Such situation has led large hospitals to introduce sequential training programs for young medical professionals, which should gradually remedy this situation.

In an American study (United States), ten heads of academic departments of internal medicine were questioned about the competencies they considered essential to successfully fulfill their mission.[5] The results highlight the following skills: the ability to develop a common vision, communicate effectively, manage change, develop systemic thinking, demonstrate emotional intelligence, take care of oneself and pursue personal development, build efficient teams, and effectively manage the department. These leaders underline the importance of *emotional intelligence*, which they considered a key ability for effective leadership.

Emotional intelligence, an essential ability

Emotional intelligence (EI) includes a broad range of personal and social capacities and competences concerning self-awareness and awareness of others (social intelligence) and self-management, including behavior management, emotional management, and interpersonal interactions.[4,6] This type of intelligence is composed of measurable abilities and skills, defined by the emotional quotient (EQ); they are quite different from those of the usual cognitive intelligence, defined by the intelligence quotient (IQ). EQ includes a set of skills and abilities that have developed in parallel with the evolution of human societies. Extensive research has shown that the level of EI of leaders influences not only the productivity, performance, and profits of the company but also the satisfaction and personal development of employees.[7] A survey of 110 senior managers showed a strong relationship between the type of leadership (measured with a questionnaire) and the level of overall EI (also measured by a questionnaire).[6] Leaders who demonstrated transformational behaviors (supporting the needs and motivations of their employees, motivating them to exceed goals and developing themselves) had a higher level of EI than those who used a transactional mode or "laisser-faire." Positive leadership outcomes such as extra effort, greater efficiency, and greater satisfaction were all positively correlated with the overall level of EI, as well as with all of its components. By contrast, there was a strong negative correlation between "laissez-faire" leadership and the leader's level of overall EI.

A new chef eager to broaden his social intelligence

Daniel is a young leader appointed two years ago to a hospital division previously directed by a doctor at the end of her career. He inherited an inactive division that was thus threatened with elimination. Daniel works enthusiastically, but his insufficient experience and his impatience play tricks on him. Tensions emerge with the nursing team, and families have reported his incompetence. A coaching is instituted at his request, supported by the medical director. The first three coaching sessions are assigned to the first work objective: a well-organized leader who can manage his priorities. The second objective is achieved in a team coaching with the medical attendings, which aimed to reorganize the department conduct by introducing a system of participatory management and delegation of tasks. The third goal is a personal goal for Daniel and focuses on human relationships: he aims to be able to have a more balanced exchange with his colleagues, starting with the young in-training doctors.

Daniel: The in-training residents are not fully satisfied. I used the last evaluations for them to give me an assessment. They reported that they have little contact with me, and I feel that I am a little rough with them. I want to do something to improve myself.

Coach: Does this only apply to these young doctors?

Daniel: Actually, I do not really know, but I imagine that it could also affect other collaborators of the division. I had previous conflicts with the chief nurse, but today it's settled.

Coach: How do you feel about this situation and these tensions? What are your feelings and emotions, and how do you perceive them?

Daniel: I try to have as few emotions as possible; I think I've been blocking them forever.

Coach: Have you ever heard of social or emotional intelligence?

> *Daniel:* I have a vague idea of what that means; I recently attended a half-day postgraduate training on the topic of personal development.
>
> *Coach:* How about working on the perception and management of emotions in the context of the meetings of the medical team?

The theme of EI among medical leaders is fashionable in the United States and supported in the literature. Recent work has suggested that EI decreases throughout medical studies, as if exposure to the clinic and the medical world reinforces the rationalism and cynicism of doctors in training.[8] This finding is particularly unfortunate because EI and the empathy of care providers are among the most appreciated qualities by patients. They both contribute to improving the effectiveness of care and preventing exhaustion and burnout in care providers and are associated with success in academic careers.[9] Studies have demonstrated that it is possible to increase the level of EI in a sustainable manner among doctors, by using simple means[10,11]: a training limited to a four-session group workshop, each two and half hours long, produced positive effects on different components of EI that persisted six months later.[10] Coaching also aims to sensitize leaders to the importance of EI and work with them to significantly improve their abilities and skills in this field.

I cannot stand my substitute

Julian runs the laboratory of a large hospital. He is a top scientist, very active in all areas of the hospital laboratory. An indefatigable worker, he is considered to be a particularly demanding man, feared by most of his collaborators. Several reports about him have been received by the general director. After informing Julian of this situation three times, the director offers him a coaching. During the tripartite meeting (Julian, the director, and the coach), Julian recognizes that he is a chief who stresses his colleagues. He agrees to start the coaching. After the first session, his general aim is "to improve my relationships with my colleagues, as well as the functioning and dynamics of the medical team." It is decided to start with individual coaching and eventually to continue with team coaching. The first meeting with the coach highlights some elements of Julian's world map: "We are paid to work, the salary is worth it, I am not interested in the personal problems of my collaborators, just as I do not tell them my life."

Coach:	One of the general goals of our coaching is to improve your relationships with your colleagues. How do you imagine that occurring?
Julian:	Actually, I don't know how to approach this question. Notably, could I meet each of them two or three times per year to perform their assessment and oversee the progress of their roadmap? I imagine that I could also discuss non-professional topics with them: their hobbies, their families?
Coach:	It's a good start, which you could possibly develop and expand. And how do you recognize their successes and failures?
Julian:	I do not take care of their successes, but I help them to correct their failures.
Coach:	And what type of feedback do you give them?
Julian:	When I notice difficulties, I give them instructions to improve their performance.
Coach:	Do you see other strategies to improve your relationship with them?
Julian:	Perhaps in participating more often in discussions and exchanges in the cafeteria.
Coach:	If we imagine a magic wand that can help you achieve your goal, what would be the ideal relationship with your collaborators?
Julian:	Everyone works at their best; I don't need to make negative comments; I share coffee and some meals with them every month.
Coach:	And let's talk about your substitute, Georgia; you told me that you are not satisfied?
Julian:	With her, it's more difficult. Today, I gave her a bad score for her overall performance. Instead of helping me, she makes my job more difficult. Some days, I could even "twist her neck".
Coach:	Has she always been like this?
Sébastien:	No, when I named her as a substitute, she gave me satisfaction. But after one year, it is a disaster.
Coach:	Did you talk to her about it?
Julian:	I made several remarks to express my dissatisfaction. She just gave me an excuse about her family problems; I think

she is getting divorced. She was even in tears, which I do not appreciate. It's often more difficult with women.

Coach: And with a magic wand?

Julian: it would take a real magic wand, because the task is really difficult!

The coach questions Julian about his preferences for his leadership style. For now, he wants to maintain a system in which everyone is responsible for managing his files. He is nevertheless ready to become more involved in social relations within the management group and in general with his collaborators.

Personal and spiritual development

Strengthening personal identity and conducting self-care are on the list of the abilities that any leader should develop. This development applies (more or less) all the senior medical and nursing heads, especially academic executives, whose multiplicity of tasks strongly exposes them to burnout and loss of meaning.[12] The acquisition of such abilities is the real work of personal development in the long run, and essential to the survival and fulfillment of individuals. This broad, multimodal, and prolonged approach includes many elements, e.g.,

- Awareness of the demands and hardship of the medical profession.
- Health maintenance disease prevention: a recent French survey showed that many hospital physicians are negligent in this respect.[13]
- Mental hygiene, time spent on body–mind balance (e.g., mindfulness, yoga, reiki, meditation), and lifestyle (e.g., food, sleep, exercise, sports).
- Moments for oneself and balance between profession and personal life.
- Sharing with colleagues and group work.
- Social relations and friends.
- Activities in specific areas of personal development, for example, speaking groups and development groups.

Personal development has long been considered a private initiative, conducted outside the hospital. It was practiced by only a small number of executives, aware of the importance of this work for both themselves and their employees. In the European medical world, personal development was largely ignored until recently, contrasting with US university hospitals, where leaders wanting to engage in personal development have the opportunity to participate in seminars or ad hoc groups established by the institution.[14,15] Self-development contributes to improving the well-being of care providers, doctors, and nurses and reducing the frequency of burnout and other mental health problems at work. Unfortunately, in most Swiss and European hospitals, individuals interested in such work must search outside the institution.

Developing the spirituality of executives has been recommended by many authors, but it should be noted that there is no universal definition of spirituality. The confusion between spirituality and religion has long complicated the separation between these two fields. Abraham Lincoln, in 1861, in a speech to the United States, alludes to the highest aspects of the human personality and uses the phrase "the better angels of our nature." Today, spirituality is a broad multidimensional concept that encompasses the whole person, her behaviors, and her values.[16] Belief in transcendence is insufficient to define spirituality unless the belief influences the whole person, that is, what she thinks and feels and how she behaves.[16] Spirituality concerns the relationship with oneself (search for authenticity and identity); relationships and interactions with others; the searches for meaning, high goals, hope, and purpose; and the implicit or explicit opening to a higher supra-human authority.[16,17] It constitutes an essential dimension of human existence, which is expressed in at least three fields: beliefs, values, and behaviors and practices.

Beliefs mainly refer to a higher dimension, expressed in forms ranging from secular conceptions of societal attitudes and searches for meaning (e.g., fraternity, equality, solidarity, respect for human rights) to faith in higher powers inaccessible to human beings or religious doctrines. *Values* related to spirituality include altruism, empathy, compassion, generosity, and sharing. The *behaviors and practices* are directly observable, and they concern, for example, the moral rules (which should be high), respect of the other, honesty, and sometimes, the vision of the executives as "role models" (key value in the enterprise).

According to my intensive care experience, spirituality is a major factor in the ability of care providers to accept the painful, emotionally charged situations they encounter in everyday work. Spirituality allows them to accept the suffering of their patients, maintain compassion and empathy despite the constant stress at work, and make sense of seemingly hopeless situations.

Caring for a killer may be difficult

This 32-year-old patient is being treated in an intensive care unit for post-operative care after extensive thorax surgery after a gunshot wound. His story includes being accused of domestic violence: his wife was about to leave him and planned to take their 6-year-old daughter. He then threatened his wife, assaulted her, and shoot her twice in the head. After a police chase and exchange of gunfire, he is wounded and then rushed to the hospital. Emergency surgery is performed to save his life. Upon waking, this patient is agitated and sometimes aggressive. The nursing team is uncomfortable and disturbed by the reports of his history before arriving at the hospital and their moral obligation to provide this patient with care. Many questions are raised: "Why should a patient such as this benefit from the progress of medicine? How can we remain empathetic in this case of violence such that we allow the patient to retain his dignity while taking the necessary distance to provide this support"? The team discussion helps determine the appropriate distance for them to feel comfortable performing their duties in this situation. The legitimacy of the team's questioning is underlined: It is normal to ask questions in such a situation; all the care providers of the team were concerned about this situation. Some fundamentals about care are discussed: can the team imagine not treating this patient, who is a human being? What would justify such an attitude? Respect for the dignity of this so-called "bad" person deeply hurts the ethical rules and the care providers' dignity. The profound values of care providers are also evoked: to do good and the values of compassion and love. Finally, many care providers underline the benefit of being able to share this reflection with the other members of the team to overcome their emotional state, to find positive outcomes, and make sense of the unacceptable. The work is resumed; the atmosphere lightens; the patient makes a rapid, positive evolution; he is transferred four days later to the hospital ward.

Treating terminal patients or during their last days of life is a difficult experience for professionals. It puts them in touch with the human finitude that preoccupies patients and care providers, and which has been a part of fundamental philosophical questions of human existence since the beginning of times.[18] None of this has changed today, despite the tremendous development of medicine and human activities. The experience of death confronts care providers with their limits, failures, and mistakes, and those of medicine. Some specialties are particularly exposed to this reality, such as intensive care medicine, oncology, and palliative care, where there is daily contact with the end of life and the limits of medicine. Care providers are questioned by patients and their relatives: "Why is this happening to me? Why to me, rather than to another? Will I still suffer more? What will occur to me after death? Will my loved ones remember me? Will I miss them? Have you done everything possible? Are you hiding something …?" It is difficult to answer all these questions without including them in a spiritual approach, which makes it possible to give meaning to situations that at first seem meaningless. Notably, most patients with serious chronic diseases, such as cancer, or otherwise at the end of their life wish to receive spiritual support, including from their physicians. Surveys conducted in North America and Europe show that 60%–90% of patients want—but often do not receive—their doctor to fulfill their spiritual needs. This has led some countries to add training in spirituality from the beginning of medical studies. In Switzerland, certain specialties, such as oncology and intensive care medicine, also provide education in this field for in-training residents.

Care providers also require spiritual support to cope with the suffering of their patients; treat them compassionately until their last days; manage their emotions; and make sense of their activities, difficulties, and failures.[19] Teamwork, debriefing of difficult situations, exchanges, and daily sharing offer effective means to maintain teams in good condition and avoid burnout.

A difficult death

A young patient is being transferred into the intensive care department of a university hospital after serious complications related to cardiac surgery in another hospital. The situation seems catastrophic, the cardiac failure is very marked, and the patient requires mechanical circulatory assistance (i.e., to replace the defective heart by an external pump to maintain the circulation).

The family situation is difficult: the patient, aged 38 years, has been a widow for six months; she raises 5-year-old twins, who have been cared for by their grandparents since the cardiac procedure. After five days without significant progress, a last-chance intervention is attempted, but without success. It is now necessary to announce to the family (i.e., twins, grandparents, brothers, and sisters) that their loved one will die in a few hours. The care providers accompany the family to say their last goodbyes to the patient. Everyone suffers, the medical team is aghast and experiences a strong sense of failure and guilt. The patient's parents are angry and overwhelm the care providers: "What occurred is simply unacceptable. See those children who have already lost their dad and are now losing their mom to medical errors." The patient dies, and the atmosphere is heavy.

A debriefing is organized. After a long silence, the senior physician in charge of the patients that day begins by providing some preformulated explanations. The nursing team acknowledges their leader's sadness while stating that sometimes at the end of life, difficult things must be accepted. The attending attempts to argue and finally lets go and recognizes his sadness with tears in his voice. The discussion allows the team to regain serenity: "Thanks to the team, because of sharing, we can rely on each other; we are there to care for others, to allow them often to heal, but not always; this story reminds us of our finitude; it's sometimes painful, but it makes a lot of sense for us ..."

The importance of spiritual development can overcome the sometimes painful and stony course of the leader and give meaning to his work. The recent literature shows the value of being able to give meaning not only to the action but also to the difficulties, crises, and failures of this journey; it is the same for the loneliness of the leader. This allows him to bounce back, learn lessons, and continue his personal development.[20]

For 30 years, a concept called *spiritual leadership* has been used in the corporate world. It aims to apply to the management of the company and teams an approach including a spiritual dimension and influences the management and methods of team-leading.[16,21] The foundations of this model can be summarized as follows:

- Inspire a shared vision between management and employees, combined with a benevolent corporate culture.
- Promote a set of shared values at all levels of the company.
- Promote respect and consideration of employees, justice, social equality, well-being.
- Increase the autonomy of employees. Motivate employees to be active, interested in the progress of the company, to take initiatives and a place in the company.
- Offer everyone the possibility of continuous learning and improvement.

Spiritual leadership seems to be associated with indisputable benefits for managers and employees: increased satisfaction and improved well-being of managers and employees, improved motivation, learning, and reduced risk of burnout.[16,21] Such benefits have also been observed among medical students and hospital physicians.[22,23] This approach is not well known among hospital executives, despite its well-established benefits.

A closer look at medical leadership

This section considers situations in which failed leadership has led to the implementation of coaching. It must be underlined that in my experience, coaching is prescribed in the most serious situations of leadership failure while many other hospital departments function satisfactorily. Does this mean that neither management nor the leadership of the teams can be improved? The answer to this question seems clear, at least based on the available literature and my personal experience: substantial progress can occur in most hospital departments to evolve from a traditional management system to a system that fulfills the highest standards. The following examples have been treated in various chapters of this book (a non-exhaustive list):

- Medical and nursing organization: governance, distribution of roles and tasks.
- Promoting participatory and transformational leadership.
- Improving leadership, particularly of the executive teams.
- Conflict management, management, and prevention of violence in hospitals.
- Management of prolonged crises.
- Prevention of burnout and management of the well-being of care providers: establishment of an institutional system such as that of the Mayo Clinic (chapter 10).

Establishing driving systems adapted to the practice of medicine and care at a hospital has become a priority, guaranteeing not only the quality of the services and the satisfaction of the patients but also the satisfaction, well-being, and development of care providers (chapter 12).

Conclusion

The skills and abilities of medical and nursing leaders play a key role in the functioning of a hospital's care teams and departments and condition the quality of care to patients. Although the nursing profession has long understood the importance of providing the new managers with adequate specific training in the areas of management and team leadership, this is often not the case in the medical profession, focused on peak clinical and academic performances. The outcomes are failures of the medical organization and leadership, which sometimes severely disrupt the operation of departments, interdisciplinary relationships, and the quality of care. This situation offers a broad field of activity to the hospital coach, who must have sufficient knowledge of hospital operations and the field of care to effectively support medical and nursing executives. The importance of personal and spiritual development is emphasized, which makes it possible to manage the loneliness of the leader and to provide meaning to the difficulties and failures of professional life.

Bibliography

1 Stoller JK. Developing physician-leaders: a call to action. *J Gen Intern Med* 2009;24(7):876–878.
2 Kotter JP. What leaders really do. *Harv Bus Rev* 1990;1–11.
3 Vimr M, Dickens P. Building physician capacity for transformational leadership – revisited. *Healthc Manage Forum* 2013;26(1):16–19.

4 Strycharczyk D, Clough P, Heffernan N. The integrated leadership model. *In*: Passmore J. *Leadership Coaching: Working with Leaders to Develop Elite Performance*; 2010, pp. 35–53. Kogan Page, London UK.

5 Lobas JG. Leadership in academic medicine: capabilities and conditions for organizational success. *Am J Med* 2006;119(7):617–621.

6 Gardner L, Stough C. Examining the relationship between leadership and emotional intelligence in senior level managers. *Leadership & Organization Development Journal* 2002;23(2):68–78

7 Schutte N, Malouff J, Thorsteinsson E. Increasing emotional intelligence through training: current status and future directions. *Int J Emot Educ* 2013;56–72.

8 Neumann M, Edelhäuser F, Tauschel D, *et al*. Empathy decline and its reasons: a systematic review of studies with medical students and residents. *Acad Med* 2011;86(8): 996–1009.

9 Bertram K, Randazzo J, Alabi N, Levenson J, Doucett J, Barbosa P. Strong correlations between empathy, emotional intelligence, and personality traits among podiatric medical students: a cross-sectional study. *Educ Health* 2016;29(3):186–194.

10 Nelis D, Quoidbach J, Mikolajczak M, Hansenne M. Increasing emotional intelligence: (how) is it possible? *Personal Individ Differ* 2009;47(1):36–41.

11 Cerrone SA, Adelman P, Akbar S, Yacht AC, Fornari A. Using objective structured teaching encounters (OSTEs) to prepare chief residents to be emotionally intelligent leaders. *Med Educ Online* 2017;22(1):1320186.

12 Saleh KJ. The prevalence and severity of burnout among academic orthopaedic departmental leaders. *J Bone Joint Surg Am* 2007;89(4):896.

13 Doppia MA, Lieutaud T, Mertes PM, Arzalier-Daret S. Congrès EAPH: le CFAR et la campagne #DIDOC récompensés au niveau européen. Available from: https://cfar. org/congres-eaph-le-cfar-et-la-campagne-didoc-recompenses-au-niveau-europeen/

14 Shanafelt TD, Noseworthy JH. Executive leadership and physician well-being. *Mayo Clin Proc* 2017;92(1):129–146.

15 Thomas LR, Ripp JA, West CP. Charter on physician well-being. *JAMA*. Available from: http://jama.jamanetwork.com/article.aspx?doi=10.1001/jama.2018.1331

16 Strack G, Fottler F, Myron D, Wheatley MJ, Sodomka P. Spirituality and effective leadership in healthcare: is there a connection?/Commentaries/Replies. *Front Health Serv Manag Chic* 2002;18(4):3–18.

17 Allison ST, Kocher KT, Goethals GR. Spiritual leadership: a fresh look at an ancient human issue. *In*: Scott A, Kocher C, Goethals G. *Frontiers in Spiritual Leadership: Discovering the Better Angels of Our Nature*. Palgrave Macmillan, New York; 2016, pp. 1–12.

18 Puchalski CM. Spirituality and the care of patients at the end-of-life: an essential component of care. *Omega* 2007;56(1):33–46.

19 Sanchez-Reilly S, Morrison LJ, Carey E, *et al*. Caring for oneself to care for others: physicians and their self-care. *J Support Oncol* 2013;11(2):75–81.

20 VanderWeele TJ, Balboni TA, Koh HK. Health and spirituality. *JAMA* 2017; 318(6):519.

21 Meng Y. Spiritual leadership at the workplace: perspectives and theories. *Biomed Rep* 2016;5(4):408–412.

22 Wachholtz A, Rogoff M. The relationship between spirituality and burnout among medical students. *J Contemp Med Educ* 2013;1(2):83.

23 Holland JM, Neimeyer RA. Reducing the risk of burnout in end-of-life care settings: the role of daily spiritual experiences and training. *Palliat Support Care* [Internet] 2005 [cited April 3, 2018];3(03). Available from: www.journals.cambridge.org/abstract_ S1478951505050297

Further readings

Hawkins P. *Leadership Team Coaching. Developing Collective Transformational Leadership.* Kogan Page Limited, London, Philadelphia, New Delhi, 2017.

Marturano J. *Finding the Spade to Lead. A Practical Guide to Mindful Leadership.* Bloomsbury, New York; 2014.

7 Life coaching

René Chioléro and Véronique Haynal

Introduction

The request for *individual* coaching at the hospital is usually initiated by the hospital management to remedy a failure of leadership or management or a personal crisis. A request for *life coaching* is infrequent in the hospital context; it is usually initiated by the care providers and occurs in a private setting, outside the institution. It often follows a coaching prescribed by management, which has allowed leaders to become more aware of themselves and their problems, a process that encourages them to make changes in their life. In other cases, the beneficiaries realize the benefit of being supported for a long time and having benevolent external support.

This chapter aims to describe the specific elements of life coaching of physicians, and reports the experience of the authors in this field of support, including the professional and life transitions.

The beginning and first sessions

The initial phases of coaching that precede the effective start of the support have been explained in detail in chapter 5. Some basic knowledge about life coaching have been described in chapter 1.

The *demands* for existential coaching from the medical profession are varied and cover all fields of life, e.g.,

- personal development;
- management of work stress;
- work–life balance;
- give meaning to one's activity, one's failures, or one's life;
- management of professional failures;
- well-being and satisfaction at work or in other fields of life;
- loneliness at work and sometimes in the private setting;
- couple and family problems and crisis;

DOI: 10.4324/9781003291831-10

- preparation and management of major transitions, e.g., retirement, career changes, and divorce;
- financial problems (rarely).

Notably, for some doctors, it is easier to consider being supported by a coach than by a psychiatrist. For these doctors, the image of psychiatry is inseparable from mental illnesses and distant from personal development. For them, it is therefore more difficult to consider psychotherapy, regarded as a treatment, rather than coaching, considered personal development, away from any mental health problem. Physicians who know the type of support practiced by the coach understand that it differs from that offered by a psychiatrist. With a psychiatrist, they may fear being in the lower position (ill, suffering), often poorly tolerated by doctors, while with a coach, clients are not expected to be sick and remain the master of their life.

A painful separation

Georgia is a senior physician in a university hospital. She has been going through a prolonged crisis for several months in connection with a difficult divorce. Her chief, who has noticed a decrease in her professional performance and an increase in absenteeism, proposes to her, with the approval of the medical director, a coaching "to regain her full professional abilities." Georgia is fully aware of her professional shortcomings; she accepts this proposal with relief. Her situation is difficult, she discusses her progressive exhaustion, shared custody of her children, and hostile ex-husband, with whom she must regularly negotiate regarding their children; she also evokes her difficulty in performing all her hospital tasks.

The beginning of the coaching is arduous, Georgia goes round in circles and ruminates on her inadequacies, showing a lack of self-esteem several times: "I am not able to overcome this crisis, I will lose my hospital job ... ." Asked by the coach, she declares right away that she refuses psychiatric support: "I do not need a psychiatrist; I'm not crazy; what will I tell my colleagues if they learn that?" The development of work goals is painstaking, as is the search for personal resources, despite her two specialist degrees and a successful hospital career to date.

The coach then changes strategy and questions Georgia about her ability to be resilient:

Coach: How did you manage to cope with such a situation, continuing your hospital activity and your mothering duties?

Georgia: To be honest, I do not really know, but I did it.

Coach: This is remarkable, especially since you are engaged on several levels.

Georgia: In any case, it was not easy is the least that I can say. It is probably for all that I feel exhausted and without energy.

Coach: Tell me about crises that have complicated your life.

Georgia: Actually, it's not the first one, but it's probably the most difficult to overcome.

Coach: Most difficult ..., can you tell me more about that?
Silence ...

Georgia: I remember when my mother died, I was 16 years old. It was difficult, especially since I did not expect it. Fortunately, my father was there to support me; I managed to get the upper hand and finish my studies on time.

Coach: Good! Other difficult situations?

Georgia: At 24, I had a painful separation from my boyfriend. I felt that I did not get along with this man, but I had to mobilize all my energy to make this difficult but necessary decision.

Coach: And in your situation, how could you imagine to get out of this crisis?

Georgia: Difficult, but probably not impossible. That's why I immediately accepted this coaching.

Coach: And if today we consider a small positive change to move forward, in what area can you imagine it?

Georgia: I don't know ... I might imagine a change of attitude with the colleagues who offer me help, which I always refused, and I don't know why.

Coach: For example?

Georgia: I have an older colleague, who has also gone through a divorce. She offered me help several times, that is, to see the most complicated patients I treat. I think I will accept it because it will probably reassure me and reduce my anxiety.

Coach: Excellent!

This vignette illustrates the path followed by a senior doctor, sinking into a prolonged crisis. Despite the severity of the crisis and the importance of the personal and professional repercussions, the client refuses to accept the support of a psychiatrist and asks for a coaching. For her, the discovery of her ability to survive a major crisis in the past because of somebody's help (her father when she was 16 years old) allows her to accept the support of a colleague.

The opposite situation can occur, in which the doctor does not bear the coaching work method. This situation is not necessarily a quiet path either, as all coaches know. In critical moments, tensions can develop or anxiety when the client steps out of her comfort zone, especially when she widens her consciousness and discovers other aspects of reality, or when she falls on limiting beliefs or an unexpected difficulty.

A coaching is not always easy to undergo!

Christopher is a 51-year-old attending physician in a large hospital department. He contacts a coach to "advance in the resolution of some problems that ruin his life." In his hospital activity, he does not report any particular problem.

Christopher: I love my job; I get on well with my department head and with my colleagues; I am satisfied. It's my private life that does not work. Since my divorce, I have not been able to settle down, and that weighs on me. Despite my busy hospital life, I suffer from loneliness and dissatisfaction.

Coach: I understand that it's difficult to work as hard as you do and find yourself alone at the end of the day. Do you have other sources of dissatisfaction that you would like to talk about?

Christopher: I have problems with my 14 years old daughter who lives with her mother. She keeps her distance and is sometimes hostile. In addition, she has had school difficulties for two years. Overall, I do not know how to help her; I sometimes have the impression that a wall separates us.

Coach: I understand that the relationship with teenagers is sometimes terribly complicated ...

Christopher: I'm also getting lost in my love life. I had several partners, but each time it was a failure; I feel increasingly lonely.

Coach: You have made an appointment with me to move forward in all these problems. Can you clarify what you expect from me? Why did you choose a coach to assist you in resolving some of your problems?

> *Christopher:*   I have been in intermittent psychotherapy for seven or eight years. I'm tired of this type of support and would prefer a less medical approach.
>
> *Coach:*   Do you have an idea of what coaching is?
>
> *Christopher:*   Not really, but it is unlike psychotherapy.

The coach explains some fundamentals of coaching, highlighting the role of coach and coachee. At the end of the session, Christopher agrees to five coaching sessions to discover this type of support. At each meeting, Christopher arrives 5–10 minutes late and gives excuses. He decides to work first on two objectives: improve his relations with his daughter and explore his relationships with women. The development of operational objectives is laborious. Christopher finds it difficult to delineate the elements and interactions that he has control of from those that depend on his partners. He gets lost in the details and does not bear some of the questions of the coach, who tries unsuccessfully to refocus him. He realizes gradually that coaching can be a difficult method of support for a person like him, whose attitude is often passive and dependent. After four sessions, he concludes with his coach that he is not ready to continue the ongoing coaching and interrupts it.

This vignette illustrates the difficulty for a doctor to participate in a coaching, which he is unable to endure. Shortly after stopping the coaching, Christopher informs his coach that he is starting a few psychotherapy sessions before considering resuming the coaching, which he did not do. The coach had noted from the first session the difficulties of supporting this client, and he thus proposed a trial period.

A similar approach can be used with physicians in crisis or suffering from chronic burnout, for whom it is often difficult to predict their ability to work effectively in coaching. Once the coach observes that his client has significant mental health problems, she needs to tactfully discuss it and propose a consultation with a psychologist or psychiatrist. Notably, doctors can suffer not only from burnout in their hospital job but also from addiction and other mental health disorders that require specific care. Clearly, supporting such clients is not possible in the context of a coaching.

When the client is strongly interested in coaching and simultaneously in psychotherapy, it is possible to carefully start a few coaching sessions to determine her tolerance to this type of double support. We have worked with health care professionals in such situations on multiple occasions, without noticeable problems.

Crisis coaching, difficult but effective

Mary, a senior physician at the hospital, emerges from a family cataclysm. Her husband left home six months ago, and divorce proceedings are ongoing. She suffered a lot during this crisis because his leaving was a surprise. She had anxiety attacks, an acute depressive state of short duration, and went for six weeks without working. She sees a psychiatrist but wishes to pursue personal development outside the setting that she associates with her crisis and recent mental health problems.

A coaching is started with the general aim of finding means to rebuild her life and improve her autonomy. The setting up of objectives is laborious because Mary ruminates on her rancor and sadness. This confusion between the present, the *here and now*, and the *past* complicates and delays the discovery of her current needs and desires. The search for Mary's strengths and favorite activities moves the process ahead:

- professional successes (she completed her studies easily, had an exemplary medical career with many successes, and is recognized in her medical specialty);
- favorite activities (cooking, culture, reading, walking).

Once this step is complete, the coaching progresses smoothly. Three months later, Mary stops her psychotherapy.

This vignette confirms the hypothesis of the coach: it can be fruitful in some cases to have parallel support, namely, coaching and psychotherapy. In this case, the client convinced the coach to start this dual approach that could have ended in failure. Notably, it is important to re-emphasize the importance of the coach's specific skills and experience that will enable the client to accept such a mandate. Authors underlined that there is no clear boundary between life coaching and therapy.[1] This is not the case when the client has specific needs that require therapeutic treatment. In our experience, practicing concomitantly a coaching and a therapy may be considered, provided that the client can withstand the tensions related to the coaching work as the coach provokes the client out her comfort zone.

A request for coaching head physicians with a difficult personality is not an exceptional situation in health care institutions, especially in the university hospital where some famous doctors behave similar to kings or dictators. Such requests usually come from general or medical management and often refused by the beneficiary. Surprisingly, we have sometimes received spontaneous requests for individual coaching by doctors considered by their colleagues as having inappropriate behavior.

Starting coaching and setting objectives

The main objective of the first coaching session(s) is to establish a relationship of trust, partnership, and collaboration with the coachee. As explained in chapter 2, a well-established coaching relationship is a major factor for success: without this relationship, no real support is possible. This is especially important in the practice of life coaching, which necessitates a strong, genuine, and trusting bond between coaches and their clients. The aim is to progressively establish a working climate based on listening, transparent communication and exchange, full information, and confidentiality. This will help the coachee to feel safe, comfortable, respected, and willing to collaborate with the coach.

The development and formulation of objectives reflect elements of the client world map. A very action-oriented and successful surgeon will not formulate her goal in the same manner as a fearful, hesitant, or pessimistic and defeatist executive. To prepare goals in life coaching, it is important to start by detecting the client's value and aspirations, a process that sometimes requires more than one session. This will allow to determine what's really important for the client, what she wants, *now* and for the *future*? And where she wants to go?

It's difficult, even at a 1000 km distance

John, chief resident in a regional hospital, is asking for a coaching because he wants to open a medical office and prepare a project to organize this installation. He aims to work on the general vague about his aspirations and hopes.

The wheel of life exercise[a] reveals nothing particular at this stage. By contrast, the work on logical levels,[b] another simple tool, is particularly productive (chapter 10). At the level of the environment, there is no particular element: John sees himself working with pleasure in a medical office full of light. It is the same at the second level, which explores activities and behaviors: John enjoys most of his activities as a doctor, except perhaps the paperwork. At the level of capabilities, John raises problems. He describes several crises in his life during the last ten years: a painful and conflictual separation with a partner and tensions with one of his bosses. He underlines the difficulty of considering the opening of an office. "It's not easy to be alone in making the right decisions for your patients." He reports that he left home just over a decade ago because of a difficult family environment. He adds: "I am convinced that today this still weighs on me. My family is an 'assembly of doctors,' and I struggle to take my place among them."

John:	My mother is a particularly dominant woman, she has the same medical specialty as me. I had to often support my father during my adolescence, also a doctor, but who works in a laboratory. My sister also trained in the same specialty, she works in a regional hospital. I ended up leaving this environment and my family. I first went to the north of Germany eight years ago to get away from them; and now I find myself approximately 1000 km from my family.
Coach:	What do you mean, explain me that?
John:	The "family tribe" still disturbs me, even at a distance. Every time I come home, my father makes me understand that he is suffering from my absence and that he would prefer me to be closer to him. My mother does not care.
Coach:	And ...?
John:	Actually, I do not feel completely autonomous. I have the feeling that my father prevents me from being free despite the 1000 km distance. In addition, I always feel that I have to give something back to others.
Coach:	What could you imagine that helps you take a little space and freedom from them?
John:	I need to be at a sufficient distance from all of them.
Coach:	In reality or in your head?
John (surprised):	... probably in my head. I feel that it's up to me to do the work.
Coach:	Well, let's go!

The ecological analysis is important because it aims to ensure that the change envisioned is beneficial to the client, not driving toward irreplaceable loss, and supportive for colleagues and family members. An example is described in the following vignette.

Leaving my job for a better future?

This mid-career division head plans to leave her job at a large public hospital. It is becoming increasingly difficult for her to endure the increasing hospital administration control over her management, with its procession of time-consuming bureaucracy, "I am tired of this administrative terrorism and to work with this gang of incompetent people." She plans to leave the hospital and move to private practice with other colleagues and asks for coaching to evaluate the relevance of her project, as well as her ability to achieve it.

The analysis of the various components of the project is performed: What are possible advantages? Disadvantages? What are the consequences: finances, pleasure at work, workload, family ... The project reveals several weaknesses that complicate its accomplishment:

- the financial plan and financial viability are uncertain, as shown by the bank's analysis; and
- the possible partners, essential to the realization of her project, are hesitant.

Finally, the coach observes that his client is hesitant. Why give up a good job situation for an uncertain future? After much hesitation, she decides to abandon the project.

One aspect of goal-based work is verifying the achievement of each goal when the end of the process is complete: *How will you know that you have achieved your goal?* This question requires some simple criteria for success, as shown in the previous vignette. Setting up repeated goals, which the client never achieves is another pitfall. It corresponds to real "short circuits of thought," which become a repetitive loop of a new goal or new project, without leading to its realization.[2] Such short circuit reflects the perpetual desire and imagination to change something but is a dream that never comes true.

Using a wide approach and an efficient technique

The hospital environment offers a particularly wide field of accompaniment demands, according to the needs of physicians and nurses. As said, this support can take many forms. Notably, there is no clear boundary among these practices. The client's needs and the coach's training determine the method and strategy of support. It is important though to be clear about the method used and to mention it to coachees. Although some coaching experts re-commend a practice strictly based on a pure coaching approach (which excludes any mentoring or expert advice), others believe that as long as the coach's skills and experience are sufficient, he may expand the support according to the needs of the beneficiary and circumstances. We do use such extended practice, attempting to enlarge the method, when justified, as in the support of people suffering from crisis or burnout, in whom the capacities of adaptation and change are initially reduced. Notably, a return to a practice based on the classic coaching-type relationship should be adopted as soon as possible. Such a wide approach of coaching depends on the training and ex-perience of coaches, provided that they know and respect their limits and benefit from supervision.

In our practice, we use many methods of support, often drawn from psy-chotherapy: neuro-linguistic programming (NLP), transactional analysis, cognitive behavioral therapy (CBT), solution-oriented techniques, and brief therapy.[c] These methods provide strategies and a framework, as well as a dynamic of action that structures the course of the sessions. In this book, we do not detail the techniques available to the coach, but do comment on their use in the hospital setting. In general, we prefer to use "solution-focused coaching" methods (from solution-oriented short therapy[3] and cognitive be-havioral therapy[4]), which have the advantage of putting the problems at a distance and focusing from the start on the desired change. In prescribed coaching, such an approach allows the spectrum of the "punitive prescription" to be evacuated and usually helps the coachee to leave her blockade and turn herself toward a solution search.

A prolonged support

Life coaching is sometimes a long-term endeavor. We regularly have clients who work for periods exceeding one year or more who return to take a new look at their life problems. In such cases, gradual changes in the relationship between the coach and the beneficiary usually occur: there is a deepening of mutual knowledge, trust, complicity, and intimacy that can influence work dynamic. Notably, life coaching should always be a professional relationship and not a personal, friendly relationship. To avoid this drift, the coach must respect the following points:

• work with defined objectives of changes;
• establish a work plan with the client, with a predefined rhythm and number of sessions and periodic intermediate assessments at the end of the coaching;
• work within the framework of a recognized method of support (e.g., solution-oriented approach, classical coaching, NLP); and
• ask for supervision when necessary to assess the relevance of the approach.

A succession of consecutive goals imprints a usual dynamic in the progression of coaching. Once a goal of change is achieved, it is possible to consider other developments. This is particularly the case in crisis coaching, set in motion in a difficult or stalled situation. Once the crisis is over, it is then possible to envisage deeper changes.

I want to change my relationship with my husband

Bella is asking for an urgent appointment to undertake a coaching. She has just learned that her husband, a senior physician, must leave the hospital because of "inappropriate harassment behavior." Complaints from several nurses were sent to the management, who dismissed him. Bella is initially overwhelmed by strong emotions: stupor, shock, disapproval, and anger. Bella admits, "I am unable to get out of this ordeal alone, I need help." A coaching is started with two initial goals: "get out of the crisis and regain my equilibrium, and negotiate with my husband a balanced relationship with him, if that's possible."

After four months of difficult work, Bella feels better: she has regained energy and reestablished a dialogue with her husband. The coach talks about either continuing coaching or completing it. Bella is not enthusiastic about this proposal but asks for further coaching: "I still have to progress. I want to become more independent, increase my professional activity, and continue working on my relationship with my husband." Coaching continues for over one year.

This vignette illustrates the dynamics of prolonged life coaching, which starts in a mode of crisis and continues in the manner of coaching and personal development.

Professional transitions

Two transitions are frequently coached: the *appointment of a new leader* for promotion and the *preparation for retirement*. The arrival of a new leader after a promotion causes a period of instability that is often difficult to overcome. This is particularly the case if this leader is an insider from the team, she must now lead. An additional difficulty is linked to the specific professional culture of the medical world: accepting the support of a coach when somebody has just been appointed chief requires a sufficient degree of humility, often absent in senior doctors. Once this obstacle is overcome, the coach may focus on the purpose of the demand, often linked to insufficient experience and skills in management and leadership. Another difficulty is caused by the complexity of the hospital organization and contemporary medical practice.

Retirement is an uneasy part of life for many medical leaders. How can a leader possibly imagine retiring and thus disappearing from the workplace after many years of running a hospital department, working 60–70 hours per week, being recognized in clinical practice, conducting research at the international level, and training young doctors? In our experience, most of the coaching requests in this area are from senior doctors sensitized by this question and who want to be supported to organize this transition. Their aims are to prepare for the future, develop a retirement plan, define priorities, and give meaning to this stage of life that heralds old age and other sometimes threatening perspectives. We present here two vignettes to illustrate the distinct aspects of this theme.

Farewell speech

Dan makes an appointment by phone for an urgent coaching: "I decided to quickly leave my position of head of department; I cannot stand the way the hospital is run; I'm sick of the administrative harassment. My decision is made, but I am stuck in writing my farewell speech. What do I say?" The coach gives him an appointment to explain his request.

The beginning of the session comprises a quasi-15-minute monologue: Dan explains that he is 64 years old, runs a large hospital department (15 senior doctors), and has decided to quit his position more than three months ago. This decision is "irremediable and is not the subject of coaching." What brings him to the coach is the farewell session, in front of the hospital management and his colleagues and heads of departments and divisions. For a long time, he has contacted neither the hospital's director general nor the new medical director, who has been in office for one year.

Coach: And what are the messages you would like to convey in your speech?
Dan: I prepared a speech where I will tell them what I think and feel about this unbearable system.
Coach: Can you clarify what you mean?
Dan: I'll tell them frankly that their system is unbearable and that I regret the time when the department heads had more freedom and less administrative burdens. I am going to suggest to the general and medical directors that they are tyrannical and do not realize what it is to work here.
Coach: and what's the right manner and time to talk to them about it?

Dan: Hey, that's a good question, I did not think about it …

Coach: I propose a short exercise to clarify your expectations and your goals in relation to this initial speech.

Dan: Okay.

Coach: Can you give three or four objectives for the content of your speech?

Dan: Can you give me an example that would help me do this task?

Coach: For example, satisfying your anger, your old anger could be a goal.

Dan: I see …

Coach: I suggest you start this work on your side to prepare for the next session. This exercise should allow you to quickly finalize your goals and prepare the speech.

Dan: OK, I'll see what I can do …

The next session, four days later, is lively. Dan worked well, he first expressed his satisfaction at having realized that his anger was a bad counselor.

Dan: I first wondered if I really wanted to leave this hospital, and the answer has not changed: I think it's time to go. Regarding the farewell meeting, I think this is not the place to convey my anger. I have spent 30 years in this hospital and had good relationships with most departments and department heads; I do not want to ruin all that.

Coach: What are your expectations for this session?

Dan: Actually, I have changed my mind about the farewell speech. I first would like to explain to you my new objectives for this speech. I'd like to have fun and talk freely; I think it's a better way to say goodbye.

Coach: Well, have fun and talk freely. What about the messages that you want to send?

Dan: I realize that if I want to be listened to, I have to change my messages and abandon my bitter critiques.

Coach: How close would you like to be to your colleagues, the chief physicians?

Dan: I would prefer to be close to them to express my gratitude; I want to describe the pleasure I have had in collaborating with them during years, rather than being distant and sarcastic.

Coach: What else?
Dan: Nothing.

Five days later, the coach receives the outline of the speech, completely different from the first version.

Final feedback: The goal is achieved, the coachee had fun, the audience was attentive, and Dan received a standing ovation.

In this case, a manager was about to leave the hospital angry and disillusioned. By talking in detail about his anger and his frustrations, then by preparing a concrete project, the doctor realizes what he is going to provoke. He can clearly imagine the scene. The reframing makes him see goal and endeavor from a different perspective.

Escape from retirement

Kate is head of the department and a professor in a university hospital. She contacts a coach to discuss possible work "to prepare for this difficult stage of life that is retirement."

Kate: I'm in great shape and very active in my field; I cannot imagine retiring and letting go, what a horrible prospect!
Coach: So, retiring is difficult when you're as active and knowledgeable as you are.
Kate: Yes, indeed. In addition to my department, I head the Swiss and the European societies of my specialty. Every year I organize an international symposium, which is in the world's top ten for participation.
Coach: I see; it's not easy to stop it all at once and get into the ranks.
Kate: Yes, especially since there is no good candidate in my department to take over.
Coach: How many doctors do you have in the department?
Kate: Three full professors and ten senior physicians.
Coach: Does anyone show interest in replacing you?
Kate: In fact, two will probably apply. I predict that when they take over, they will effectively run the department, as I did for 18 years.
Coach: I understand. And what would be your goals for this coaching?

Kate:	I would like to prepare a retirement plan that allows me to maintain the same pace of work outside the department. I have already been asked by the European society to organize training modules, and I contacted two private clinics where I can treat my Swiss and foreign patients.
Coach:	How much free time do you allot to do other activities, for example, leisure and travel?
Kate:	Well, that's what I don't want because I want to stay visible and recognized.

The development of objectives is particularly laborious: any reference to retirement is experienced as impossible and rejected outright. For Kate, the only possibility is to prepare a program of activities of the same types that govern her current professional life. No opening is planned at this stage regarding free time for her or family activities.

Again, we observe the great difficulty for this professor, head of the department, to engage in the personal work necessary for the transition to retirement. For her, it is unimaginable to think to her successor, change her life, reduce her working hours, and start other activities. The course of the coaching is difficult; it is interrupted after three sessions.

Ending a life coaching

The end-of-coaching process is an important step for both beneficiary and coach. They decide by mutual agreement to end coaching, after assessing the progress of the objectives and concrete results of the support. If they are satisfactory and the client's expectations are fulfilled, this step is easy. It enables them to look into the future and consider the value of the experience and learning and the possibility to transfer them.

In group coaching, this process is often more complex because of the inevitable individual differences in the experience of coaching and the evaluation of results. It is important for the coach to put energy into this step and not skip the end-of-coaching process, to leave the group without regrets. On some occasions, we have not been able to complete a team coaching with doctors, which resulted in unresolved questions, the feeling of unfinished work, and regrets.

Any coaching has an end, even when prolonged. We usually address the end of coaching at each intermediate review, emphasizing the importance of autonomy for the beneficiary. For the last session, we prepare an overall assessment of the work accomplished throughout the coaching and ask the client to do the same, emphasizing the importance of highlighting the changes, discoveries, and progress made. During the meeting, we discuss the end of the coaching relationship and what it means for the client and coach. A small number of clients return from time to time to solicit support during a new event in their lives. Then, the beginning of a new coaching starts in a relationship where trust has been established. In this case, coaches must again avoid working in a friendly environment and use a professional approach.

In the case of prolonged coaching, it is our practice to review all of our session notes, to follow the evolution of the support throughout the process. We note in particular the following:

- The *implementation of coaching* and the elaboration of the work objectives: how was the beginning, especially during a prescribed coaching, an initial resistance period observed? If so, what strategy was used by the coach to unlock the situation and with what result? How did the client prepare her goals? If there was a setback, what strategy was used, and with what effect?
- The *evolution and progress of the work*: the achievement of objectives, setting of new objectives, and periodic evaluations of the possibility of finishing the coaching. Has the highlighting of the client's resources been beneficial? Has the use of the "perfect future" made it possible to advance the elaboration of objectives? What are the client's main discoveries and results? Have periodic evaluations of the results been performed?
- The *evolution of the coaching relationship*: the establishment of the process; reinforcement; setting up a partnership between the coach and the coachee, with the possibility of sharing, co-constructing, and sometimes opposing. How have the coaching relationship and trust evolved? Have there been obstructions, crises, and critical moments? If so, what has been done, and with what effect? Have there been periods of complicity, proximity, and rapid advancement in achieving goals? What has been the evolution of the client's behavior? What does the coachee think today?
- *How did the coach feel* during the work, how did he overcome any difficulties? Did he ask for supervision, and if so, what did he learn? What is the quality of his relationship today with the client?

This assessment concerns not only the coach and his client but also the coach of himself. It often provides rich and useful information: assessment makes it possible to check the effect of the coaching management, the relevance of the strategies used, as well as the quality and authenticity of the coaching relationship. When a usual strategy is ineffective in several consecutive situations, it is necessary to analyze it critically to replace it with other more effective strategies. Periodic supervision provides an established means of improving the conduct of coaching, especially when the coach's assessment reveals difficulties or weaknesses in the coaching.

Conclusion

Life coaching is focused on life issues, personal development, and projects for change. Generally, it is requested by the clients themselves, rather than the hospital management. Setting goals for life coaching is often a complex process: it is about supporting clients so that they identify their personal needs, desires, and aspirations. They also have to determine whether the envisaged changes are in line with their values. Goal setting usually requires an ecological analysis, to assess the impact of expected changes on the individual and those around them. Professional transitions of senior hospital care providers, particularly retirement, frequently induce a period of crisis that can benefit from coaching.

Practice requires a high level of training, including basic competences in psychology, goal setting, and emotion management, as well as a range of working methods and techniques. Adequate supervision is mandatory.

Notes

a The *wheel of life* is a tool to assess the clients' perceived satisfaction/dissatisfaction in different domains of life, for example, career, family, spouse and partners, social life, finance, leisure, exercise, and personal development.
b The *logical level* is a tool to explore the current and future situation of a person by going through different levels of reality: environment, activities performed, capabilities, values and beliefs, identity, mission, and purpose (for details, see chapter 10).
c For a comprehensive description of coaching techniques, refer to Grant A, Cavanagh M. Life coaching. *In*: Cox E, Bachkirova T, Clutterbuck D. *The Complete Handbook of Coaching*. SAGE Publications, Los Angeles, London, New Delhi; 2010, pp. 297–310.

Bibliography

1 Grant A, Cavanagh M. Life coaching. *In:* Cox E, Bachkirova T, Clutterbuck D. *The Complete Handbook of Coaching*. SAGE Publications, Los Angeles, London, New Delhi; 2010, pp. 297–310.
2 Hawkins P. Coaching the five disciplines: systemic team coaching. *In*: Hawkins P. *Leadership Team Coaching. Developing Collective Transformational Leadership*. Kogan Page, London, Philadelphia, New Delhi; 2010, pp. 83–99.
3 Berg IK, Szabó P. *Brief Coaching for Lasting Solutions*. 1st ed. New York: W.W. Norton; 2005.
4 Beck JS. *Cognitive Behavior Therapy. Basics and Beyond*. 3rd ed. The Guilford Press, New York and London; 2020.

Further readings

Dunbar A. *Essential Life Coaching Skills*. Essential Coaching Skills and Knowledge Series. Routledge, London and New York; 2009.
Menedez DS, Patrick WD. *Becoming a Professional Life Coach: Lessons from the Institute of Life Coach Training*. W. W. Norton & Company, New York and London; 2015.

8 Coaching healthcare teams

René Chioléro

Introduction

Many medical and care hospital activities require the mobilization of groups for clinical practice, training, and research. This requisite leads care providers of all categories to spend a considerable time in various forms of collective activities. Surprisingly, despite this considerable investment in time and energy, little effort has been devoted to training hospital staff in the main aspects of teamwork, such as facilitation, organization, communication, distribution and execution of tasks, collaboration, and others.

Team coaching was introduced late in the hospital environment. In Europe, it was non-existent until the beginning of the twenty-first century, and gradually developed parallel with the development of human resource management systems, despite the lack of enthusiasm and even resistance of doctors. For doctors, coaching remains controversial and often considered a witness of the weakness or failure of many executives. Although becoming involved in the day-to-day operation of groups in the hospital is uncommon, the coach is often called upon to support executive teams in crisis or suffering from chronic conflicts or major dysfunctions.

The chapter aims to provide information on specific aspects of the functioning of hospital groups and on coaching of medical teams. This information reflects our practical experience throughout the field.

Groups and teams

In a modern work model, a team includes nurses and/or doctors from the same department with different levels of training and is often supported by other care professionals, such as physiotherapists, pharmacists, and psychologists. The National Academy of Medicine in the United States considers teamwork as belonging to the fundamental competencies of all healthcare providers: "All health professionals should be educated to deliver patient-centered care as members of an interdisciplinary team."[a]

Effective teamwork requires significant changes in the organization, especially in terms of communication, methods of collaboration, and decision-

DOI: 10.4324/9781003291831-11

making.[1] It also pertains to rethinking the mode of leadership and the role of stakeholders. Interdisciplinary teams should bring together doctors and healthcare professionals of different specialties to optimize the different modes of care and treatment. Each specialist is responsible for specific areas, and the team ensures *coordination* of all care.

The distinction between the dynamics of groups and teams has been long described; however, the usual distinction may not always apply to hospitals, where different forms of groups and teams coexist.

We propose simple definitions of groups and teams as follows:

- *A team* is formed over a long period. It precedes the beginning of coaching and continues its activity once coaching is finished. The essential characteristics of a *team* include the following:

  - At least two participants who interact in a dynamic, interdependent, and interactive manner to achieve a common goal that federates them (goal/activity/mission) and requires the participation of all members. Managing a hospitalized patient without the help of colleagues and leading a medical division without effective collaboration between the head of department, senior physicians, and head nurses are all impossible feats.
  - A specific and stable cultural envelope, which includes values and common beliefs, patterns of communication, interactions, and connectivity.

- *A group* brings together people from different backgrounds to accomplish a defined task during a specific period. This period can be short (a few sessions for a few weeks) or longer, as is the case for a patient referral group for organ transplantation or a development group for the hospital. The members are non-permanent; the objectives of the group are focused on task(s) and not on individual objectives; the common cultural envelope is limited; and members may even lose awareness of the group, particularly when working at a distance.

In general, a team has a more complex dynamics than a simple group. To achieve its goal, a team requires extensive interaction, collaboration, and sharing. Compared to an individual or group of individuals with little cooperation, an effective team offers many advantages. It enables the performance of complex tasks, which are inaccessible to a single individual. It has the potential to provide better adaptability, productivity, and creativity for solving complex problems.[2] Alternatively, when a team has an inefficient organization or is dysfunctional, the consequences may be serious or catastrophic if the team is occupying a key sector. This case is especially true in the hospital that relies on the labor of care and non-health care teams for the day-to-day operations of its key sectors. How then should one work effectively in a hospital division when vital departments, such as the operating, emergency, intensive care, radiology, or laboratory malfunction?

Two operative rooms must be closed in the operating room

The session at the surgery department is stormy. The head of the main operating room announces that two operating theaters will be closed due to the unexpected departure of several technicians. Discussion comes alive, and several heads of surgery are furious: "Impossible to work in this hospital; it is always the same thing; this time we are fed up! We must summon the general director general at our next meeting ... ." The head of the operating room tries to provide explanations: "Indeed conflicts and fights occurred in the team of technicians for over a year. In addition, the head nurse who was excellent in planning but weak in team management was kicked out. The position is open and we hope that the new head will be up to it. Unfortunately, no valid candidate has been identified internally, and we must probably wait a few weeks."

Comments: Running an operating room without a team of efficient and supportive instrumentalists is impossible. Solidarity within the team is essential to overcome unforeseen absences and ensure the introduction of new staff. However, why was this foreseeable situation not anticipated for several months?

The team consists of individuals who, through conscious and unconscious interactions, create a real living and unique social system. For the coach, the objective is to take such a system into account in its entirety and complexity.

Three main factors influence the effectiveness of teamwork[3]:

- Team structure, which refers to the stable elements of its functioning, such as missions, tasks, leadership, roles of members and distribution of tasks, and cultural elements.
- Team processes, which define how members work together in terms of communication, interaction, and management of joint activities, problem solving, decision-making, and disagreement management.
- Active context of the team, such as the hospital or healthcare facility.

These factors not only play a decisive role in the functioning, effectiveness, and performance of the team but also influence its ability to create an environment that promotes learning and development (i.e., "learning organization"). In this context, each member may develop and learn. Team structure and processes are factors directly influenced by group members and the leader. They will mobilize the energy and competence of the coach to manage the changes. Alternatively, the context of the team, which is related to external factors, such as the hospital organization, is not under the direct influence of group members. This setup may limit the coach in his action when a failing hospital organization is a determining factor in the crisis observed in a department, which is only a symptom. In such a case, the coach should transmit his observation to the hospital management to correct it if possible.

Shared mental models

Working effectively as a team means sharing common mental models about team processes, especially goals, communication, professional behavior, task distribution, roles, team coordination, and elements of the cultural envelope.[2] These models create a common framework of thought. If they are weak or absent, then sharing common goals, communicating effectively, synchronizing work, and organizing mutual aid becomes difficult. The team leader conducts the buildup of this type of common mental models and can be facilitated by coaching.

Executives with diverging views on the organization of work

A coaching is initiated in a department of a regional hospital to improve the functioning of the medical team. The department head devotes a substantial amount of time for clinical activity and teaching, but neglects the management of the medical team, which is an activity she does not prefer and underestimates. Over time, many disagreements emerge between senior physicians especially about the organization of work and distribution of tasks among them.

From the beginning of coaching, the coach observes the extent of the differences in opinion between a few attendings on the organization of clinical work.

- For the chief and most young professionals, setting up specialized areas of medical practice and assigning their organization to specifically trained attendings are necessary. The purpose of such initiatives is to raise the level of clinical services and improve the teaching of residents.

- This idea is fiercely opposed by a few of the former attendings, who find no reason to leave to their colleagues a part of their field of specialty.

For several months, the head of department has been hindered by this disagreement, which prevents improving the functioning of the department and cooperation in the medical team. The nursing team, which directly suffers from the lack of consensus among the medical team, complains that it cannot provide high-quality care if the physicians fail to agree on a shared model of work organization.

This vignette illustrates the dysfunction of a team composed of excellent specialists. The combination of a weak leadership coupled with the team's inability to resolve disputes and conflicts prevents the team from adhering to a shared model of clinical organization. The rivalry between attendings, lack of mutual trust, and weight of unresolved conflicts prevent the development of such a "shared mental model." The coach realizes that working from the outset is impossible on this point but recognizes that the first urgent need is restoring confidence and establishing an effective leadership.

Medical teams: a cultural envelope

The functioning and effectiveness of the medical teams are conditioned by the abovementioned general factors. However, the dynamics of these teams is also influenced by many elements of the medical and nurse professional culture and by the functioning of the hierarchies.

We have described the main elements of the professional culture of care providers in detail in a dedicated chapter (chapter 4). We will here briefly summarize some key elements, which influence the functioning of the teams.

- A strong commitment to work and limitless dedication to a certain extent (i.e., until exhaustion and burnout).
- Marked individualism.
- Culture of confidentiality and secrecy.
- Respect for authority, which is acquired at the beginning of medical studies. This culture leads young doctors to incorporate the judgment of their elders without questioning.
- Strong power relations at all levels.

- Marked rivalries, which are often exacerbated in the academic world and go hand in hand with a critical, even devaluing, vision of colleagues.
- Persistence of a patriarchal system (in comparison with other professions) as expressed by the search for a high position in human relations in all circumstances, which complicates relationships with the nursing staff.
- Corporatist spirit (particularly in opposition to the administration and other professions).
- Limited capacity for empathy and compassion (contrasting with nurses).
- Difficulty in working and cooperating in groups.
- A tendency to reject the importance of internal processes within the team, especially conflicts.

In human relations, the physician adopts a high and dominant position of "the one who knows," as learned in clinical practice: "The doctor knows, the patient suffers and does not know." This attitude is reflected in the functioning of medical hierarchies in which the weight of hierarchical and academic positions plays a determining and crippling role that may disrupt all communication and collaboration processes. The frequent lack of familiarity with the team processes leads to various dysfunctions that are often poorly managed by the executives. The culture of secrecy, which is learned in clinical practice to ensure confidentiality, is frequently reproduced in groups. It prevents the sharing of information and establishment of a true participatory system.

The culture of physicians differs significantly from that of the nursing profession because nurses have long built shared mental models for group work and care processes that promote cooperation and collaboration. This relationship is in contrast with that of the medical profession, which remains highly individualistic. In North America, many medical professional organizations have called for a reform in medical studies to integrate the learning of group work and interdisciplinarity, which goes hand in hand with a change in professional culture.[4] Many medical and nursing schools have created joint training modules for medical and nursing students, which are designed to teach interdisciplinarity.

You and your nurses!

A professor, a renowned surgeon, performed organ transplant on a patient. The postoperative course is complicated: hemorrhage requiring reintervention, prolonged renal failure, and serial infections. After two months in the intensive care unit, a high-intensity rejection of the organ required a new transplant. A month later, the situation is catastrophic as the patient suffers from infection and multiple organ failure. Following the insistence of the nursing team and the family, who suggested giving up maximum therapy to offer the patient a peaceful end, palliative therapy is proposed. The surgeon is strongly opposed to it. Nevertheless, he agrees to meet the nursing team.

The meeting takes place in a tense atmosphere because the nursing team no longer supports the therapeutic project, which is labeled "futile" while the operator is stubborn.

Nurse: How can you accept such futility in overtreating this patient and letting the family suffer?

Surgeon: In your place I would be silent. You do not know what you are talking about. The transplant specialist here is me, not you!

Nurse: You exaggerate, we look after the most seriously ill patients in the hospital, including transplant patients, and we know the situation. We believe that we have a say in the management of this patient who is suffering and who we consider to be a victim of therapeutic futility.

Surgeon: In my department, I take important decisions with my senior physicians and inform the nursing team, who decides nothing and does not impose diktats!

Two days later, following a new request from the family, the surgeon is forced to let go and accept palliative treatment. Subsequently, he complains of feeling "humiliated" in front of the nursing team.

A month later, when the head of the intensive care unit tries to communicate with the surgeon to refrain from remaining in a sense of mutual incomprehension, the surgeon admits to having a hard time accepting the decision to provide palliative care. "You and your nurses do not understand how attached we are to our patients and how we see ourselves as their best advocates in the face of fatality. We fight death with tenacity and loyalty."

This vignette illustrates the image of the "savior doctor," who fights death, which is a common position in transplant surgeons. We also note the posture of the surgeon in the high position of one who "knows," makes all vital decisions, and faces the nursing team in the ancillary position of a performer. Such a posture, which is typical of vertical hierarchy, prevents real collaboration and hinders any possibility of exchange and reciprocal learning. Moreover, such attitude promotes the deep loneliness often overserved in such leaders.

The death of a friend is a difficult experience even for a doctor

An article published in 2017 in the *Journal of the American Medical Association* (*JAMA*) describes the experience of a young in-training anesthetist who is confronted with the tragic death of a young colleague and friend, who suffered from severe burnout. Furthermore, the anesthetist died from opiate overdose, which he took to bear the weight of his medical activity.[5] In this situation, the young physician then discovers his vulnerability and how much he ignored the painful experience of losing a loved one as he feels helpless. Although he thought he could comfort his friend's family, he realized that he could not. In fact, he was the one who needed to be surrounded. and the bereaved family was the one that soothed him.

This vignette illustrates the discovery of a young doctor about his vulnerability to death. He realizes that he is unable to provide the desired relief despite the supposed superiority related to his profession. In addition, it illustrates the dramatic consequences of burnout on the mental health of in-training physicians who are facing a hard-core environment with little empathy and no inclination for self-criticism.

A medical team divided into two opposed groups

The coach is requested to assist the head of a medical department following the proposal of the medical director. After five sessions of individual support of the head physician, coaching begins with the team of senior physicians. The coach meets each senior physician.

The team is divided into two groups spread over two hospitals with different salary regimes that result in substantial wage inequalities. The least paid group is dissatisfied, which is associated with tension and multiple dysfunctions in the department's medical team. This subject, which does not appear in the initial coaching objectives, is tackled late in coaching at the fourth team session. The salary issue was mentioned that day as the discussion was focused on another objective. The coach immediately noted discomfort within the members of the two groups. The discussion was carried on without addressing the subject directly. The coach eventually intervened to set the issue on the table: "Explain to me, please, the system of remuneration in the two hospitals."

The answer shows that a substantial difference in wages is clear.

Coach: Can you give me figures about your salaries such that I can get an idea of the difference?

After an initial silence, the doctors receiving the lowest salary then cite figures.

Coach: And in the other hospital?

The coach continues to ask a series of questions to finally obtain an answer that clarifies the problem. The difference is very consistent! Recognizing this fact and its importance may take several working sessions for both groups. They painstakingly develop an agreement that preserves the functioning and solidarity of the team. Several solutions are mentioned to mitigate these differences before a choice is made.

This vignette illustrates three aspects of the medical culture, namely, individualism, weak solidarity, and a culture of secrecy. This team of doctors shares many common activities but is stuck with the simple problem of salary inequality among physicians. For the coach, clarifying the numbers about salaries meets resistance because this information is considered private. Moreover, the mindset "every man for himself" seems to prevail.

Weight of the medical hierarchy

A single model of hospital hierarchy does not exist because it is influenced by many factors, such as:

- Size of the hospital.
- Department missions (clinical and/or research and/or teaching).
- Academic or non-academic hospital.
- Medical culture specific to the hospital or department.
- Type of leadership and personality of the head of department.
- Geographical location and its specific cultural aspects. In general, hospital hierarchies in Europe are more vertical and authoritarian than those in North America. Substantial differences also exist in the hospital culture between Northern and Southern Europe.

Several studies show that professional culture and organization of medical hierarchies may hinder the possibility of working effectively in teams.[6] The first reason is related to the verticality of such hierarchies with important differences in the role and status of the various categories of physicians, such as medical residents versus chief residents and physicians without academic titles versus physicians with academic titles. These differences often negatively influence the functioning and dynamics of teams. The same phenomenon applies across professional categories of healthcare professionals, such as doctors versus nurses versus physiotherapists, etc. Such barriers disrupt communication, collaboration, and cooperation and reduce the participation of all care providers in the management of difficult patients and learning opportunities during team activities.

A common observation in clinical practice is that doctors in a junior position are reluctant to express themselves and give their opinion especially if it contradicts that of the chief. In contrast, attendings frequently consider working hard, becoming fit for the purpose, low salary, and being held accountable for a few medical failures are normal for in-training residents.

Residents in training must reduce their work schedules

In the early 2000s, a change in the labor law in Switzerland led to a reduction in the working hours of doctors in training. As a result, the medical activity in all medical departments required reorganization.

In a meeting of the surgical departmental council, which brings together the head of departments and divisions, the discussion began with remarks, such as "How is this possible? How to do and manage our units? It is an attack on our authority. It was better in the past ... ."

In my notes of meetings (I was then the secretary of the group), I wrote the elements of the discussion between the head of department and heads of divisions.

Head of division A:	Changing the way we work is impossible, and I will not apply the new rules.
Head of department:	I think we have no choice because it is the new Swiss law, and we must now find solutions.
Head of division B:	I do not understand why the director of the hospital does not defend us.
Head of division C:	Could the department head obtain a waiver for our sector?
Head of department:	I will try, but I am pessimistic because it is the law.
Head of division A:	This situation will certainly increase the work of the attendings, idem for ourselves!

Finally, only two department heads implemented the new regulation, whereas the others were forced by the hospital management to obey afterward.

This observation highlights the very vertical culture of the surgical department, in which residents and chief residents obey without participating in the organization of departments and divisions.

Unexpected meeting in the elevator of a Swiss university hospital (story experienced in 2017)

During a recent visit to a university hospital, I found a visitor and a medical attending assisted by four residents in the elevator. The attending, who seems angry, speaks to his team of residents:

Attending: This time, it is enough. "The morning hand job" is over. I am tired of repeated delays and lack of participation. The visit starts at 7:30 am.

Visitor: I am surprised to hear how you talk like that to your young physicians. Now, I understand better the article I recently read in the paper on the abuse on residents and nurses in training …

Attending: I apologize. I did not see you … . But, you know, nowadays, dealing with young in-training doctors is difficult.

These vignettes illustrate the functioning of certain hospital hierarchies. Although data regarding burnout of in-training doctors are well known, many department heads fail to consider this reality. In their representations, that young people should work more is normal (similar to their chiefs) instead of complaining and obeying without discussing with their superiors who are responsible for all decisions. We also note the lack of respect and vulgarity that characterize the chief's speech to his doctors.

Team coaching: getting started

Coaching medical teams can be a difficult task. Coaching is not prescribed in well-functioning hospital departments, contrasting with "dysfunctional units," such as those with inadequate leadership, poor performance, repeated conflicts, and complaints from the nursing team or other departments.

The coach's mission is managing the group to achieve its goals. Duties include leading the coaching process, such as:

- Assisting the group, establishing operating rules, managing the agenda, managing time and its use by various participants (hierarchy), and distributing the floor inside the group.
- Managing participants' interactions to give them opportunities for change and learning.[7]
- Limiting destructive and conflictual individual or group behaviors (i.e., domination, aggression, obstructions, obstructions, and scapegoat).
- Managing tension and possible conflicts.

Similar to individual assistance, group coaching is usually initiated by the hospital management and rarely by the department head. If initiated by management, then it is "prescribed coaching" that aims to overcome issues or shortcomings of the team and less to assist a transition or a major change. In the first case, the coach must be particularly respectful of the steps of prescribed coaching to mitigate potential negative consequences. He must take into account the mistrust and even hostility of the head of department or division as well as the wariness of the team who fears being placed under guardianship and lose liberty. The coach should therefore pay particular attention to carefully following the initial stages of coaching, namely, analysis of request, meeting with all interested parties (i.e., management, head of department, senior physician, and nurse in charge), elaboration of work objectives, and preparation of the contract. He will also need to mobilize his capabilities and experience to establish a relationship of trust with the team and its leader as soon as possible.

If coaching is initiated by the leader, it often follows prescribed individual coaching to strengthen the leadership. At that point, the coach has generally gained the trust of the leader but not that of the team. He must then focus on undergoing the initial processes with the team to gain its confidence. Importantly, he must meet each member individually. This step is vital if the team is suffering from conflict. Obviously, the development of objectives cannot come from the sole head of department but must be part of a genuine team project.

A suspicious team

The general manager of a regional hospital is requesting coaching to improve the functioning of the medical team of a key division of the institution. Recent complaints from executives of other departments lead him to think that support is required for the team and its leader to improve functioning. According to his analysis, reviewing the organization and functioning of the team are urgent, whose tasks are constantly increasing.

The coach initially meets the head of department, Kevin, who abruptly announces that he is upset by the director's proposal. "Up to this day I have not encountered any problem running this division. I get on well with my colleagues, and everything is running smoothly. I do not see why we should waste our time for this coaching. I have already given this message to the director twice." Asked about his leadership and team management, Kevin recognizes that everything is challenging. "I get along particularly well with two of my attendings but less well with others who have formed a rather oppositional group. I have difficulty delegating certain tasks because these persons are reluctant to accept communal activities, such as supervision of young physicians, preparation of training seminars, and quality of care follow-up." After giving the head of the department information about coaching, the coach summarizes the discussion to help determine the leader's position. At the end of the interview, Kevin's motivation seems to change. He finally agrees to undertake coaching sessions with the team to evaluate the effect.

The coach meets all members of the executive teams who support the idea to organize team coaching to improve functioning as a team and particularly communication within the group and relationships with the department head.

The first meeting of the coach with the team is difficult because a few of the executives are silent or reserved. The coach solicits the opinion of everyone. Two executives seem favorable to the proposal, whereas three attendings are not in favor because:

- "We are suspicious of the hospital management and express fears about the possible consequences of coaching."
- "The director wants to put us in step. We are weak in the face of management, especially because we disagree with one another."
- "You are paid by the management; thus, you will have to follow instructions. The assistance could thus weaken us."

This vignette illustrates typical elements of the first steps of a team coaching prescribed in a hospital environment, such as power relations between hierarchical levels, divergences of points of view and interest, and uncomfortable position of the coach when the expectations of the members differ. Table 8.1 summarizes important points to consider when setting up team coaching.

Table 8.1 Coach analysis grid for starting team coaching

- Did the coach meet individually with the leader and each team member?
- Does the leader understand what the proposed coaching approach means, the role of the coach, and the guarantee of confidentiality? Does he agree to engage in the proposed assistance?
- Do team members understand what the proposed coaching approach means? Do they agree? Are they ready to play an active role in the process beginning with goal setting?
- How do the members of the group communicate in terms of overall quality of communication? Is it non-violent or violent communication? What is the level of psychological security of the members? Are they capable of expressing oneself and sharing and giving opinions? Are clans present?
- What is the behavior of the leader, i.e., assertive, authoritarian, dominant, participatory, passive, careless, empathic …?
- Is the leadership model participatory or non-participatory?
- What is the level of effectiveness of leadership?
- Does effective communication exist between the leader and members of the group?
- What is the behavior of the team members, i.e., active, assertive, participatory, non-interested, passive, aggressive, hostile …?
- What is the general atmosphere of team work sessions, i.e., relaxed, productive, or tense and not very productive? Are the participants active or passive? Is humor present?
- What is the level of confidence within the group? Do people speak out and give their opinions? Do they criticize themselves or others? Is it done openly or indirectly? Is the presence of a scapegoat noted (although sometimes difficult to discern)?
- Are disagreements and conflicts discussed and put on the table or obscured?
- Are common culture and shared values present?
- Are delegated tasks executed? Does each member feel responsible for carrying out his tasks? Is the task delegation process defined and known to all? Do the senior physicians have specifications? Are the tasks of the leader known to everyone?
- What is the assessment process for each participant organized (including the chief)?

Carrying on coaching

Unlike other types of businesses, organizing sessions with the entire medical team in the hospital setting is often difficult and nearly impossible at times, given the many activities of physicians and high number of meetings they attend. We have recently experienced this situation with the medical team of a department severely disrupted by the prolonged absence of two attendings. Starting of coaching on top of the weekly team meetings was nearly impossible. We accommodated ourselves to this situation and agreed to intervene within the actual team meetings, emphasizing the need to spend time for discussion and feedback. During these time slots, we focused on the ongoing processes, such as communication, mode of leadership, decision-making processes, exchanges between the department head and attendings, or between the attendings. In addition to the planned interventions at the beginning and end of each meeting, the coach played an active role in an impromptu manner when topics or interactions between the physicians emerged related to the objectives of coaching (e.g., managing the divergence of opinion or distribution of task). Such interruption enabled the coach and the team to work in the *here and now*, a metacommunication to progress in the coaching goals.

In such a condition, we propose to complete the course of coaching during the team sessions by organizing meetings specifically devoted to coaching and ongoing projects at regular intervals and, if possible, in a non-hospital setting. Only then can deepening the development of coaching goals becomes possible.

The mode and course of coaching must be specified at the first session of work. Defining the roles of the coach, head of unit, senior physicians, and other participants (e.g., chief residents) and the rules of conduct during coaching and activities of the group are necessary. The head of department is a key element of medical hierarchies regardless of the type of leadership. Understanding that the coach does not play in any case the role of a substitute of the leader or a subordinate is a necessary concept that must be understood by the head of department.

Jupiter wants to improve his communication

The head of a university research laboratory is seeking coaching to improve the functioning of the management team. Apart from the head, the team is composed of executives from different fields, such as physicians, biologists, a project manager, a quality manager, a computer scientist, a finance manager, and an administrative manager. While acknowledging the excellence of the research carried out in the laboratory, the head complains of the insufficient collaboration of various executives, frequency of minor conflicts, lack of shared vision, and low level of interest shown for the activities of other sectors. For him, coaching will enable "the management team to wake up, to encourage the collaboration of the teams, and to warm up the working climate." He is immediately ready to review the governance and distribution of tasks in the management group.

The interviews of the members of the team confirm the general picture. In addition, most of them emphasize the image of a rather distant leader ("Jupiter on Olympus"), that is, authoritarian but fleeing conflicts or playing a role that favors them. All executives seem to agree to undertake coaching.

The first coaching session begins by providing information on the coaching project given by the head of department. After explaining the basics of coaching, the coach goes around the table. A short discussion is opened focused on the method of coaching work.

> Coach, addressing the chief: Do you agree with the working method and operating rules that I propose?
>
> *Chief:* No problem, but I fail to see what my role is during this work.
>
> *Coach:* You put yourself in the shoes of a department head who agrees to work in a particular setting with a coach at his side. You prepare the agenda of the sessions, and you animate as usual. Having time slots to intervene during discussions is necessary for me. As explained, I hope that all executives will take the floor and actively participate in the sessions to advance in the collective work. For the next session, I propose that everyone develop a sketch of the coaching work objectives. For your convenience, I suggest that we prepare the next meeting together for approximately 30 minutes before the arrival of the team.
>
> *Chief:* In practice, does this mean that I lose certain levels of authority and attributes?
>
> *Coach:* Not at all. This option means that the management sessions will take place in a setting different from the one you are used to. You will find that everything will come into place without problems and without threatening your prerogatives as a leader.
>
> *Chief:* For decisions, can I keep my authority?
>
> *Coach:* Yes, of course. However, I will regularly solicit feedback from your colleagues, such that they can express their opinion and make proposals.

This vignette describes the difficulty experienced by a department head to agree to work using a different mode of operation within the framework of the executives' team. His stance at a distance has allowed him to govern his department alone but affirmed the opposite. The preparation of the sessions with the coach enables him to become familiar with a new way of leading and be reassured at the same time.

Start with a submissive chief of division

The medical director offers Andrew (head of division) coaching to improve the dynamics of the medical team and the operation of the entire division. The first meeting with the medical team is set up in two stages. The first is devoted to information concerning the proposal of the director to undertake coaching. The second pertains to explanations about the coaching approach, different processes, and the role of the coach. A heated debate on the usefulness of such an assistance follows: "What can we expect? Is it not a waste of time and energy?" The coach notes that Andrew seems nearly absent from this discussion. The coach questions him about the information that has been given to the team.

Coach:	Following our meeting with the management, did you inform your team on this project and prepare with them a sketch of the work objectives?
Andrew:	No, not really, I did not tell them about the discussions we had with the hospital management. What should be done?
Coach:	I suggest you lead the session for the next 30 minutes and work on the team's goals for coaching.
Andrew (embarrassed silence):	... I would prefer you to lead the beginning of the discussion.
Coach:	Okay, I will start for a short while as long as you are in charge.

Andrew gradually regains his place and exposes the fruit of his reflection about the process of coaching (already discussed with the coach): to work initially on three axes, namely, distribution of tasks, organization of the medical call system, and relationships with the nursing team. At the end of the session, the participants confirm their interest in coaching.

This vignette illustrates the possible confusion of roles between the leader, coach, and medical team. At the onset, the coach strives to avoid the triangulation that can take place and disrupt the course of coaching. In this situation, the leader is withdrawn and prefers the coach to lead the session. In the case of an assertive head or a blocking hierarchy, which is common in the medical world, leaders often take the floor instead of attendings, who withdraw into a passive posture. Such a situation requires to be tackled face-to-face to avoid an impasse of the dynamics of coaching from the beginning. The first step is to establish a clear definition of roles during the first session. The coach supports the work and manages the coaching process. He is the guarantor of the establishment of a safe and respectful work environment for all, including the head of division. Andrew eventually actively participates in the work, retains his role as leader, and agrees that team members play an active role in the process. The team members also actively participate in the coaching process and achievement of objectives. Going regularly around the table at each major transaction and at the beginning and end of the session gives everyone a voice.

Preparing the sessions with the head of department at the beginning of the assistance is beneficial for developing a bond of trust with him. The process also helps to convince him to accept that team members speak up and take an active place in the discussions in the respectful environment of his person. In the case of participative leadership with less pronounced hierarchical positions, issues can be rarely observed.

The drama triangle: a trap to avoid

The role confusion between the head of department and coach favors the emergence of a negative triangulation dynamics, as described by Stephen Karpman, a transactional analysis psychologist.[8] In its classical form, this dynamics involves three people who play different, interchangeable roles, namely, the *persecutor, victim,* and *savior.* Each role goes hand in hand with an incomplete and biased view of reality called *misunderstanding*[b] in transactional analysis. The persecutor is in a high position and dictates his wishes, exercises power, and even mistreats the victim. The latter is in a low position and seeks a savior she solicits without making an explicit request. The savior, meanwhile, wants to help others whenever possible even without being asked. This biased dynamics between needs, expectations, and lack of demand goes hand in hand with an unexpected reversal of roles: the victim then turns into a persecutor or savior; the persecutor becomes the victim or savior and so on. The coach can be trapped in the dramatic triangle and finds himself in a position of savior of the chief of division. He then advises the chief and whispers what he must do and thus risks seeing the head of division turn against him at the first opportunity.

Start with a submissive chief of division (continued)

During the first three coaching sessions, Andrew is withdrawn. On each occasion, he questions the coach to ask his opinion or to take a stand on a particular point. The coach stimulates the senior physicians to intervene and be active in the discussion. After six sessions, a first assessment is presented to the medical director.

Medical Director:	I am anxious to know how you are doing. Describe the work done.
Andrew:	Here is our list of objectives in line with what has been discussed with you during the first session. I am asking the coach to comment on the development of the objectives.
Coach:	I note the involvement of all executives in the process.
Andrew:	That is right, but it embarrassed me many times.
Coach:	I'm surprised. What do you mean by that statement?
Andrew:	At this point, I think I feel misled about the development of coaching? On several occasions, you have supported the requests of my executives. How do you want me to run the division in these conditions?
Medical Director:	I am surprised, because it is not the mission of the coach to replace the head of division, and it goes without saying.

Coach, on the defensive: I have neither taken the position of the head of the department nor interfere in the decisions he makes.

This vignette illustrates the risk incurred by the coach in occupying the high position of the "savior," the one who knows, in front of a passive and resigned head of division. The latter, which is most often in a low position during the first coaching sessions, takes this opportunity to trip his coach and move into the position of a "persecutor." This dynamics is a typical example of Karpman's triangle even if the coach challenges the version of the head of division.

Team dynamics

The first sessions allow the coach to identify the fundamental elements of the functioning of the group and its internal processes, such as rules of operation, internal culture, type of leadership, and weight of the hierarchy. Initial analysis can hold many surprises at all levels in terms of the behavior of the leader and executives, relationships between residents in training and senior physicians and between doctors and nurses, and open or hidden conflicts.

A new team leader

A senior physician without previous experience is appointed to lead a department in a regional hospital. He begins his new activity in a difficult context by being linked to the unexpected departure of his predecessor whose failing management had long been known. This poor team leadership resulted in tension between the medical and nursing teams, which disrupted the functioning of the department. The medical director offers the new leader coaching for the medical executive group to "get off on a good start," which is accepted. The coach meets the head of department and head nurse. The interviews confirm the initial diagnosis: the department operates sub-optimally and reviewing medical practices and patient management protocols is necessary. The nursing team lacks resources and should train new specialists to respond to development projects and ensure an equitable distribution of workload between the old and new staff.

The first two sessions highlight several significant elements. The head of department is authoritarian and less open to dialogue. The senior physicians are passive and resigned. Lastly, the head nurse is less open and is fiercely defending her territory against the medical team. A general mistrust ensues, which results in the poor circulation of information and lack of shared culture and common objectives. The development of coaching goals is laborious. Working on the strengths of care teams, which are recognized in other departments (high level of competence of senior physicians and a few nurses) and difficult to emerge, enables the elaboration of the first shared goal, that is, "to create a medical and nursing direction system promoting collaboration and joint projects."

This vignette illustrates the behavior of a management team in a long-standing stuck system. As the new physician head wants to change things quickly, he has opted for authoritarian and obstructive leadership. This scheme prevents the establishment of a new team dynamics. At the start, coaching is painstaking, but working on the team processes releases the initial block.

A new team leader (continued)

To encourage the stakeholders to open up to one another and promote proactive discussion, the coach goes around the table and questions the participants about the functioning of the department management and their expectations. All, including the senior physicians, report being dissatisfied with the current operation of the head physician. This view is not shared by the new department head who believes that he must first "strengthen his authority to put a system in place allowing him to change things quickly." A lively debate follows, which is a first for the coach with this team! Questioned about the role he imagines for other members of the management, the head of department ends up changing his views and admits the establishment of a system that is more open, in which "we can say things and everyone is active and speaks up." He notes that this approach should contribute to "promoting the system functioning and its management." This agreement marks an important step forward in achieving the first goal. At the next session, the debates, which remain animated and intense, finally lead to the development of a new objective in terms of improving the organization of the department in three fields, namely, medical and nursing organization and medical–nursing interface. To move quickly toward these goals, developing a department project based on such objectives was agreed.

Supporting a medical team, particularly bringing together senior physicians, can be difficult as described earlier. Facing the stalling power of the medical hierarchy is often necessary to succeed in this step and implies that the coach is actively developing a relationship of trust with the leader, which will serve as a lever for the remainder of the process. This relationship must be part of the coaching relationship with the team, excluding any special relationship between the coach and team members or the head of department. In this context, the coach is not the *adviser of the prince*; he should not experience any conflict of loyalty during possible tension in the team and thus keeps his freedom of action.

The development of objectives shared by the majority of the team members, which is essential to the coaching work, can be painstaking especially in a department suffering from chronic conflicts or inadequate leadership. To make the head aware that his version of the objectives may not be shared by the entire team requires work with the sole manager. The coach has typically started the coaching with the latter and prepared temporary goals, although not explicitly shared by all team members. They were finalized in subsequent sessions with the team members. Supporting the medical team during weekly sessions and starting the coaching by focusing on the ongoing processes during these meetings (i.e., information, communication, leadership, and decision-making) makes better aligning the head with the team possible.

You will address the hospital management

The merger of two medical divisions has significantly increased the size of a medical team. However, a year later, the team remains divided into two groups and struggling to develop a shared culture, collaborate, and even clash. The medical director initiates coaching. Goal setting is difficult as two sessions are required for a majority of physicians to align with the work objectives. After four sessions, during which the coach gradually takes his place, a half-day workshop is planned to advance in teambuilding. The main theme is "Identifying the strengths of the team."

The workshop begins with a "game" in which the team is divided into two subgroups. These groups were formed (with the help of the head of department) with the idea of mixing the doctors from the two opposed groups. The instruction to both is to sketch a draft letter to the management (maximum two pages) on an actual hot topic in the hospital: "What to answer to the hospital management that plans to increase the deductions on our private fees?" The answer must focus on the strengths and successes of the medical team.

The two groups work and write two relatively different texts that describe the rapid development of the department, commitment, and strengths of the direction team, which are not always recognized by the hospital management. Together, the groups finally elaborate a text that summarizes the viewpoints of all senior physicians. They suggest that they are ready to mobilize to defend their interests.

The remainder of the afternoon shows a substantial improvement in the working climate and group dynamics. A first assessment of the coaching is drawn, which leads to a revision of the work objectives.

Trust is a complex feeling that is difficult to identify and measure in groups, but it is essential for effective and efficient teamwork. Without having a solid mutual trust, communicating effectively, giving personal opinions, managing conflicts, adhering to decisions, developing a common cultural envelope, and cooperating and collaborating will become impossible. A lack of trust disrupts work climate, interdisciplinary relationships, satisfaction of team members, and their ability to learn and develop personally. For Lencioni, reciprocal trust forms the foundation on which the main processes governing teamwork are based.[9]

How then should the level of trust in a team be rated? In a team with a strong atmosphere of trust, the information circulates, members speak up freely and are able to describe their difficulties, their errors, and even their weaknesses and occasional failures. The reaction of other members including their understanding and level of empathy also express their confidence. Such groups are usually led by a chief with effective and participative leadership and with strong human qualities. As such, they are rarely the subject of a coaching request. In groups with low levels of trust, the coach observes a completely different scenario: the discussions are restrained; description of facts or difficulties is withheld, and the participants do not report their dissatisfaction or failures. Leadership is often inadequate, either weighing an excessive hierarchical weight or, rarely, leaving the direction in a laissez-faire fashion.

Trust in the teams corresponds to a large extent to the level of psychological safety felt by the members in their activities within the team: "Am I at ease in the group? Is my place recognized? Can I express myself freely? Can I give opinions that differ from those of the majority? Can I oppose the chief's ideas?" The leadership style of the head and the behavior of all members of the hierarchy play predominant roles because they directly influence the members' sense of security.[6] When the weight of the hierarchy is excessive, people in a low position tend not to speak up, not to give their opinion, and not to contest the opinion of their superiors even if they disapprove of it.[6] Reinforcing the feeling of security is a priority task of the coach in such conditions, which can take a considerable amount of time and energy.

The coach is also concerned and the target of the trust factor: How will a team be effectively coached if trust is missing and if members prefer to hide their opinions rather than express them? As we have observed, trust is worthy, and the coach does not escape this reality. He must be particularly attentive to his interactions with the leader, which must be transparent especially if he prepares sessions with him. In other words, all information exchanged during these preparation sessions must be reported to the group, except for personal matters. The same is true of his interactions with the management who prescribed coaching. In our hospital experience, being assisted by the head of unit for meetings with the hospital management regarding the coaching in progress is wise.

Work on the department project

When the manager of our university hospital center decided to merge the two adult intensive care units (medicine and surgery), she asked the medical and nursing leaders to prepare a department project, which describes the main processes governing the operation of the department at all levels. Emphasis was placed on the leadership model at the medical and nursing levels, decision-making processes, definition of roles and distribution of tasks, communication, and medical–nursing relationships. The medical and nursing executives went to work with enthusiasm and took them approximately six months to prepare a model accepted by all senior care providers and finally by the hospital management with minimal changes. This realization required a long process, repeated negotiations, and compromises, to align the divergent points of view and identify the structuring of shared values. It highlighted the value of collective work accomplished by two teams involved in the co-construction of a joint project, whose success was far from being guaranteed at the beginning of the process. All of the care providers benefited from it in many ways as confidence grew within the medical and nursing teams, as well as between the medical and nursing staff. The different categories of care providers have developed mutual recognition; many care providers committed to the merger and change processes. Enriched by this founding experience, we propose to the management teams to carry out this approach in their own way. It allows them to approve together the main elements of medical organization and team management.

Creating a new management system as part of a merger

The merger of the two adult intensive care divisions required a fundamental rethinking of the management system: it was about building a new, larger department, including approximately 300 employees and a team of more than 30 physicians. In addition, the project involved bringing together two models of medical and nursing organizations and two types of leadership. Agreement from the medical staff of the new department was needed to obtain the green light from the hospital management. This step required motivation, considerable work, time, and compromise on both sides. The process was simple at the level of the nursing team; however, it was more centralized and more hierarchical than the medical corps.

The discussions, led by the two head physicians (supported by their senior physicians) and by the two chief nurses, made building an innovative system that was approved by all managers possible.

- a medical–nursing directorate, including the two chief physicians and the two head nurses who were responsible for the medical–nursing coordination;
- two chief physicians, where one is responsible for management and the other for education and training;
- two head nurses with complementary missions;
- a participative leadership system at the medical level centered on a medical executive group. The latter is made up of the two chief doctors and all senior physicians. The clinical activities are under the control of the medical executive group. One of the senior physicians coordinates the research activities, whereas others coordinate the main specialized areas of management (i.e., quality, information technology, and data collection);

- a medical–nursing group is created to distribute information to middle managers (i.e., chief residents, representatives of nurses, and other health professionals) and enable them to participate in decisions;
- a medical–nursing group for quality assurance is created assisted by a quality manager to conduct accreditation in the ISO system.[c]

Such an organization has made possible the setting up in a collaborative atmosphere of a high-performance system that is recognized by users. The various executives managed differences and conflicts without difficulty during the first three years after the merger.

In a public hospital, governance and model of general organization are determined by the State, which holds ultimate responsibility and is the funder. A substantial freedom is usually given to the medical and nursing managers to set up their organization (i.e., department, division, and unit), team leadership, and specific management processes. We will describe three essential elements of such a model.

Leadership

In this chapter, we will focus on certain aspects of leadership concerned with team coaching. Addressing this issue openly in the context of team coaching and in front of the head and senior physicians can be challenging. However, it is necessary when leadership and management are faulty, which is often the case when coaching is undertaken. The coach must first address this point with the department head to convince him to put it in discussion in front of the senior physicians and make him understand that an open leadership can improve operations and simplify his duties as manager.

The discussion within the medical team invariably shows the desire of senior physicians to be able to work in a participative system and to actively collaborate in the management and decision-making.

Changing a solitary type of leadership

The medical head of division, Bill, leads his team remotely and alone. He prefers not to take a stand to avoid difficult decisions and flee conflict. The work on the division project is launched at the third session. Interviews with the attendings and chief residents unanimously express a desire to introduce a more participative system. Bill agrees to present the results of the interviews to the team. Conversely, he is reluctant to discuss the assessment of his leadership by the senior physicians for fear of losing face. The preparation of the team meeting with the coach gradually reassures him.

Coach: The medical director feels that your style of leading the division is sub-optimal. To prepare for the next team session, I propose that we analyze certain positive characteristics of your leadership and others that may be counterproductive and complicate your life.
Bill: OK, as long as it stays between you and me.
Coach: What are you afraid of?
Bill: I am afraid it will weaken my position again.
Coach: How do you feel about starting by analyzing your leadership in the preparation sessions? This analysis could shed light on your strong sides as well as your difficulties. You can then make the decision to talk about it or not with your team.
Bill: Okay.

After two preparatory sessions, Bill is convinced that building a new model of management with his team is in his best interest. He begins to realize that he might feel more comfortable in a system where he will be supported by his team in the management rather than left to himself and even contested. However, he hopes that clear rules of operation will be established to facilitate his mission as leader.

This vignette illustrates the difficulty of a leader in a field of highly specialized medicine in directing his division, which is an activity that he does not appreciate and in which he recognizes being not very effective. It also shows the fear of this chief to question himself and accept that his leadership is put in discussion. Once this door is opened, it is a matter of setting up a new system to manage the main processes of the division.

Decision-making processes

The question now is *who decides what and how*. When the head of department has opted for an authoritarian mode, the decision-making process is simple: he is the one who decides after hearing or not his team deliberates on the decision to take. In more participative models, the fact that in the current hospital medical world, the definition of roles and the sharing of authority often remain unclear and vary according to circumstances should be underlined: without a clear decision-making process, certain decisions are made by the chief alone, whereas others are shared.

In practice, three main decision areas should be considered:

- The department head's domain pertains to the representation of the department, hiring of medical executives, evaluation of senior physicians, management of conflicts between senior physicians, and conflicts with other departments. In this area, the chief can inform and consult his executives, but he remains the person responsible for the decision.
- The domain of shared decisions with the executive medical team. For a truly participatory system, the respective roles of the chief and executive team have to be determined. The chief has to distribute information, organize discussions, and define the final decision mode.
- Areas delegated to senior physicians (e.g., organization of the training program, supervision of in-training physicians, and supervision of quality assurance). Defining the domain, mission of the person in charge, and feedback to give back to the management team is necessary.

Changing a solitary type of leadership (continued)

The delimitation of Bill's decision-making area raises an animated discussion.

Coach: To move forward in the decision areas of the head and management team, I propose to listen to the views of the chief.

Bill: As my own field, I retain the duties of a division head that I must assume myself according to my specifications, that is, the representation of the department at all levels, preparation of the budget, annual reports, and management of legal complaints. In addition, I want to continue hiring and promoting the senior physicians and academics.

Attending A: Why not share with the team the recruitment of attendings or their hospital promotion? Requests for academic promotions could also be finalized with the medical executive team!

Bill: I do not think that is a good idea because it can lead to tension or even fights in the team. In the department of surgery, my colleagues are the ones who settle these questions.

Attending B: I can understand the position of the head, but how do you ensure minimal transparency? The previous hospital appointment was conducted during a cloudy climate, which is detrimental to the team's goodwill and the candidate. I propose that this area remains in the hands of our chief, who should inform the team in real time.

Coach: As I understand, it is about finding reasonable equilibrium between the necessary authority of the head and the right of the executives to participate in decision-making. It is a question of leadership style. It is also necessary that the chief feels at ease in his new clothes.

Coach, to Bill: How do you feel in hearing these proposals?

Bill: Actually, I do not feel threatened. I am looking for balance that suits me and my colleagues. I agree to inform the executive team during academic promotion as it is a sensitive point, and transparency is necessary. I think we should continue the discussion to move toward a solution.

The following session allows the team to come to an agreement about a system of shared leadership that is accepted by all.

In this situation, we see an effective work of co-construction involving all executives and their leader, who elaborated a balanced solution acceptable to all parties. Such a compromise is not always possible.

Defining roles and delegating tasks

In a small medical division, the chief usually performs the majority of management tasks. In large departments, however, he cannot assume all management and supervision tasks in the fields of clinical, teaching, and research activities, in addition to his management tasks. Therefore, he has to delegate part of his tasks to his colleagues. Thus, designating attendings in charge of delegated tasks is necessary. For example, in the clinical field, the drafting of treatment protocols, quality assurance, establishment of the medical call plan (i.e., residents, chief residents, and attendings), supervision of patient discharge letters, and control of clinical records should be taken up by designated colleagues. In the field of training, the development of a postgraduate training program, supervision of the assessment of medical students, supervision and evaluation of residents, and supervision of the training institution should also be handled by senior physicians.

The definition of roles, delegation, and the follow-up of tasks are important processes for the functioning of the department, as well as for the motivation of the chief and executives. The difficulty in effectively delegating tasks to attendings (such that they lead to the expected results) is at the top of the complaint list of many department heads. From the perspective of the attendings, two complaints are frequent, namely, unequal distribution of tasks and authoritarian delegation of tasks that are not negotiated between the chief and his subordinates. Frustration and tension emerge, where the chief complains of the "bad will of his executives to carry out the tasks he delegates," whereas the attendings complain of being considered as "mere performers," and recognized little for their work.

Task delegation to the attendings: a difficult job

Charles is the head of a large hospital department and complains, among other things, of his difficulty in delegating tasks to his senior physicians.

Charles: I experience no problems with the chief residents, and delegation is simple. They perform their tasks effectively within the allotted time. The executives, however, are another story, especially with those who were appointed before I arrived three years ago.

Coach: Can you explain how you delegate?

Charles: Most often in the weekly meeting. I briefly describe the task and designate someone.

Coach: And then ...?

Charles: We do not have time to discuss it in detail during the meeting given the limited time available. I send an email to the designated person to explain the work to be done and the deadline. In addition, I always give the indication that I am ready to discuss or help the person if necessary.

Coach: Could you imagine a more interactive method?

Charles: Why not, but I would be afraid of losing control of the delegation. It is already difficult given the current situation, and it could become worse.

> *Coach:*   How then will you give the attendings the possibility of
>   expressing their opinion and preferences regarding the
>   tasks?
> *Charles:*   I see what you are alluding to, and why not? I will think about
>   it before the next meeting.
>
> The question of delegation is on the agenda of the next meeting. A
> lively discussion ensues, which highlights the frustration of the
> executives to undergo such a delegation mode. The attendees finally
> decided to set up a participative system and to make each executive
> responsible for the accomplishment of his tasks to the team (and
> not to the head solely). After a moment of hesitation, Charles agrees.

The opening up of the head of department, who is rather fearful in front of his executives, makes it possible to find a common solution to this recurring problem. A roadmap is established for the follow-up of the delegation of tasks, thus allowing the head of department and managers to share an overall vision of the distribution of these duties and their accomplishment.

When the coach has difficulties or is defeated

Group coaching is a difficult art, especially with groups of physicians, whose individualistic character and difficulty in participating in group activities are well established. The organization of the particularly vertical medical hierarchies in Europe subjects the coach to the constant risk of being stuck or being an "idiot." After several experiences, we can affirm that this process requires a certain number of qualities on the part of the coach, such as flexibility, sense of humor, self-confidence, and capacity to recognize his difficulties. Adequate posture made of trust and openness is required, thus avoiding the high position of the one who knows. Positioning oneself appropriately when managing tension and conflicts in the team is essential to show authority when necessary. In short, the coach must have a good experience of working with groups before rubbing against medical teams during crises in the hospital.

In the most difficult cases, we ask for supervision especially when we feel tension or discomfort with the group or even nervousness or discouragement. The same is true if we envisage putting pressure and actively pushing the process forward to escape the feeling of failure. Supervision gives the coach the opportunity to take stock, broaden, identify parallel processes, modify his posture, discover new strategies, and finally recharge his batteries and make his work more enjoyable. Finally, it reiterates the importance of the quality of the relationship between the coach and the group, which is built on the ability of the coach to be accepted and to promote trust, ensure the safety of all participants, bring out empathy and benevolence, and bounce when necessary.

A coach struggling against a divided team

Coaching is being undertaken to improve the leadership of the department head and address the problem of a team of senior physicians that split into two clans and remain disrupted by long-standing conflicts. The chief and the team of attendings are committed to working on the department project and find solutions to their disagreements and improve the functioning and cohesion of the team. After five sessions, a first assessment of the progress of the objectives is proposed. The coach is quickly hooked by one of the executives, who refutes the support deemed excessive for the head of department.

Attending A: I am sorry to tell you, but I do not find your attitude as neutral. In my opinion, you always support the head when it comes to making decisions.

Coach: I'm surprised at what you are saying. Can you name one case where I took a stand for someone?

Attending A: I recently attended a seminar on coaching, in which the benevolence of the facilitator astonished me. I cannot find this quality in your behavior.

Attending B: How can you say such things? I do not agree with you and find that the coach does his job well. In my opinion, we are a difficult group, and the problem is not the coach.

Coach: You need to have broad shoulders to lead a group coaching. In addition, remember that the coach is entitled to make mistakes once or twice ... .

The head of department does not intervene. The coach asks him:

Coach: Why are you so silent?

Chief: During the last months, I was rather able to solve the conflicts that are being voiced again today and believe me, it was difficult. To be honest, I do not like this kind of human emotional overflow. Finally, I would like to disapprove those who accuse the coach of taking a stand in this debate.

> *Coach:* I would like to emphasize the great individual qualities of the team members in their clinical practice, who would nevertheless benefit from learning to live together, collaborate, and develop their team spirit.
>
> A round is started, which shows that the interaction between the coach and the executives did not have a negative effect. Nevertheless, the coach leaves the session with mixed feelings.

In this situation, we see a coach who gets caught by a rather virulent executive who tries to destabilize him. He is unconsciously used in the group process to continue the splitting situation and be associated with one side.

Notably, the head of department only speaks up, describes her difficulty with conflictual relationships, and finally takes a position to support the coach only when the coach addresses her. This scenario is a true critical event that the coach will use in the following sessions to improve trust and relationship with the head (see critical events in chapter 12).

Building a climate of trust and abandoning old quarrels will take more than six months of work for this team. Conversely, two supervision sessions occurred before the coach could feel fully at ease in this coaching.

Conclusion

Current medicine is practiced by teams at the hospital. This statement is true for physicians and nurses who perform an increasing number of activities not only within their professional group but also in an interprofessional setting, in which care providers from diverse backgrounds work together. This chapter focuses on the coaching of medical management teams whose operation is sub-optimal. Many factors may explain this finding, such as weak leadership, weight of the medical hierarchy, and poor organization of the medical units. Leading a coaching in dysfunctional teams is a difficult task and requires good skills and experience in team life. Adequate posture made of trust and openness is needed, thus avoiding the high position of one who knows. Furthermore, flexibility, sense of humor, self-confidence, and capacity to recognize his difficulties are useful capabilities. Elements to be considered and difficulties and pitfalls (many) are analyzed and illustrated. Appropriate solutions in the hospital setting are proposed.

Notes

a The Core Competencies Needed for Health Care Professionals. In *Health Professions Education: A Bridge to Quality.* Greiner AC, Knebel E, editors. National Academic; 2003.

b Misunderstanding refers to an unconscious omission of an information, which would enable the resolution of a problem.

c ISO stands for "International Organization for Standardization." ISO develops standards that apply to products and services.

Bibliography

1 Doherty RB, Crowley RA. Health and Public Policy Committee of the American College of Physicians. Principles supporting dynamic clinical care teams: an American College of Physicians position paper. *Ann Intern Med* 2013; 159(9): 620–626.

2 Salas E, Sims DE, Burke CS. Is there a "Big Five" in teamwork?. *Small Group Res* 2005; 36(5): 555–599.

3 Schwarz R, Davidson A, Carlson P, McKinney S. *The Skilled Facilitator Fieldbook*. Jossey-Bass, San Francisco; 2005.

4 Hall P. Interprofessional teamwork: professional cultures as barriers. *J Interprof Care* 2005; 19(Suppl 1): 188–196.

5 Khan A. A death in the family. *JAMA* 2017; 318(16): 1543–1544.

6 Nembhard IM, Edmondson A. Making it safe: the effects of leader inclusiveness and professional status on psychological safety and improvement efforts in health care teams. *J Organ Behav* 2006; 27(7): 941–966. Available from: www.hbs.edu/faculty/Pages/item.aspx?num=21122 [cited April 5, 2018].

7 Thornton C. Looking deeper: the secret life of groups. *In: Group and Team Coaching: The Essential Guide*. Routledge, London and New York; 2010, pp. 44–63.

8 Joines V, Stewart I. *TA Today: A New Introduction to Transactional Analysis*. Lifespace Publishing, New Barn, UK and Chapel Hill; 2012.

9 Lencioni P. *Overcoming the Five Dysfunctions of a Team: A Field Guide for Leaders, Managers, and Facilitators*. Jossey-Bass, San Francisco; 2005.

Further readings

Lencioni P. *The Five Dysfunctions of a Team*. Jossey-Bass, San Francisco; 2005.

Schwarz R, Davidson A, Carlson P, *et al*. *The Skilled Facilitator Fieldbook*. Jossey-Bass, San Francisco; 2005.

Senge P. *The Fifth Discipline: The Art & Practice of The Learning Organization*. Currency Double Day London, New York, London, Toronto, Sidney, Auckland; 2006.

Thornton C. *Group and Team Coaching. The Essential Guide*. Routledge, London and New York; 2016.

9 Coaching through crisis

René Chioléro

Introduction

Change is part of the daily life of care providers who—similar to most humans—are naturally armed to adapt to most disturbances in their environment. Transitions, which accompany changes of state (e.g., promotion, transfer of hospital division, change of hospital), are less frequent and more challenging; they sometimes require external support to ensure that things run smoothly. Crises are characterized by the overflow and breakdown of systems of operation and the conduct and adaptation of a person, a group of people, or a company. They are caused by events of internal or external origin that exceed the means and resources of the involved individuals at that time. The most common forms of crises are quickly controlled and part of daily life in hospitals. When a crisis is intense or prolonged, the crisis becomes a significant event, which can induce marked stress on all employees and serious dysfunction in teams and activities. Such protracted crises may require external intervention.

Starting a coaching in a crisis is often a difficult undertaking because it is part of an unstable, changing reality, where the normal functioning of the individuals and groups is impaired. This case is particularly notable with care providers, who often delay requesting help (internal or external), which can seriously complicate the conduct of coaching. The use of appropriate methods makes overcoming these obstacles possible.

The purpose of this chapter is to describe the salient features of a crisis situation in the hospital context and analyze its impact on health care professionals. Crisis also affects the coaching course, which we describe in this chapter. Notable professional transitions, associated or not with an individual crisis, are also discussed.

Crisis: types and impact

Hospital systems can have *many types of crises*, for example, low-intensity crises occur almost daily in the busiest services of the hospital (e.g., emergency room, intensive care, operating rooms). The care providers who work to

DOI: 10.4324/9781003291831-12

provide these services know how to cope with the peaks of activity and daily disturbances such that they are of little consequence to them, except a feeling of high stress in some of them. There is no place for a coach in this context. The situation differs for serious or prolonged crises, which cause marked stress and exhaust care professionals and their leaders and may profoundly disturb a department's operation. Although care providers are naturally equipped to successfully manage daily professional and non-professional changes of all types (e.g., overload, promotion, change of leader, family change), the individual or group may be overwhelmed, and a crisis occurs. Crisis can be triggered by external factors affecting the hospital environment, such as imposing mandatory budget reductions stipulated by a government. It may also be caused by internal causes such as prolonged conflict or personal factors, for example, an illness or family crisis. The result is an overflow of the usual adaptation mechanisms of individuals or groups, which could disrupt their functioning, activities, or mission.

The *impact of a crisis* on individuals can be significant and cause psychological stress, dysfunction, tension, and conflict. If the crisis is serious and prolonged, it may induce a burnout, with all its attendant troubles and be the cause of absenteeism and dismissal. For the company, serious and prolonged crises are synonymous with disorganization, loss of productivity, financial loss, and can even destroy a company. For a hospital, a serious, prolonged crisis may threaten the delivery and quality of care.

By definition, personal crises affect only one person, even if they can negatively impact the functioning of the entire team. These crises may be related to that individual's work or private life or a combination of factors. Family crises, separation, divorce, and serious conflict all have repercussions that may disturb the whole functioning of the person involved, including her hospital duties and personal relationships at all levels.

Help, I'm drowning!

I receive a phone call on Monday morning at 7:30 from Elisabeth, medical head in a regional hospital. She immediately tells me that she is going through a difficult period.

Elisabeth: I'm not feeling well; I'm going through a terrible crisis; my life is rocking in all areas. My husband found a former girlfriend and left home. At work, it's not much better: my division is in crisis, and I cannot cope with the multitude problems of management and medical team functioning. In addition, I suffer from severe insomnia, and wake up at night with anxiety. Finally, I am summoned to the management in one week. This convocation led me to consider that I might need a coach to support me. Can you receive me quickly so that I can explain my problems and my heartbreaks? This time, I am forced to find solutions to get out of this crisis.

Coach: I'm sorry that this is a terrible time for you. I understand that you need help as soon as possible. I agree to meet with you for a first discussion to consider the work we can do together.

The first open appointment is the following Sunday. Elisabeth schedules her appointment at 5 pm.

This vignette illustrates the often special introduction of crisis coaching. In this case, there is a serious family crisis with severe professional repercussions and wide multilevel consequences.

At hospitals, common causes of crises include leadership failure, inadequate management, sudden team overload (e.g., illness, flu epidemic), interpersonal conflicts, transitions and promotions, medico–nursing relationships, and extensive reorganization.

Merging two intensive care unit divisions

René faced two major organizational changes during his career at the Lausanne University Hospital Center. During the 1990s, the anesthesiology department experienced a protracted crisis, initiated by a serious, prolonged leadership failure, with recurring medical conflicts and several changes at the head. In 2000, this situation led the hospital management to separate the surgical intensive care division from the anesthesiology department. This parting, in a climate of tension and conflict, represented a major transition for medical and nursing staffs. The mission was difficult and delicate: organize the new intensive care division and operate it seven days per week and 24 hours per day with a reduced medical team in a complex, uncertain, and unstable environment. This major change occurred without serious problems: the few crises encountered were quickly settled by the executives, and no major incident disturbed the work of the medical and nursing teams.

In 2004, the hospital management initiated a new project to merge the medical and surgical intensive care divisions, to create a large intensive care department and professionalize patient care as much as possible. The medical and nursing heads of the divisions, their six senior physicians, and seven senior nurses actively prepared the merger plan for the next 12 months. They had the support of a management specialist, incorporated into the new department for two years. A steering committee was established under the leadership of the medical director, to facilitate change processes. In this case, too, several crises were quickly overcome because of the strong involvement of all the nurses and medical executives; most of them were enthusiastic about merging the medical and surgical divisions of critical care.

During this experiment, we realized the importance of having support from a professional experienced with change, to ensure the success of the transition, a situation that had no room for failure. This support helped to reduce the stress of managers and collaborators related to this unstable period. The accompaniment also helped to improve our adaptability and flexibility of action in managing the inevitable disturbances and uncertainties of the merger.

In such a major transition, crises were expected in many fields. The involvement of a manager-coach prevented both a catastrophe and long-term dysfunction. Because of this support, transitional problems were resolved by the management of the department, without dire consequences for the users.

Alteration of cognition

Stress significantly modifies all the higher cerebral functions: attention, memorization, and cognitive performance.[1] This modification is related to the emotional and physiological repercussions of stress that influence (positively or negatively) memory and all cognitive functions.[2] Analytical capacity and the ability to make decisions are also impaired.[3] This reality is easily observed when an untrained person must give an impromptu presentation to an assembly. Overall impairment of cognitive abilities is also observed during a high-intensity crisis in most untrained physicians and nurses. This usually returns to normal thereafter.[1,4] When testing the cognitive performances in low- to medium-intensity crises, alterations can be observed, although of weaker intensity. In human groups, this phenomenon can be amplified by group dynamics, particularly by the processes of mirroring, resonance, and condensation.[5]

Work with fear in the chest

The medical director solicits a coaching for a senior physician, Dr. Michael B, active in a leading a medical–technical specialty. This doctor has to perform complex and invasive technical procedures daily. The medical director considers Michael to be an excellent physician, probably the most dexterous of his medical team. By contrast, his temper is sometimes difficult, similar to that of his chief of department. The relationship between these two colleagues has gradually deteriorated over the last year, and the current situation seems explosive. Michael's boss has even threatened several times to fire him if he does not make amends. The medical director is eager to resolve this recurring problem. He suggests that Michael start an individual coaching, which might be followed by a mediation. The coach's first meeting with Michael is instructive. Michael confirms that he is negatively affected by his difficult relationship with his boss. He adds that the latter often has a threatening attitude toward him and sometimes ignores him in the sessions of the medical team.

Michael: I must tell you that in fact, I'm afraid of my boss; it was already the case when I was chief resident, before my appointment as attending. I am also afraid of being thrown out of this hospital, a place I like very much.

Coach: How does your fear manifest, what do you feel?

Michael: This fear disturbs me a lot, even during the interventions. When I'm scared, I get angry easily and doubt my ability to set the indications for a treatment and apply them correctly and without complication. I sometimes work with the feeling of fear in my stomach, which disrupts my actions and even my judgment.

Coach: How do you overcome your fear and be able to work?

Michael: It's difficult, especially since I try to hide this fear as much as possible.

Coach: I see, I understand your difficulty in doing delicate and potentially dangerous medico-technical intervention for patients in such conditions. And how do you imagine that a coaching may help you overcoming these difficulties?

Michael: In fact, I have thought that coaching may help me to make two changes: first, to tame my fear and to control it, and second, to learn how to better manage my relationship with my boss.

Coach: That's a good place to start …

These two goals will require more than 12 months of coaching to achieve a satisfactory result.

The alterations of cognitive functions during intense stress can be summarized as follows[1,3,4]:

- Reduction in the ability to process several pieces of information in parallel: under normal conditions, this capacity amounts to approximately seven simultaneous messages, and under marked stress conditions, this can be reduced to three to four or even less.
- Decreased overall cognitive capacity, for example, decreased attention, reduced understanding, slower thinking, misinterpretation, and sometimes confusion.
- Increased reaction time and selective attention, which can result in "attentional and auditory blindness."
- Impairment of higher cognitive functions, for example, calculation, reading, use of foreign languages, listening, comprehension, reasoning, ability to assess a situation, and decision-making ability.

In a perfectly quiet state, some people have difficulty processing several pieces of information in parallel, others always have a long reaction time. However, stress intensifies cognitive dysfunctions and induces several of these impairments simultaneously. All these symptoms do not simultaneously appear in every stressed person, or with the same intensity. Because of the magnitude of these alterations and the high-intensity stress environment in which care providers are immersed daily, stress management should be systematically taught.

The usual process of action and learning include four main components (Kolb's learning cycle)[6]:

- Concrete experience (acting, experiencing): live an experience, doing.
- Reflective observation (reviewing): analysis of the action, what worked and what did not work.
- Thinking, problem-solving: analysis and thought processes help create new and abstract concepts, new solutions.
- Active experimentation: planning and testing concepts in new experiments and drawing conclusions.

This learning model is logical: It allows reflecting after experiencing to define an objective, draw a realization plan, act, and then evaluate the effect. In crises, short circuits of thought often occur, which disturb the whole process.[7] The most common short circuits include the following[7]:

a   The "plan-do-plan-do trap," in which the subject acts and directly makes a correction if it does not work, without going through the initial assessment and reflection; this corresponds to a trial-error strategy.
b   The "do-review-do-review" short circuit, where the cycle is focused on action and reviewing the errors, skipping problem-solving and planning.
c   The iterative "reviewing-planning-reviewing-planning" cycle, in which the subject is looping between reviewing and thinking about how things could be improved, without planning and acting.

The following vignette describes a division head in acute stress and is a striking example of this phenomenon.

I am not myself anymore

Emily arrives angry at the coaching session because she just had an altercation with her co-worker who "hurted her a lot." She says: "He has the ability to upset me so much; I'm no longer myself and unable to answer calmly. After the last altercation, I was irritated enough that I didn't remember what I said, what he said, and who started to quarrel; this has never occurred between me and a colleague. I don't feel myself anymore."

In this vignette, there is a leader, generally calm and decided, who loses her means, after an acute confrontation with a colleague. She becomes increasingly upset, causing major cognitive impairment that completely disrupts her thinking.

The following vignette describes an overreaction after an attack of anger by a chief physician:

Today, I am quite upset

I receive an email from a chief of division with whom coaching, proposed by the medical director, is in its initial phase:

Dear coach, I am writing to you, even if what follows will not concern you directly. Today, I was very upset by the head of department, who made me nice promises that he did not keep and shamelessly supported a colleague with whom I have a conflict. This occurs despite my written warnings to him. Investing time outside the hospital to prepare projects that no one reads simply makes no sense to me. I reflected on this situation; I warn you, that I propose canceling our remaining coaching sessions. This is regrettable, but today, I don't see any way out of the problems that agitate our division. An official letter will follow to announce this decision to the medical director.

After a long phone call with the coach, the chief of division had to think about all this, and shortly thereafter, she changed her mind and decided to pursue coaching. She acknowledged the importance of continuing the effort to manage her time and control her stress.

All of these alterations significantly disrupt the management of acute, high-intensity crises, preventing meaningful analysis and rational decision-making. This is why emergency professionals (e.g., firefighters, police, military, emergency doctors, nurses) benefit from specific training to improve their general and cognitive performance in the most difficult situations. The effectiveness of such training has been widely documented in situations such as cardiopulmonary resuscitation situations on the street and in emergency departments.[8] The cognitive impairments resulting from high-intensity crises also affect the coach, who must be able to identify and adapt to them, to help the client to overcome them. The coach may be directly affected and, for example, become upset or lose his composure in front of a group in an acute situation or when he is contested by one or more participants.

Coaching progress

Assessing the capability of the client

Coaching a client in a state of acute crisis can pose many problems because she is usually less able or unable to endorse her normal role: to present a clear request, set work goals, make decisions, and take actions, with many similarities to states of acute stress. In such a state, she may need assistance, support, understanding, and empathy. Her emotional response must be considered; if the response is strong, the first contact and first sessions can be hectic; otherwise, when the client can better hide her symptoms, the coach may, at first, not observe anything particular, only to realize later that the client was indeed in crisis. Next, we present an example of this situation: a description of the first session with a manager who is exhibiting a "reactive" behavior, experiencing chronic burnout, and overwhelmed by a day full of unforeseen events:

Here we all run.

Alexander leads the cardiology department of a large regional hospital. He has multiple activities and runs from one task to another throughout the day, for example, practice in the cardiac catheterization room, with emergencies that require immediate availability (e.g., undertaking coronary angioplasty); visits; direction of the service; and teaching.

Constantly under pressure, he shows signs of exhaustion. His availability for his colleagues is weak; some days his impatience and poor ability to listen are evident. A coaching is proposed by the human resources manager to improve his leadership, particularly the conduct of the medical team and his time management. Despite his reluctance to accept a coaching, Alexander says that he is "interested in discovering something new, as long as it does not take too much time."

The first session is scheduled at the height of the problem: his beeper, placed on the table, rings several times because a patient must be admitted to the emergency room catheterization.

Coach: Is it possible to give this beeper to your secretary for at least the next 45 minutes?

Alexandre: Yes; ok; she will pick me up when the patient is ready.

Alexandre describes how the division works, his problems with his colleagues, and his great difficulty in developing a shared vision with the attendings.

Alexandre: Everyone runs in the division; it is not only me who is concerned. It is exhausting, and I really want to find solutions to lower the pressure.

Coach: How do you organize the team of senior executives?

Alexandre: It's a bit the same as today: the beeper rings several times, and the discussions within the team are sometimes difficult to follow.

Coach: Team life is often disturbed as it is today, I guess?

Alexandre: Probably ... moreover, my colleagues complain that they don't receive all the information about the division and don't participate in all important decisions.

Coach: How would it be to work on these topics in our coaching?

Alexandre: Well, probably interesting, but I must think in order to clarify my expectations.

After 45 minutes, the session is interrupted because the patient is now lying on the catheterization table and Alexandre leaves the session.

A person in serious crisis may be too fragile to undertake or bear a coaching that could put her in front of her difficulties or inadequacies. Determining an individual's ability to participate in coaching ("coachability") can be difficult in such a condition. When in doubt, a good strategy is to organize a 3–5-session coaching test, to reduce the intensity of the crisis and assess the capacity of the beneficiary (psychological comfort, progress, problems encountered). When this is not possible, the appropriate action is to refuse this "impossible coaching" and suggest the help of a psychiatrist or psychotherapist.

Initial strategies

The coach's initial strategy is to provide a reassuring atmosphere based on trust, support, and active listening. The goal is to allow the client to find as soon as possible her usual normal functioning (i.e., to fall on her feet), advance in crisis resolution, and promote the recovery of autonomy. This is the framework of supportive coaching: an initial focus on alleviating tension and suffering, as well as building resilience.[9] As soon as possible, the coach engages the client to work on her resources, strengths, skills, and ability to withstand the challenges of life. Studies have demonstrated that most adults have experienced many transitions and crises leading to significant changes in their lives: according to Hopson, adults in their mid-thirties have usually endured at least 30–40 crises related to important changes.[10] This experience can be assessed by using the exercise the "lifeline," which shows the peaks and lows of existence and illustrates the practical familiarity that any human has with ordinary crisis management.[a] Such an experience forms a real resources bank that can be activated during difficult times or crises; these resources must be sought for each one, based on her life history and experiences; therefore, they are not directly transferable to another person. As philosopher Ken Wilber, from the United States, says: *Even if we possessed the perfect integral map of the Cosmos, a map that was all-inclusive and unerringly holistic, that map itself would not transform people. We don't just need a map; we need to change the mapmaker.*[11]

Help, I'm drowning! (continuation)

Elisabeth arrives at her first meeting the following Sunday. I see that she looked very badly, and I ask her how she is doing.

Elisabeth: I'm not doing well; the nightmare continues. I slept badly these last days; I feel like I'm sinking. I cannot cope alone with my personal situation; the division is in crisis; I don't know how to manage all these problems, I'm totally unable to find solutions ....

Coach: I see .... This must be a terrible time, costing you considerable energy. However, by the way, why do you want to be supported by a coach, what do you expect from me?

Elisabeth, immediate answer: I need support from someone who knows the hospital environment; that's why I thought of you. In fact, I think that I especially need to be listened to and treated with benevolence, which will help me resolve this difficult situation as soon as possible.

The coach asks some exploratory questions to further understand the situation.

Elisabeth: I am having increasing trouble managing my hospital division, which has been in a serious crisis for several weeks. The nurses have complained to the management. The residents have also complained. I have lost all motivation for my job.

Coach: And your family?

Elisabeth: I live half the week without my children, who are with their dad; it's difficult. I am very sad in their absence, and I suffer.

She asks me questions about what coaching is and how it differs from psychotherapy. She is treated by a psychiatrist but is not satisfied with this therapy because "it does not move much." I provide her with brief information on coaching and explain the active role of the client, who develops objectives, makes the decisions, and conducts the agreed-on tasks.

Elisabeth is referring to the psychiatric support she is currently receiving, which has helped her sometimes cope with the situation. She confesses to me that she is unsure she will "be able to bear a coaching."

Elisabeth relates her situation step by step. She is 48 years old and runs a hospital division in a large regional hospital. As soon as she began her work, she was caught up in clinical tasks that prevented her from reviewing the organization of the division and being close to her family. Nothing seemed to be wrong until one year ago. At that time, she discovered that her husband had been having an affair with one of his—supposedly—former friends. He told her that he wanted to divorce quickly. The divorce was pronounced rapidly, with shared custody of the children.

Coach: And if you consider the evolution of the crisis, how is it going, and where do you see improvements?

Elisabeth: I don't see many, which worries me a lot. Two weeks ago, I was summoned by the medical and general directors, who sent me several remarks on the division's poor operation. They warned me that they expected me to improve the situation. I informed them of my personal situation, which surprised them a lot. They nevertheless told me that I had to find a solution to regain the normal functioning of the division, even if that meant delegating more tasks to my attendings. For the directors, I must now improve the management of the division, letting go is no longer possible.

Coach: I now better understand your distress and your difficulty in going up the slope.

Elisabeth: I am very touched, deep inside me. I feel overwhelmed and without energy; some days I feel destroyed. I have to get back on my feet to find my balance. I feel seriously threatened in my professional activities.

Coach: What makes you think that coaching could help when you already see a psychiatrist? To be honest, there is no guarantee that a coaching will fulfill your expectations and current needs … As I told you at the beginning of the interview, coaching requires a number of conditions; in particular, a coachee must be aware of her situation and be able to develop goals for change, mobilize resources, and make decisions. As you already know, coaching differs from psychological support in which the therapist is available to take care of you. Do you think you can withstand the coaching approach?

Elisabeth: Actually, I'm not sure. Nevertheless, I know that I want to try.

Coach: What crisis have you already successfully overcome in your life?

Elisabeth: Many, but none as serious as this one.

Coach: Can you tell me about one that affected you?

Elisabeth: I was sued by the family of a deceased patient, who I treated for several months. This difficult story affected me a lot because I was afraid of going to court. I never managed to make this family understand the difficulty of the situation. I expended substantial energy for a miserable result.

Coach: I see, and what resources did you mobilize to resolve this situation?

Elisabeth: I was able to accept the reality that the family is dissatisfied and has the right to file a complaint. After discussions with my colleagues, I managed to accept that I didn't make a mistake and that the death of the patient was inevitable. I then regained confidence and handled the family.

Coach: Good! How would it be to do the same today with the help of your coach?

Elisabeth: Well, good; that's what led me to seek your help.

Coach: So shall we get to work?

Elisabeth: Yes, I want to apply all my energy to this task. Let's move forward, and we'll see.

Feedback at the end of the session:

Coach: How are you feeling, what occurred today?

Elisabeth: I feel rather reassured by what occurred today; I have the feeling that for the first time in several months, I see a little light at the end of the tunnel, but a lot of darkness remains. In any case, I have the sensation of having deposited something and having fewer stones in my bag.

The coach suggests starting with four sessions, followed by a simple evaluation. For the next session, they agree to prepare a list of general purpose and coaching goals; they also decide to elaborate a list of her achievements in the areas of family, profession, and social relationships. In addition, the coach "prescribes" three sessions per week of at least 20 minutes of jogging, which she has not done for a few weeks.

To effectively support a client experiencing a crisis, a coach needs a certain amount of information, particularly the context, nature, effects, and severity of the crisis and the impact on the client, on her work capacity, family life, and health. This information is most often provided by the client and more rarely by the prescriber of coaching. Sometimes, this information is incomplete, biased, or erroneous and requires complements and adjustments during sessions. Is it a crisis or a simple disagreement that is easily surmountable? The story told by the client, and the emotional and cognitive changes observed by the coach, allows the latter to discover and understand the situation. The client and her coach should first assess the impact of the crisis and her ability to withstand and overcome it (i.e., to be resilient); then, the client can recover her normal functioning as soon as possible and advance effectively in coaching.

Developing resilience

According to Erick Haan and Anthony Kasozi, there are six critical resiliency capabilities that successfully address stress and crisis situations[12]:

- Controlling emotions, feeling responsible for thoughts and behaviors.
- Being self-confident.
- Being able to develop goals of change and implement them.
- Demonstrate flexibility and adaptability during change.
- Understand the situation, be aware of oneself, abilities, and limitations, as well as of opportunities offered by team activity
- Become actively involved in the crisis, for example, analysis and development of own opinions, options, and choices.

When these capacities are insufficient to cope with the situation, the person often requires more direct support and going beyond the usual framework of a professional coaching, to take the position of mentor, expert, or more rarely, caregiver, to progress in the crisis management.

Studies have shown that it is possible to develop resilience, through active development work, which requires a prolonged period of training. The US Army's Comprehensive Soldier and Family Fitness Program is designed for soldiers and their relatives who are subject to the crises of military life. The program is taught in several modules that span several months.[13] The outcomes show an increase in the resilience and psychological health after soldiers' training, compared with soldiers without training. This training induces a significant reduction in stress-related mental health problems in military life (e.g., involvement, activities in extreme climates, sleep deprivation, prolonged physical exertion, prolonged separation from family, uncertainties of war such as threats of injury and death).

Relying on the client's experiences and successes, particularly crises effectively overcome, is a useful strategy for crisis coaching. It makes it possible to turn away from accumulated problems, stressful situations, and associated blockages to obtain a positive view of the situation, favoring the search for solutions. Recalling the ability to cope in previous situations frequently allows the client to become aware of her strengths and resources and to move toward positive mental strategies.

Crisis with management

Jack, head of division at a large university hospital, accepted a coaching prescribed by the medical director. The overall goal was to develop his leadership and ability to manage his team. His relations with his head of department were bad. After five coaching sessions without problems, he is summoned by his boss, and quickly, the discussion goes awry. Three days later, he calls his coach unexpectedly and declares: "I am summoned by the medical director and the head of department, without mentioning any particular subject." Jack calls his coach unexpectedly to prepare for this session, and they have the following conversation:

Jack: I'm summoned this afternoon at 4 pm to the medical director and the head of department—without a clear reason. This worries me; I'm afraid of being stuck, not knowing what to say … I feel very anxious, and I don't know what to do. An appointment with the coach is organized 90 minutes before the session.

Coach: How should you prepare this session? What are your needs?

Jack: I feel bad; I'm afraid to fall apart in front of my boss and the medical director; I feel like a child who is afraid.

Coach: I understand it must be very unpleasant for you. Do you have any idea what would make you more comfortable? I am available for you, and we have a good stretch of time to work.

The rest of the discussion is difficult because Jack has trouble concentrating, and his speech is interrupted by emotions, tears in his voice, and silences. He ruminates on the theme "it's difficult, I don't feel it, I'm afraid of not getting there … ."

After approximately 20 minutes of support, the coach interrupts the discussion to question Jack.

Coach: Do you really want to go to this session? Couldn't you decide not to go there on the pretext of a last-minute impediment?

Jack stops, is silent, then reflects, and ends up saying:

Jack: If I don't go today, I should go in the days to come. That, I don't want at all. I think it's better to go today; I'll try to do my best.

Coach: What if we started with a few minutes of *relaxation*, as we already did?

Jack: Okay, that may be good for me.

After five minutes of relaxation, Jack gives a sign to the coach indicating that he is ready for resuming the active work.

The coach and client briefly review the list of professional successes and events, established during previous sessions, that Jack is most proud of.

Coach: That's good; you feel stuck but have many resources that must be mobilized now. Have you ever had crises in your medical practice?

Jack: Yes, of course, but never like that one. This time, I feel much more affected.

Coach: How did you resolve it?

Jack: I always find a solution, even if I ask my colleagues for help.

Coach: And this time?

Jack: My colleagues support me a little; it's better than nothing; it helps me feel less alone and reassures me.

Coach: Let's speak about you, the head of division; you have high-level specialist skills, and you have accumulated success in sometimes difficult conditions. What do you think about that?

Jack: That's right, I tend to forget everything I've done, all my successes.

The use of scale questions (scaling) allows the coach to initiate progression in small steps.

Coach: What would you rate your current level of preparation and confidence for the upcoming session, on a 10-point scale (1, I'm absolutely not ready; 10, I feel completely ready; I'm going to succeed)?

Jack: At the beginning of the session, I was at 3/10; now, I feel a little better, and I'm almost at 5–6/10.

Coach: What does it take to go to 7/10?
Jack: I'll have to continue my preparation with you during the minutes that remain and position myself in the shoes of a confident person.

The coach finally proposes a few minutes of "meditation of love and benevolence" (see chapter 10 and chapter 2), which reinforces Jack's calm state.

Coach: How are you feeling; are you ready to go to this session?
Jack: Yes, almost. I feel better, but I'm still worried about what might occur.

The client goes to his meeting. At the end of the session, he calls the coach to tell him that things went rather well, despite the difficulty and his initial stress.

This vignette illustrates the difficulty of this leader in crisis to manage his obligations. The accumulation of problems at all levels has overwhelmed his ability to lead his division and manage his relationship with his department head (probably a difficult person). The call to an impromptu session is sufficient to trigger an anxiety crisis, which cuts all his means. The organization of an "emergency coaching session" calms the situation and helps him to find lost resources, because of anxiety related to the crisis. This allows the client to reconnect with reality, improve his perception and analysis of the situation, and finally be able to confront the medical director and his department head.

Selfcare

Unlike short-term and low-level crises, which can be swiftly overcome, longer-lasting and high-intensity crises have deleterious effects on individuals as a whole. The latter can progressively alter health in all its aspects—physical, mental, emotional, and spiritual—and invade and disrupt his functioning in his professional field and many other fields of his existence. When a crisis is intense and prolonged, it may lead to "system failure" that can be permanently overwhelming.

In addition to specific measures aimed at resolving the causes of a crisis, which might be from the direct environment or external factors, the coachee should improve her work's ergonomics (e.g., definition of priorities, delegation, hours of work) and lifestyle (e.g., time available for herself, family and social activities, sports practice, nutrition, body-mind work, personal development).

Post-crisis growth

The concept of post-crisis growth, also called "post-traumatic growth," was developed by proponents of positive psychology. The idea that a crisis provokes an existential awareness capable of causing development and maturation has been supported by abundant literature. These studies demonstrated that after a major crisis, 30%–80% of people demonstrate growth[14]. This maturation mainly concerns five fields:

- Consolidation of psychological strength and trust
- Development of relations with others, which tend to become closer and warmer
- Discovery of new possibilities of life
- Appreciation of life (value of life) with a change in priorities
- Spiritual development

Post-traumatic growth can occur after many different situations experienced as trauma, for example, a physical injury, unexpected illness, a terrorist attack, sexual abuse, separation, and bereavement. For example, one study assessed this affective growth in a population of 66 adults with acute leukemia, an oncological disease with an uncertain prognosis and particularly painful therapy[15]. The severity of symptoms, quality of sleep, level of well-being, tendency to ruminate, and perceived threat were measured throughout the treatment. Patients were evaluated at the beginning of cancer chemotherapy, after five to six weeks, and after nine to 13 weeks, using a questionnaire to assess the physical and mental health indicators and quality of life. The results showed an improvement in well-being and signs of post-traumatic growth five to six weeks after the start of therapy. There was also a significant decrease in the symptoms of psychological distress. The highest growth scores were observed in the youngest patients, in those who had a longer duration of disease progression (since the date of diagnosis), and who had a higher tendency to deliberately ruminate. Conversely, older patients, with a short duration of evolution and a greater sense of threat, showed more limited growth.

The same phenomenon can be observed in beneficiaries of crisis coaching, as well as among coachees who can cope with particularly severe burnout or bereavement.[16] We also observe post-crisis growth in care providers who successfully go through professional or non-professional crises. Post-traumatic growth provides a rich experience, which may remain unconscious, at least during the initial phase of the crisis, and is often in parallel with the development of a new existential cycle.

Jack, crisis with the management (continued)

Three months after the beginning of the coaching, Jack seizes an opportunity to leave his difficult situation: a position with an academic promotion is offered to him in a university hospital, which allows him to abandon his activity in the regional hospital. He accepts this proposal after discussing this project with his coach.

This decision interrupts the coaching. After the last session, Jack sends an email to his coach:

"Dear coach, here I am ready to make a big jump into another job that could lead me to hire you to prepare for this change. I want to thank you for your work, your availability, and your point of view, which I requested when necessary. By contrast, I regret that we did not have the opportunity to complete our work, because we could have progressed with a series of essential changes. I re-read my "coaching book," where I noticed once again all that I learned during this coaching. Today, I am doing much better, I feel like a new man who is looking forward to grappling with the rest of his career. Thank you"!

This vignette illustrates the path of a chief physician who has experienced a prolonged hospital crisis. Working with the coach allowed him to conduct a course focused on personal development, the discovery of his capacity for resilience, and the possibility of giving meaning to his difficulties. This path allowed him to somewhat improve his difficult relationship with his boss and finally to succeed in obtaining an academic promotion.

The same observation can be made during team coaching. During my hospital career, I have repeatedly experienced major crises with different groups of colleagues or hospital managers. This experience allowed me to acquire significant experience in navigating crises, despite my limited knowledge of the topic. I have also observed many times the "hidden gift" of post-traumatic growth in individuals and positive changes in group cohesion, emotional sharing, and the development of common values. Notably, large groups and even whole companies can benefit from the unexpected gains after a crisis. The same is true for humanity, which has learned to adapt to all the circumstances of history (or almost all!) and grow despite the intrinsic weakness and vulnerability of man and the political systems.

Analysis grids: individual and team coaching

Grid for individual coaching

This grid proposes elements for the systematic analysis of a crisis during an individual coaching.

- Is it a crisis: how do you recognize that your client is in crisis?
- Level of crisis: person, team(s), company?
- What are the manifestations of the crisis?
- How serious is the crisis: are there vital threats to the individual or immediate actions to take?
- What is the emotional impact on the client?
- Is the client able to manage with the crisis herself or does she need support?
- Is the client able to develop goals and make decisions?
- Is a therapist (psychologist or psychiatrist) preferable to a coach?
- What are the most appropriate coaching strategies?
- At the end of the crisis, is the client aware of the possible benefits of overcoming the crisis, namely, the post-crisis growth?

Grid for team coaching

For team coaching in crisis, the analysis grid is more complex than that for individual coaching because it must include elements related to leadership, team composition, culture, and history.

- Is it a crisis: how do you recognize that the team is in crisis?
- What are the manifestations of the crisis within the division (department ...), regarding individual team members, the team, and department functioning?
- What are the repercussions outside the division (systemic effects at the hospital level); this point is important in case support is necessary for cross-cutting departments, such as intensive care, radiology, and pharmacy, whose dysfunction may impact the whole hospital?
- Are there implications for quality of care and patient care?
- What has been (was) the duration of the crisis?
- Is the origin internal (in the division) or external (factors related to other departments or the management of the institution)?

- How serious is the crisis? Is the group still functioning? Are there impacts on the quality of care, other divisions, departments, or hospital sectors?
- If the crisis is serious, should immediate action be taken? This question is important if the crisis is related to conflicts between individuals. It is also essential if the quality of care is impaired.
- Can the team resolve the crisis alone, or does it need external support?
- Regarding the role of leadership, what is the type of leadership and effectiveness of the leadership and the ability of the leader to solve a crisis?
- Does communication in the group appear to be impaired?
- Is it possible to undertake group coaching under these conditions, or is it better to start with an individual coaching of the leader?
- At the end of a crisis, what could be its benefits on, for example, the organization, team functioning, and leadership quality?

Conclusion

Hospitals are in a constant state of development and change. The ability of health care providers to work in an unstable environment is often sufficient to adapt to daily dysfunction and short-term crises; this is not the case in a high-intensity, prolonged crisis that may induce significant alterations of cognition and cerebral functions, leading to serious individual and team consequences. Crises are provoked by hard work, daily stress, and the frequent professional exhaustion observed among health care providers. Different aspects of crises in the hospital environment have been presented, as well as examples of individual and group coaching.

The beginning of coaching, often difficult, has been extensively described. Assisting coachees in developing their resilience and ability to care for themselves is an important goal for a coach. The *post-crisis growth* can be observed after a few coaching sessions and offers the expected benefit of any crisis, allowing the individuals to modify their maps of the world and develop and enrich their resources.

Note

a In the *lifeline* exercise, the coach asks the client to draw a continuous line across a page and map the high points of her life (i.e., success and progress) with the peaks and low points (i.e., difficulties and failures, respectively) with hollows; the events and their dates are also noted.

Bibliography

1 Sandi C. Stress and cognition. *Wiley Interdiscip Rev Cogn Sci* 2013; 4(3): 245–261.
2 Dolcos F, Denkova E. Current emotion research in cognitive neuroscience: linking enhancing and impairing effects of emotion on cognition. *Emot Rev* 2014; 6: 362–375.
3 Gok K, Atsan N. Decision-making under stress and its implications for managerial decision-making: a review of literature. *Int J Bus Soc Res* 2016; 6(3): 38–47.
4 Mandrick K, Peysakhovich V, Rémy F, Lepron E, Causse M. Neural and psychophysiological correlates of human performance under stress and high mental workload. *Biol Psychol* 2016; 121: 62–73.
5 Thornton C. Looking deeper: the secret life of groups. *In: Group and Team Coaching. The Essential Guide*. Routledge, London; New York; 2010, pp. 44–63.
6 Cassidy S. Learning styles: an overview of theories, models, and measures 2004. *Educ Psychol* 2004; 24(4): 419–444.
7 Hawkins P. Coaching the five disciplines. *In: Leadership Team Coaching. Developing Collective Transformational Leadership*. Kogan Page Limited, London; Philadelphia; New Delhi; 2014, pp. 83–102.
8 Finn JC, Bhanji F, Lockey A, *et al*. Part 8: education, implementation, and teams: 2015 international consensus on cardiopulmonary resuscitation and emergency cardiovascular care science with treatment recommendations. *Resuscitation* 2015; 95: e203–e224.
9 Hall L. *Mindful Coaching. How Mindfulness Can Transform Coaching Practice*. Kogan Page Limited, London; 2013.
10 Hopson B. Transition: understanding and managing personal change. *In*: Chapman AJ, Gale A. *Psychology and People. A Tutorial Text*. Palgrave, London; 1982, pp. 120–145. Available from: https://link.springer.com/chapter/10.1007/978-1-349-16909-2_7 [cited April 5, 2018].
11 Wilber K. *A Theory of Everything. An Integral Vision for Business, Politics, Science, and Spirituality*. 1st ed. Shambhala, Boston; 2000.
12 Haan ED, Kasozi A. Leaders in crisis: attending to the shadow side. *In*: Hall A. *Coaching in Times of Crisis and Transformation. How to Help Individuals and Organizations Flourish*. Kogan Page, London; Philadelphia; 2015, pp. 144–171.
13 Seligman MEP, Fowler RD. Comprehensive soldier fitness and the future of psychology. *Am Psychol* 2011; 66(1): 82–86.
14 Tedeschi RG, Calhoun LG. Target Article: "Posttraumatic growth: conceptual foundations and empirical evidence". *Psychol Inq* 2004; 15(1): 1–18.
15 Danhauer SC, Russell GB, Tedeschi RG, *et al*. A longitudinal investigation of posttraumatic growth in adult patients undergoing treatment for acute leukemia. *J Clin Psychol Med Settings* 2013; 20(1): 13–24.
16 Hall L. No mud, no lotus? Crisis as a catalyst for transformation. *In: Coaching in Times of Crisis and Transformation. How to Help Individuals and Organizations Flourish*. Kogan Page, London; Philadelphia; 2015, pp. 50–69.

Further readings

Hall L. *Coaching in Times of Crisis and Transformation*. Kogan Page, London; Philadelphia, New Delhi; 2015.
Jackson PZ, McKergow M. *The Solution Focus. Making Coaching & Change Simple*. Nicholas Brealey International, London; Boston; 2007.

10 Care provider: a difficult profession. Coaching in case of burnout and mental health problems

René Chioléro

Introduction

Hospital work is considered particularly difficult and painful in many ways, as evidenced by the high prevalence of burnout among doctors, and nurses. They must overcome personal difficulties and suffering in addition to daily exposure to the illness, suffering, and even death of patients. Indeed, care providers endure irregular work schedules, chronic overload, night and weekend shifts, team life with frequent interpersonal tension and conflict, with academic pressure and troubled functioning of hierarchies in academic institutions. Chronic stress, which is difficult for some to tolerate but appreciated by others, promotes burnout and occurrence of psychosomatic disorders in individuals at risk. Compared with other professions, such disorders are significantly more common among care providers.[1] Moderate forms of exhaustion and burnout are rampant, they are often discovered during the course of coaching and may be improved by the coaching accompaniment. This contrasts with the severe forms of burnout that lead to prolonged work interruptions, require active therapy, and do not belong to the field of coaching.

This chapter focuses on care providers' stress, burnout, and other frequent disruptions in their psychic life and mental health. Factors that may influence well-being are also described. Given the frequency of burnout among senior doctors, this chapter contains numerous general information on this subject to raise the awareness of hospital coaches to this issue and to provide basic tools that are useful for detection and carrying on coaching.

Burden of healthcare practice

Today, the practice of healthcare professionals remains difficult today despite the gradual evolution toward a reduction in the time and workload of doctors and nurses apart from the ever-increasing administrative tasks. This relief is reflected in several areas, such as the reduction of service hours, compensation of hours for night care and weekends, and the strengthening of the supervision of physicians in training. Furthermore, it required a progressive

DOI: 10.4324/9781003291831-13

increase in medical and nursing endowments. In 2018, the medical and nursing professions remain associated with hardship to a large extent. A recent article published in the journal of Swiss physicians (*Bulletin des Médecins Suisses*) is entitled "The physician's profession: Dream or nightmare?"[2] In this country, weekly working hours exceeding the legal limit (50 hours) are still imposed on many hospitals in training physicians. Notably, such a work schedule is lighter than US rules. Taking into account the harshness of night work and weekend duties, young doctors complain that they cannot reconcile work and family life. In addition, they suffer from numerous psychological constraints related to the frequent dysfunctions of the medical teams, strong pressure of their hierarchy to improve performance, and rivalries that oppose them to colleagues. These scenarios are common in university hospitals. Surprisingly, little is done to improve the situation and reconcile the practice of the medical profession with a normal life.

Mental and psychological health of care providers

An abundant literature demonstrated that somatic and psychic disturbances are commonly observed in doctors in Europe and North America.[3,4] The most frequent complaints include fatigue, exhaustion, insomnia, depression, anxiety disorders, obesity (especially in the United States), alcoholism, and drug addiction. Surprisingly, the prevalence of alcoholism is similar in the medical world as it is in society, whereas suicide rates are significantly higher among physicians (approximately two to three times higher).

According to Merry Miller, "The painful truth is that doctors are not invincible."[5] A longitudinal study of more than ten years (1997–2007) conducted among 9,000 physicians in Norway confirmed the observations in the North American scene, that is, certain mental disorders, such as depression and suicide are more common in the medical profession than in the general population, whereas self-medication is common.[3] This finding contrasted with their somatic health, which was similar or better than that of the general population. The reality has led many medical societies, in particular the Swiss Medical Federation, to encourage doctors to take better care of their health and to set up preventive measures. As advised by the head of the federal health promotion and prevention department in Switzerland, "Physicians should take care of their health."[6]

Burnout is the most common occupational disease among healthcare professionals following anxiety disorders, depression, alcoholism, and addiction to psychoactive substances. These alterations in mental health are promoted by the stress and heaviness of the profession, especially when the demand, as experienced by care providers (perceived stress), exceeds his capacity to cope. Burnout affects approximately 40% of nurses in hospitals and approximately 30%–60% of doctors and medical students.[7–9] It induces serious repercussions on the psychological and physical health of care providers, on professional performance and productivity, and on patient satisfaction.

A survey on 27,276 physicians from the United States collected 7,288 responses.[1] A total of 46% reported at least one symptom of burnout (according to the Maslach scale) with significant variations dependent on medical specialty. In comparison with 3,442 professionally active non-care providers, physicians were 36% more likely to display burnout symptoms, and 73% are more likely to be dissatisfied with work–life balance. As noted by the American Academy of Pediatrics, burnout sufficiently reaches the health of the sufferer to constitute *the antithesis of good health*.[4]

A similar observation can be made in the nursing profession, particularly in certain at-risk settings, such as emergency medicine, intensive care, and oncology. This reality is highlighted in an editorial of the journal of the American *Critical Care Nurses* entitled "When your work conditions are thicker than your patients."[8] The author recalled how the intensive care environment is likely to induce exhaustion, which affects approximately 50% of professionals.

I don't ask for coaching

Daniel has been head of a medical division in a big hospital for eight months. The division has experienced many crises in recent years under three consecutive leaders. Without much experience in management or team leading, Daniel arrives in a poorly organized structure undermined by dysfunctions and conflicts. Upon his arrival, the medical team has been divided for a long time into two clans. Three colleagues are behind him, whereas two others are quickly in the frontal opposition. After a few months, this conflict results in major disorganization in the division, thus causing the nursing team to complain to the hospital nursing director.

The medical director proposed a coaching, who intends to definitively solve the operating problems of the division starting with the chief physician and his lack of experience. According to medical management, the coach's mission is to assist him in the management of his division and team conduct, strengthen his leadership, and improve the functioning of the medical team.

Daniel reluctantly accepts this proposal with little enthusiasm.

Daniel: It is not me asking for a coaching; it is the idea of the medical director. I believe that a true leader must be able to run his division effectively without the need for a coach or advisor. After reflection, I finally agreed to meet to talk to you about this coaching project.

Coach: Do you know what coaching is and how it works and what the roles of the coach and client are?

Daniel: Actually, no, but I imagine that the coach is more or less in the same position as the doctor in his relation with patients.

Coach: Not at all. In coaching, the client knows what he wants, prepares goals, and makes all decisions. This position is very different from that of a sick patient.

The coach briefly explains a few coaching characteristics and provides simple examples.

Coach: Why do you think the medical director offered you coaching?

Daniel admits that he is in a difficult situation and probably needs help.

Daniel: I am exhausted, and my work is heavy. I gradually lose my enthusiasm and the pleasure of going to work. I am not moving and oftentimes feel I am stuck. Maybe with a coach, I'll find solutions?

Coach: I understand. Feeling stuck like you are must be difficult ... . Are there other things that could be work goals?

Daniel: I progressively lost contact with many colleagues in the division because they do not really support me anymore. I feel alone in performing my tasks and climbing back up the slope ... (silence). In the evening at home, I ruminate, sleep badly, and frequently wake up with anxiety. In other words, I have to do something to fall back on my feet ... In addition, I have the feeling that my head of department does not fully support me. I think he is tired of seeing problems in my division. I am stuck because if I do not change something, I'll have to leave this position to ensure survival. That aspect made me change my mind and led me to finally accept coaching.

Coach: Well, that statement changes several perspectives. I suggest that we quickly begin to work by perhaps starting with work objectives.

This conversation illustrates a manager in pain because he cannot fulfill his role as leader, manage the division, and efficiently lead the medical team. The implementation of coaching enables him to make an initial assessment and develop initial objectives, which are focused on improving leadership and managing priorities.

In terms of motivation and commitment to work, burnout, even at a low intensity, poses a serious problem because it reduces not only available energy but also personal involvement and overall efficiency in professional activities. The repercussions of this situation are strong. A decline may be observed in the quality of clinical services, such as sub-optimal care with negative consequences on the long-term prognosis of patients.[4,8,9] One may also note irritability, aggressivity, changing humor, decreased attention, and concentration associated with increased errors, impaired decision-making, empathy, and compassion. Patients often complain of inadequate communication and express a decline in trust and satisfaction with burned-out care providers and often perceive a lack of empathy. In addition, an alteration occurs in the adherence (compliance) of patients to treatments. At the institutional level, the burden of burnout is considerable, because it is associated with a marked tendency to resign (and the sources of suffering), which is a consequence associated with high costs and repercussions on hospital operations as attrition contributes to the shortage of hospital doctors in certain specialties at risk.

Many risk factors favor the onset of burnout, which can be grouped into four categories as follows:

1   type of work, workload, and organizational factors;
2   care provider's personal characteristics, such as psychological profile and personal history;
3   quality of the working relationship; and
4   exposure to significant emotional situations.

These *risk factors* include excessive workload, insufficient time to perform tasks especially during night and holiday shifts; lack of sleep; overestimation of the care provider's endurance; and lack of recognition for tasks performed. Certain medical specialties are characterized by difficult environments (i.e., tense, conflictual, or hostile) or by daily contact with death and suffering and are more affected by burnout. This case is particularly true for intensive care medicine (adult and pediatric), emergency medicine, oncology, pediatric surgery, and hospital psychiatry. In a survey on 2,392 critical care nurses, end-of-life patient care was the highest risk factor for burnout followed by quality of work relationships, organizational factors, and individual characteristics.[10]

By contrast, *clinical practice provides satisfaction* in 80%–90% of practitioners, given that it occurs in good working conditions, such as harmonious relationships with patients and their relatives, control of the clinical situation, sufficient physician autonomy (although this factor is not always guaranteed in the hospital), and a setting that favors the quality of services.[11,12] Conversely, clinical practice in high-stress specialties can become a nightmare when the doctor loses control of the clinical situation, suffers from overwork or lack of sleep, and faces relationship conflicts with patients and their families or other practitioners.

The research on burnout highlighted the importance of *meaning* that can be given by the care provider according to various activities. When the meaning is positive, it is generally associated with satisfaction and vice versa.[13] In addition, wellness at work, especially the ability to implement tasks considered favorable, protects the healthcare provider from burnout. A study conducted in the United States on 465 physicians in the Mayo Clinic illustrated a low prevalence of burnout among physicians who can focus on activities considered meaningful for them (i.e., clinical, teaching, or research).[14] Two-thirds of physicians reported preference for clinical tasks, 19% research and only 9% teaching. A total of 34% indicated signs of burnout according to the Maslach criteria. The amount of time spent doing preferred tasks was strongly correlated with risk of burnout. Physicians spending less than 20% of their time on favored tasks displayed a higher risk of burnout than those who spent more than 20% (burnout incidence: 54% versus 30%). Other studies reported that doctors often derive professional satisfaction from positive relationships with patients and colleagues as well as pleasure from daily practice and its associated intellectual stimulation.[15]

The personal characteristics of care providers, such as perfectionism, self-criticism, idealism, difficulty in coping with stress, and tendency to over-commit to work, also influence the risk of burnout and associated with higher risk of burnout. The majority of these traits are reinforced by medical training and professional culture.[9] Burnout is common among neurotic and anxious individuals. Conversely, extrovert personalities with high levels of psychological endurance (hardiness) seem to be preserved. Other risk factors include lack of sleep, prolonged imbalance between work and other activities, unhealthy lifestyle, financial worries, lack of family support, and family conflicts.

These considerations illustrate the importance of burnout in healthcare professionals and hospital management. It requires a large set of measures to humanize the medical profession, such as respect for working hours, to provide a satisfactory work–life balance, recognition of the value of care providers, improvement in training of executives for leadership, and assessment of care provider satisfaction.[12]

Although the harshness of the health professions is clear, it should nevertheless be noted that many care providers undergo their professional career without suffering from excessive stress or exhaustion and even enjoying dealing with daily tension, such as René Chioléro ("good stress"). However, this aspect does not imply that such care providers are immune to burnout, which can occur as a result of personal problems (i.e., family and finances) or health. Instead, they prefer to work actively in a tense and dynamic environment (similar to a sportsman in training).

A head physician and a marathon runner who likes stress, effort, and performance

David is 58 years old and leads a department in a university hospital. He is in direct contact with a coach because he wants to improve his time management and develop his leadership.

David:　I need a coach. As a sportsman, I know that being supervised to progress is useful. I think the same is true in professional life.

Coach:　Exactly. I regularly receive requests from leaders who wish to progress in their profession and achieve professional or personal goals of change. Do you have an idea of your goals or personal aspects you would like to change?

David:　Yes, I thought about it. First of all, I would like to better balance my professional and personal life. In addition, I want to improve my leadership, especially leadership of the medical team, which I neglected a little. I also want to involve my direct collaborators more in the management of the department.

Coach:　Regarding the first point, can you give me a quick list of your main activities?

David:　The direction of the department is a big part. I participate in clinical activities and conduct private consultation two days per week. In addition, I lead a research group. My academic activities are heavy as a professor at the faculty, vice-dean, the president of the national society of my specialty, and member of the committee of the European society. Finally, I travel a lot (i.e., congresses, conferences, and scientific committees).

Coach:　I see. What are the repercussions on your family and private life?

David:　I am married with two sons. At this level, I sense no problem, and I am very happy with my family. My wife, however, often complains about my repeated absences. I must say that, in addition to professional tasks, I practice sports relatively intensively because I feel that it is essential to my balance. I jog two to three times a week. Every year I register for one or two marathons.

Coach:　How many hours a week do you work?

David:	Oh, certainly a lot. I estimate my work time at 60—80 hours per week depending on the period. However, I say straight away that I like this life; I like my work; my multiple activities and it is very stimulating.
Coach:	… and do you feel fatigue or even signs of exhaustion?
David:	No, hardly ever. Of course, when my work schedule is heavy, I become tired, especially when traveling long distance.
Coach:	The stress, what effect does it have on you?
David:	I like feeling the pressure. It is similar to a marathon at the 30th kilometer.

David undertakes the test of the *wheel of life* (Figure 10.1). This easy-to-use tool enables the coach to complete the information gathered at the beginning of coaching and to discover relevant materials about family life, social relationships and friends, hobbies and sports, finances, and personal development. The wheel indicates that David is satisfied with his life in many areas, such as professional activity, career, family, leisure, finances, and social and friendly relations, which are all favorably evaluated. The only weak field is focused on "time for me," which is very limited, and the impossibility of engaging in personal development. These aspects are mainly what he envisages to change today.

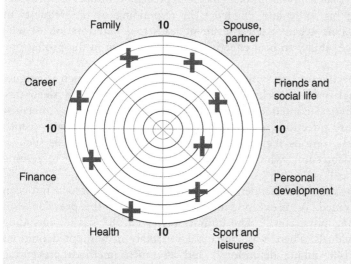

Figure 10.1 David's wheel of life.

What is burnout?

Since the 1970s and the work of the American psychologist Christina Maslach, the manifestations of burnout are generally classified into three areas, namely, emotional exhaustion, depersonalization, and loss of perception of personal accomplishment. These manifestations can be detected using specific tools (typically in the form of questionnaires), such as the Maslach Burnout Inventory (MBI).[16]

- *Emotional exhaustion* is characterized by lack of motivation and pleasure at work coupled with a feeling of inability to perform one's tasks properly. This type is followed by a further decrease in motivation and a tendency to flee the current situation and to want to leave a work-station.
- *Depersonalization* mainly influences the care provider's relationship with patients (or partners in other professions). Instead of being viewed with empathy or compassion, patients are perceived in an impersonal manner similar to things or objects instead of sick and vulnerable persons that require protection. Empathic exhaustion also occurs in this situation. Care providers with severe burnout may even "hate" their patients, as suggested by a survey conducted in Switzerland among 60 residents and chief residents of a large regional hospital.[17] A total of 34% and 14% of the residents and chief residents, respectively, admitted to often feeling a marked aversion to patients during clinical work.
- *Loss of personal achievement* refers to the appreciation of the care provider regarding his value and efficiency in responding to the requests of patients. This negative self-assessment leads to a deterioration of self-confidence, ability to heal effectively, and self-image in the profession.

Many non-specific somatic symptoms occur during burnout, such as fatigue, headache, back pain, muscle tension, digestive disorders, and sleep disturbances. Physical consequences may include abnormal glucose metabolism, respiratory infections, gastrointestinal problems, and coronary events. In severe cases, serious mental health disturbances are observed, such as anxiety and depression, which may lead to prolonged inability to resume hospital activity.

Il should be underlined that definition and criteria of burnout have not been clearly determined. A recent systematic review assessed the prevalence of burnout among physicians.[18] The authors reviewed 182 studies including 109,628 individuals. There was substantial variability in burnout definitions (more than 140 unique definitions!) and assessment methods preventing meta-analytic pooling of data.

I lost pleasure in work

William works in a regional hospital and spends many hours in the cardiology intervention room at all hours of the day and night, including weekends. In recent months, he complains of growing problems at work. After several interviews with the medical director, the latter offers him coaching to "find a solution to his difficulties and improve his ability to cooperate with colleagues."

The first meeting with the coach goes well as William recognizes that for a few months he has been undergoing a crisis that is destroying him.

William: I lost the pleasure of working and of being in contact with patients. I am struggling to occupy my place in the team. I am often tired, even in the morning, especially after the night and weekend interventions.

Coach: This must certainly worry you. How do you feel?

William: I am often irritable and tired even in the morning. I perceive much more of the stress in hospital work. In the past few months, I noticed conflicts with my boss and certain collaborators. Such encounters have never been the case before. I noticed that I am finding being relaxed and open with patients increasingly difficult, which worries me.

Coach: How long have you noticed this disturbing development?

William: It started approximately six months ago. Since then, I have felt that the difficulties are worsening. At home, I can feel tension as my wife complains that I am often in a bad mood and participates less in family life. Frequently, I even get angry with my kids. Recently, I have to force myself to go to work, which had never happened before.

Coach: How was it before?

William: I have always had fun in my work until recently. Since the past few weeks, I see a drop in my performance, and I fear such complications in my interventions. It is a very technical job, which requires a tremendous amount of concentration and precision.

Coach: Do you see any solutions?

William: Currently, no. For this reason, I accepted coaching.William's resigned and passive attitude strikes the coach.

A simple test, Christina Maslach and Susan Jackson developed the MBI based on a 22-item questionnaire.[16] An abbreviated version of the MBI that focused on emotional exhaustion and depersonalization was developed, which is available on the Internet for coaches who want to assess clients about burnout. Other similar, copyright-free tests have been developed, such as the Copenhagen Burnout Inventory.[19] A new test named The Professional Fulfillment Index has recently been evaluated in the United States for assessing burnout and job satisfaction among physicians.[20] It is based on analysis of three fields, namely, (1) professional satisfaction, (2) burnout at work, and (3) interpersonal disengagement, which is determined by self-reported medical errors (i.e., misdiagnosis, prescription of drugs, or laboratory tests). Physicians fill up the form themselves. It has been validated on a population of 250 doctors in an American university hospital. Compared with MBI, it has the advantage of directly assessing job satisfaction.

The intensity of burnout greatly varies from one situation to another. Symptoms can be mild to moderate and prolonged or of varying intensity over time. A picture of low-intensity prolonged burnout is largely observed among chronically overburdened leaders, who are accommodating it and lose awareness of its reality. These leaders state they work a lot and describe certain symptoms without emphasizing their importance. This case is particularly true among those responsible for heavy academic activities that overburden them durably in addition to actual medical activities. A survey on 282 academic orthopedics leaders in the United States showed that they worked an average of 68 hours per week, and 77% of them showed moderate or high levels of emotional exhaustion.[21] This situation is difficult to remedy given that such a life is fully accepted, considered "normal," and endured by the doctor without questioning the multiple activities.

I am tired of working too much

George has been chief of a medical department at a large regional hospital for over ten years. He also holds a part-time position in a university hospital with the title of full professor. His schedule is particularly tight with many and varied activities, such as clinical activities, supervision of in-training physicians, direction of the department, and participation in the medical call service. He organizes the postgraduate medical training program, actively participates in teaching, and maintains a research activity rewarded by publications every year. For the past three years, George has noticed tension in the medical team with strong disagreements between a few of the senior attendings, which have a severe impact on the functioning of the team. In addition, he complains of difficulty in delegating tasks, which he says contributes to the stress. After discussion with the medical director, he requests for coaching, which is approved.

George: I am tired of working in this manner. Other colleagues are reluctant to become involved in the leadership of the department. They probably prefer to increase their number of consultations and personal activities, which results in more work for me.

Coach: What made you decide to start coaching?

George: Many things. I am often tired. On other days, I am even discouraged when I notice that the more the time passes, the more the workload increases. I do not know where I am going. Today, I fail to see solutions to my situation, which is gradually but inexorably worsening.

Coach: What do you envisage as remedy?

George: Actually, I really like my work, which is exciting. My activities are diverse and interesting. However, for no reason in the world, I would like to change my job.

Coach: I wonder if you are suffering from exhaustion, which can vary in intensity from one day to the next? It is common among senior doctors.

George: It is quite possible.

The remainder of the interview highlights that George has a long history of moderate symptoms of stress, such as fatigue and multiple complaints about the painful nature of his situation, difficulties in managing priorities, regrets of being unable to deal properly with family, and long-time sleep disorders.

The coach asks him if he has any requests and if he has considered goals for the coaching. He immediately states that he wants to learn how to better delegate tasks and change his lifestyle without giving up the hospital job.

The presence of low or moderate levels of exhaustion does not necessitate a specific medical intervention but a review of style and healthy living at and outside work. This option can be selected by the client as part of coaching. If the symptomatology is more severe, with marked somatic, emotional, and empathic exhaustion, and disruption in the physician–patient relationship, then additional measures should be undertaken including therapy by a specialist. The overall manifestations may cause a serious deterioration of mental health; therefore, employing rapid measures is necessary to reduce the pressure and tension felt by doctors and to avoid a sudden worsening of the situation. In addition, doctors should be encouraged to consult their physician because burnout at this stage is a real disease that affects the whole individual and can lead to serious consequences on physicians, patients, families, as well as the institution. Doctors suffering from burnout are understandably averse to consultation with another physician (especially a psychiatrist). Frequently, they deny the seriousness of their suffering, illness, and fear to appear weak in front of colleagues. In fact, the entire medical profession acts in this manner in terms of confronting health problems of any kind. A recent abstract presented in 2016 at the Congress of the French College of Anesthetists (CFAR) illustrated that 80% of hospital physicians (for all medical specialties) lacked the services of a physician to monitor their state of health. In the case of mental health problems, 87% of the respondents reported that they preferred self-medication over medical follow-up, whereas only 40% were ready to use the hospital's occupational health department for themselves.[22] These physicians believed that in the private sector, most doctors practice the profession throughout their careers without medical supervision.

A burnout to "get crazy"

Julietta is a biologist in the clinical chemistry laboratory of a hospital. The laboratory underwent a complete reorganization following the merger of several hospital chemistry laboratories. In this merger, the entire specialized chemistry was relocated into a single hospital. The process involved a complete overhaul of the organization of work and quality control, acquisition of new equipment, and relocation and departure of several employees.

Julietta is given responsibility for the reorganization of the specialized clinical chemistry laboratory. She also had to coordinate in-call teams during the transition period (twelve months) between the old and new systems. The new functions and tasks made her feel uncomfortable, thus she became anxious and irritable. The HR Director offered support coaching with the goal of enabling her to effectively fill his new position.

From the first meeting, the coach observes that Julietta shows signs of serious burnout assisted by strong anxiety and victimization.

Coach: Tell me what seems wrong since the beginning of the new organization and what is upsetting you?

Julietta: In fact, everything started with the merger. Previously, I have always held my office without much problem, and I was appreciated by my colleagues. In the past few months, it has become much more difficult. The new managers are scrutinizing us, and I fail to get along well with them. I wonder if the new heads appreciate me. In fact, I am nearly sure they do not like me, which could eventually push them to fire me.

Coach: And what do you expect from this coaching?

Julietta: I am rather suspicious, and I had to accept it, but I am reluctant. You still need to realize that you are paid by the company, and therefore you defend its interests.

Ten days later, the coach learns that Julietta was put on sick leave by her doctor. Three months later, she did not reappear.

In this scenario, a complex merger leads this biology specialist to develop symptoms of burnout. This work-related disease rapidly evolves into a state of paranoia, thus requiring the interruption of work and the intervention of a psychiatrist. The issue was prolonged, and Julietta never resumed her activity in the laboratory.

Coaching through burnout

As previously described, burnout is common among care providers and may have serious consequences. Considering motivation and commitment to work, burnout, even of low intensity, is a significant issue because it reduces the involvement and effectiveness of entire professional activities.[23]

Such a finding has implications for the coach working in the hospital setting, which can be summarized as follows:

1   The coach must be aware of the importance of stress and burnout among care providers.
2   He must be knowledgeable about its symptomatology and capable of detecting it.
3   He must know how to identify the forms of high severity burnout that require specialized treatment by a doctor or mental health therapist. Notably, the coach is unqualified to assist a client whose request hides a disturbance in mental health: coaching is inappropriate in such cases, and the coach is in general incompetent for this form of assistance.
4   He must be trained and acquire skill and experience to support clients suffering from low or moderate intensity burnout and employ appropriate coaching techniques.

How then should coaching be done? First, listen to the client when he describes his hospital activity and other related aspects. Sessions may be difficult at times given the restraint of doctors in discussing their difficulties and suffering particularly in the professional field. Thus, questioning them about their professional and private lives, effective working hours, work–life balance, overall quality of life, pleasure and motivation at work, as well as their level of general health is often necessary to gather useful information. Such an approach should provide reliable data on the client's life balance and health at work. Furthermore, such information may lead the coach and client to review objectives and prevent or correct the factors promoting exhaustion.

This hospital is destroying me

The coach is summoned by the medical director of a regional hospital who wishes to offer a coaching to Oliver, the head doctor of a medical division. For the past six months, complaints have been increasing about this hitherto exemplary doctor: repeated tensions with a few of his colleagues, complaints from the nursing team, and possible medical complications during specialized technical procedures (undergoing investigation). Despite several interviews with the department head and medical director, the situation seems to be worsening inexorably. The goal of the coaching would be to assist Oliver in restoring his capacities as chief physician.

The first interview is difficult. Oliver is suspicious, uncommunicative, and withdrawn. He lacks complaints or any particular request to the coach. He admits that he is in a difficult situation but "does not see what a coaching could bring him." I explain in two words several characteristics of coaching, of which he admits to know nothing. I ask him about his activity at the hospital. Although still less communicative, he admits to have lost all motivation to work in the morning with a rating of 3 out of 10 for pleasure at work (10 = maximum; 1 = minimum). Oliver gradually opens up to the discussion and expresses a few words about his suffering.

> I work too much; I do not have time to play sports; I go home in the evenings exhausted from work. I find that I have increasing difficulties in performing my interventions well. I am frequently overwhelmed by the complaints of patients. My relationships with my colleagues, which were good until a few months ago, have deteriorated similar to the nursing team.

Questioned about his working time, Oliver admits to working approximately 80 hours per week at the hospital and working at home on Saturdays. He fails to see how to reduce the time spent at work and the current workload. "It is impossible; the division will not run anymore, and my colleagues will not accept it." He lives alone, has a friend whom he meets occasionally, and admits to suffering from loneliness. At the end of the interview, Oliver decides to start a coaching. He has no specific goal but says he wants to find pleasure in working and his full medical capabilities again. The coach agrees and proposes to start with three sessions before making a simple assessment. For the next session, Oliver will specify his work objectives and fill "the wheel of life."

At the next session (first coaching session), Oliver looks defeated. He is obviously not doing well and is complaining about his colleagues and insomnia. In contrast, however, his clinical activities, which he mainly appreciates, go well. "I feel satisfaction these days in my clinical work." The same is true for his relationship with the young residents. He confesses to feeling blue several times when coming home. "It is difficult, and I am not moving forward. This hospital is destroying me." He has made little progress in developing his goals. "I do not know what I want, and I am not sure I can prepare these goals without help." Conversely, he filled the "wheel of life" (Figure 10.2). This test confirms the permanent imbalance in Oliver's life and severity of his difficulties. Job satisfaction is rated at 3/10, social relations and friends at 5/10, and leisure at 4/10.

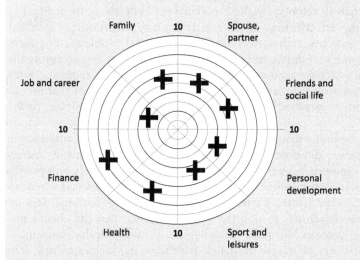

Figure 10.2 Oliver's wheel of life.

The only source of satisfaction is observed in the field of finance, which pertains to a good salary. Faced with this observation, the coach asks Oliver about simple remedies starting with a search in his resources and past professional success. After 60 minutes of work, including simple considerations about the reality of professional exhaustion in the medical world, Oliver realizes that he is indeed suffering from burnout with severe symptoms. Undertaking a plan of action is now necessary. Otherwise, the situation will inexorably worsen. However, what should be done? He refuses to consider reducing his working time any more than going to a doctor. "What would my colleagues say?" He finally agrees to consult a colleague and friend, G.P., whom he calls in front of the coach to make an appointment.

The feedback of the session is positive. Oliver declares that he is beginning to trust the coach and that he appreciates the way that the coach leads the sessions. He then decides to pursue the support and prepare his goals for the next session.

This vignette describes a serious, multisymptomatic chief physician suffering from burnout, who can no longer perform his tasks and who is anxiously observing the situation worsening. An extended coaching, in association with a medical therapy, will enable him to break out of his exhaustion gradually and regain pleasure at work.

Decreasing the factors that promote burnout, such as reduced work intensity and effective management of priorities, typically does not fall under the initial goals developed by these executives. They are more focused on improving the effectiveness of their activities and relationships with colleagues and patients, rather than alleviating personal problems. For them, recognizing one's weakness, vulnerability, and exhaustion and accepting that one may be suffering from burnout is eccentric. As such, requiring a few sessions is common practice to uncover symptoms of burnout that are not readily reported, qualified as part of the normal life of a physician, or as a weakness.

Although assuming that the coach's client is a priori capable of autonomy in making requests, developing objectives, and making decisions is deemed reasonable, exploring his personal history, state of mental health, and possible visits to a psychiatrist before or at the beginning of the assistance remains necessary. In other words, a client being a healthcare professional does not imply that the coach has to skip this step and assume that the client's professional label protects him from psychological or mental health problems.

Starting coaching, as previously stated, is delicate in clients suffering from burnout or other mental health problems. The coach should provide an empathic welcome, good listening, an effective questioning, a large space for the client, and a moderate pace of work. The initial sessions provide insights into many areas, such as the client's ability to describe the situation, difficulties, and problems and to communicate clear demands to the coach. He should develop the initial goals and a positive vision for the future, make elaborate plans, and perform his tasks. In our practice, we aim to use a "solution-oriented" approach from the beginning to stimulate the client to find his answers and solutions rather than to stay stuck on his difficulties and problems.[24,25]

Elaborating goals is often difficult in people with marked burnout who, despite complaints of being overworked, often initially seek to improve their performance and effectiveness at work rather than their well-being. "I want to do better; I want to do more; I have to improve; otherwise, the department will not work." This attitude is likely to aggravate exhaustion and symptomatology and creates a vicious circle. Ignorance of the conditions favoring burnout, specifically the internal mechanisms of the person, is common even among physicians. Furthermore, it complicates the resolution of the problem and often requires the intervention of third parties (i.e., chief, colleagues, and coach).

Requests for coaching made by the director of human resources or the medical director rarely make clear mention of burnout. At most, they recognize that the person works a lot and that it may sometimes affect professional behavior. The problems that drive demand are usually related to symptoms of burnout, such as difficulties in the relationship with colleagues, doctors in training, or nurse teams, decline in the effectiveness of leadership, and repeated complaints from patients. Once the assistance is initiated, only then can the coach perceive the presence of symptoms of exhaustion. At this point, leaving the coach's cap and pushing the client outside of his comfort zone are often necessary steps that can be taken by the coach to gain the client's awareness and acceptance and to explore burnout. This scheme will lead the client to review his initial work objectives, such as organization of work, development of priorities, reduction of schedules, maintenance of work–life balance, and lifestyle, to reduce the factors favoring exhaustion.

Working hard is normal for a surgeon

Robert, head of the surgery division, accepts the coaching proposed by the medical director. The initial goal is to improve his leadership, relationships with colleagues, and work organization. From the initial interview, Robert appears to suffer from significant work overload. In addition to the organization of the division, he is in the operating room from three to four days, organizes the training of residents, teaches students, and participates in many hospital commissions. He is saying that he loves his job while complaining about lacking time for himself and his family. He deems that devoting a considerable amount of time to his activities is normal for his profession and position: "For a surgeon, it's perfectly normal."

The coach offers him to write down his daily activities for four consecutive weeks to appreciate the volume and types of his tasks. The coach also proposes that he fill the "wheel of life" to visualize his activities. Analysis of the wheel of life clearly shows a significant imbalance between professional invasive but rewarding tasks and non-professional activities (i.e., family, social and friendly relations, leisure time, and personal time). A more targeted questioning of the coach highlights symptoms of chronic low-intensity burnout, which Robert did not perceive. This discovery will lead him to introduce a goal on the control of his activities as well as lifestyle.

To facilitate the *preparation of objectives*, instructing the coachee to prepare a list of her personal resources and strengths on which she relies to adapt to the changes and difficulties of daily life is useful.[24,25] These strong points include the following:

- Skills, professional and non-professional knowledge, and abilities.
- Professional (and non-professional) experience: "What I learned during my career; what I can do effectively."
- Successes: "What I'm proud of; what I accomplished."
- Interests: What I like to do, where I find pleasure.
- Values: What values and things are most important for her and guide her action.

Articulating these strong points leads to an incentive to think of a "solution," which makes envisioning the initiation of changes and preparation of a different positive future possible. In addition, they stimulate the client to realize that he is better armed than he expects given the situation.

No time for coaching; I have other priorities

Mark runs a department in a regional hospital. In recent months, he has had to increase hours of work due to prolonged illnesses of an attending and a chief resident. He did not consider for once that he could reduce department activities by transferring other patients to the university hospital and postponing the department development plan. As a result, the medical team gets tired, many executives protest, and finalizing the plan of on-call physicians becomes increasingly difficult. The nursing team complains that medical attendance on weekends is insufficient to meet the needs of patients. Pushed by a colleague, the medical director, who fears the occurrence of a serious crisis in the department, Mark agrees to undertake coaching.

At the onset, the coach notices that Mark is not motivated to start the process. "I'm already short of time. I do not want to waste more of these precious hours on coaching because I have other priorities." However, he quickly opens during the initial discussion and recognizes that he can benefit from coaching to "better manage my time and put energy on the conduct of the medical team. In fact, enabling the department to run efficiently is most important to me. Today, I find that we can do better." The following discussion indicates that Mark has been suffering from moderate burnout for a long time as indicated by less pleasure at work, less contact with patients and the nursing team, increase in conflicts with colleagues, families and management, and no improvement of the situation in view. Preparing objectives is difficult because Mark is passive and does not consider the possibility of change. Identifying his strengths and resources, however, stimulates him and makes him consider changes.

- My professional resources are elevated: two specialist titles; a title of professor of medicine. I am recognized in my field of specialty, in which I have more than ten years of experience. I have a good list of publications and received two awards for my research in recent years. Indeed, I did a good job, and I realize all the work accomplished for 20 years.
- I think I am a good clinician, and I like contact with patients. In fact, I would like to focus more on clinical activities and less on management. I may consider delegating management tasks to one of the executive physicians who enjoys it.
- I am proud of my children, but I lack the time to take care of them. I would like more time, but how?
- I was a good sportsman. However, the last time I practiced was over five years ago. I would certainly like to resume, but it is difficult and takes time ....

Identifying his strong points enables Mark to imagine that he can improve his situation in many fields, particularly his lifestyle, and especially to better control his working time and priorities.

Another strategy that is mainly effective in the face of a work objective is transporting the coachee to an imaginative better future (*a perfect future*).[24,25] The current problems that may be life-threatening are solved, all aspects are improved, and life resumes in a pleasant manner. This transposition gives the coachee imaginary avenues for resolution once the impasse related to the current problems has been removed. However, not everyone can do the exercise, especially clients with burnout associated with depressive symptoms and limiting beliefs ("I am unable to succeed, and it never worked …"). In such a condition, the coach may use another method of changing perspective (reframing) by explaining the capacity of our brain to imagine a positive scenario similar to a novel, such as focusing on previous achievements.

I lost my pleasure at work, and I plan to leave

Stephen is the head physician-in-charge of a medical–technical center and head of a medical department in a big hospital. Although the center is performing well, the department is critically dysfunctional. The misunderstanding between several senior doctors is eroding the life and functioning of the department with negative repercussions on bed management, doctor–nurse relationships, medical training, and administrative management. The medical director is worried about the situation, puts pressure on Stephen, and eventually imposes coaching to "settle definitely the problems and conflicts of this department."

During the first meeting with the coach, Stephen expresses his difficulties and tiredness: "I cannot force my colleagues to work differently. I am exhausted, and I lost pleasure at work. As such, I plan to leave." He is working a lot, including weekends, in an attempt to solve department issues by himself. However, he now doubts being able to succeed and increasingly feels that a better future is non-existent.

Stephen: I would like to improve my relationships with my colleagues, review the functioning of the department, and find again pleasure at work again.

Achieving goals into operational objectives is challenging because he does not precisely and concretely know what he wants and loses himself in unproductive details.

Coach: What about your successes and resources .... What would you like to do and what do you do well?

Until three years ago, he lived a flawless medical career that is full of diplomas and successes. He has successfully completed his medical studies and acquired a specialist degree and many skills specific to his area of expertise. He says he is happy at home, married, and a father to four children but has little time to take care of them. He practiced sports (mountain) at a good level until the birth of his third son. According to him, he never suffered from burnout. His medical studies and years of training as resident and chief resident were smooth and happy. He regrets lacking the same success and the loss of this vitality and ability to ride the wave.

Coach: Please describe four success stories of your life of which you are particularly proud.

After a long reflection, he quotes his children, his doctor's degree, his medal at the cycling University Championships, and his current clinical research project, which is supported by the National Fund for Scientific Research and awarded by the national society. He says: "Recalling these successes makes me feel good, and I feel that my energy is regained."

The exercise of the "perfect future" surprises him. How can one imagine that in a year everything or nearly everything can be solved? Yet, he sees himself smiling with colleagues and discussing the distribution of tasks in the department .... Indeed, a possibility of developing a shared system for the management of the department with his senior colleagues exists. This perspective leads to a modification of the first objective, that is, "to develop a shared management system with colleagues and the support of the medical director."

When a client with significant burnout is stuck in the development of his goals, useful information can be collected using a tool called the "logical levels"[26] developed by Robert Dilts, an expert in Neuro-Linguistic Programming (NLP). The concept was initially described by Gregory Bateson who was Dilts's teacher at the University of California.

Briefly, it is about exploring the current situation and the desired change by going through various levels of reality. The test is carried out in a standing position, and the client successively steps on six determined fields on the floor one after the other (Figure 10.3):

- (Field 1) *Environment*: in which the client lives and interacts: description of the situation (i.e., place, setting, people involved, and business), atmosphere (how the client feels about it), benefits, problems.
- (Field 2) *Behaviors*: activities performed by the client in that environment (what I do; what I say; what I appreciate; my problem, etc.).
- (Field 3) *Capabilities*: how to do one's activities and how to adapt (i.e., strategies, skills, and learning): my skills and competences in the tasks and how to develop myself and learn.
- (Field 4) *Values and beliefs* of the person (the principles that lead my life and give meaning to what I do; their coherence with my actual and future activities and what I believe to be important): "Do these activities make sense to me?" or "Am I uncomfortable with these activities?"
- (Field 5) *Identity*: Does it correspond to who I am, the unique person I am, and to my way? Are the previous logical levels (i.e., environment, behaviors, capabilities, and values and beliefs) in accordance with my identity (myself)?
- (Field 6) *Purpose and mission* (highest level): "What are my long-term vision, purpose, and goal?" and "What is the meaning of my mission, spirituality, and religious beliefs?"

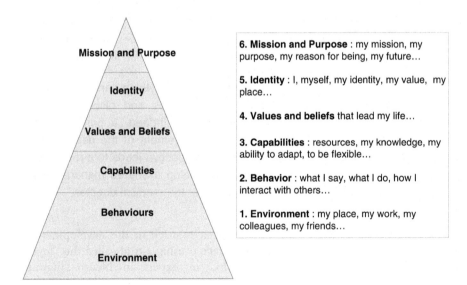

Figure 10.3 Logical levels, according to Robert Dilts.

The work can be illustrated by a triangle (Figure 10.3). In each field, the client describes his situation, the positive and negative aspects, and his feelings (see the following vignette).

I cannot continue like this

John is a doctor in charge of a large hospital division. Near the end of his career, he asked to reduce his working time to 60%, such that he could take part in missions with the International Committee of the Red Cross (ICRC) in Africa. This initiative implies that he will leave his position as head of division. Thus, a new 38-year-old chief physician is appointed. During the first weeks, the relationship between the two doctors goes awry, and a strong rivalry sets in. The new leader seems to ignore the presence of John, who is a competent man, hyperactive, and engaged in multiple projects. The latter notices from the outset that the new colleague, who is very competent in certain advanced areas of the specialty, lacks training in general clinical practice. The situation is gradually worsening as medical and nursing teams complain about tension between the leaders. The medical director is worried.

John makes contact with the coach to evaluate if a coaching could be useful to him. During the first session, he immediately declares that he comes for professional worries:

> I work too much, and it kills my weekends. I do not live anymore. Fortunately, I have a lovely wife (doctor). However, hospital life is becoming increasingly complicated, and we become real function-aries, pawns. I live in a system of influences that lacks respect for people. Moreover, I do not get along with my colleague, who in everyday practice, is incompetent. Currently, our relationship is very bad, and talking to each other is impossible. The medical manage-ment is aware but does not move. The boat is sinking, but I would not want to be blamed for this inevitable failure. In other words, continuing in this manner is impossible. I need change and to find solutions. I even plan to leave the hospital if it does not work out because I do not feel recognized, and I do not work with pleasure anymore.

John is a talkative client, who sometimes gets lost in his speech, which compels the coach to occasionally interrupt to understand his words and refocus.

Coach: What do you expect from coaching?
John: Help me out of this bad situation, find peace, and fall back on my feet.

Today, he is considering two solutions, namely, leaving the hospital and refocusing on other activities or finding a way to get his successor off. However, he admits to not knowing what he really wants.

The coach first gives a short information on coaching and its course and on the roles of the client and coach. He then questions John again about his needs. After discussion, they decide to carry out 3–4 sessions, then make a first assessment. John will prepare a sketch of his objectives for the next session, as well as a non-exhaustive list of achievements and resources (professional and non-professional).

Second session

John arrives tense at the meeting because he just had an altercation with his colleague, who "hurt him a lot."

> She has the capacity to upset me so much, I am not myself anymore and unable to answer calmly. After the last argument, I was irritated enough to forget what I said, what she said, and who began to quarrel with the other. It never happened to me with a colleague beforehand.

John repeats his feelings of ill-being and his complaints, such as feeling of uneasiness, destruction, harm, hopeless situation, and ruminations. He feels less effective at work, such that he even happens to rush other patients and their parents. His main need is to quickly find a solution to his professional nightmare. For the remainder of his concerns, he was unable to progress in his objectives. Alternatively, he worked on his "wheel of life" (a version focused on professional activities), which clearly illustrates the current problems: poor rating in career prospects, relations with the chief, leisure activities, physical exercise, personal time, and health, whereas other fields are balanced or less affected.

John is stuck in setting coaching goals because he does not know what he really wants, final professional goal, and even where his future is. Even the ICRC project is of little interest to him.

The coach proposes an exploration of John's situation by means of the "logical levels of Robert Dilts" (Table 10.1).

- At the first level (environment), John was perfectly at ease in his hospital environment before the arrival of the new boss. Today, the only element that disturbs him in today's environment is the presence of the new leader, which is difficult or impossible to continue without change.
- At the second level (behavior), John's activities are not a problem as he has always been motivated for work that he likes and at ease in his tasks.
- The third level (capabilities) again demonstrates John's inability to adjust to the arrival of the new leader: "She is unable to do all the work of a good physician, even if she is excellent in her field of specialty."

Coach: Have you ever had to adapt to a similar situation in your career or in your life?

John: No.

Coach: What is your experience in managing professional, family, or even other conflicts?

John: Very little. I managed the division without problems for 20 years and could always impose my point of view in the disagreements with the medical team, as well as with the nursing team.

Coach: Who would benefit from adapting to actively lower the pressure: the new leader or yourself?

John: (thinking ...) Probably both. I wonder if I should add to my work goals *learning to position myself in front of a difficult colleague* without increasing the pressure?

Table 10.1 John's logical levels

---

1 **Environment**: OK, except my boss ...
2 **Behavior**: I love my job, but I'm disappointed and blocked
3 **Capabilities**: OK, except my incapacity to collaborate with my boss
4 **Values and beliefs**: I'm old style physician, I have no shared values with my new boss
5 **Identity**: I lose my sense of identity, I feel destroyed, I do not know who I am
6 **Mission and purpose**: I don't know where I go. what is my purpose ...
   After the *future perfect*: I think I've found my identity, my values, and the meaning of my mission

---

Coach: Well done, excellent!

- At the fourth level (i.e., values and beliefs), John is in a strong opposition to his base of values and beliefs: "I have always worked in systems where the leader was competent and able to treat all patients with the support of specialists if necessary. I deeply disagree with the new organization that does not guarantee optimal patient care."

Coach: How should the organization and quality of care be improved?
John: We have to collaborate. It is the only practical solution, or I have to leave.
Coach: Do you want to work on this option and find ways to collaborate with your colleague?
John: Yes, I can make it a goal.

- At the fifth level (identity), John admits to feeling a deep discomfort: "Even if my professional identity is that of a doctor, without a doubt, today I do not know who I am and what my role is in my professional environment. I have never experienced this feeling in the past. I am stuck on this aspect ... ."
- At the last level (vision and mission), John first declares that he does not know where he is going to and mission and purpose in his profession and in his life. The coach then proposes to imagine a "perfect future," where everything will be set in 12 or 18 months ... . After a few minutes of reflection, John says to the coach in a low voice:

John: I still work at the hospital (part-time), and I have found pleasure at work. A new chief who respects the quality standards and his collaborators is in place. My activity at the ICRC appeals to me and I am contemplating of increasing it.
Coach: And your identity as a doctor?
John: I think I've found my identity and the values, and meaning of my mission. However, I still need time to really realize what they mean to me.

Prevention of burnout

Prevention of burnout should be a major concern for any care provider given the frequency and consequences of burnout. It should be the subject of a specific training starting from medical studies and be continued thereafter. Furthermore, prevention should be complemented by active measures of the hospital, which holds the responsibility and interest to preserve its employees. These schemes are unfortunately not yet in place.

Creating an environment that promotes the well-being of care providers and taking measures to support doctors affected by exhaustion or other work-related issues constitute the moral *duties of the hospital management*. This new task has recently emerged for the area of hospital management, which has learned about the catastrophic effects of burnout. A shortage of care providers in certain key areas of medicine related to occurrences of burnout disrupts daily hospital functioning. This shortage is aggravated by the long-term absences of care providers with severe burnout and by the significant costs associated with the replacement of out-of-division professionals. In the United States, the total costs of a discharged physician are estimated to be two to three times his annual salary.[4,12]

Mayo Clinic, a prestigious university institution, has established an assessment of the professional satisfaction of physicians and other employees since 1998.[12,27] In 2007, a program was launched on the well-being of physicians. The program was completed in 2010 by assessing the level of burnout among all healthcare professionals using specific instruments. This assessment was initially carried out every two years, then yearly because of interest in the results. The level of commitment of care providers in their professional activity and satisfaction with work–life integration was also measured. In a study on 2,000 physicians, every 1-point increase in the severity scale of burnout (scale of 7 points maximum) or every 1-point reduction on the job satisfaction scale (5-point scale) was associated with a 30–40% reduction in work effort over the next two years. The CEO of Mayo Clinic, a physician, is personally involved in this project. He proposes that burnout prevention is a task that should be shared between care providers and the hospital and should no longer be left to the care providers alone. In this regard, a position of Director of the Physician Welfare Program has been created with a direct link to the general manager. The two managers developed an action plan for nine intervention strategies as follows[27]:

- Recognition and evaluation of the problem.
- Improvement of team leadership (training and supervision of head physicians).
- Development of targeted interventions by the heads of the unit affected by excessive burnout.
- Use of incentives.

- Work on culture and common values; for example, developing a sense of community at work.
- Promoting flexibility and work–life integration.
- Providing resources to promote resilience and the ability of care providers to take care of themselves.
- Supporting research in the field of burnout and mental health of care providers.

The training and mentoring of physician leaders to improve their leadership, particularly the department heads, are key elements of the program. A study conducted at this clinic in a population on 2,800 physicians showed that each point of elevation of the direct supervisor's leadership score (on a 60-point scale) was associated with a 3.3% decrease in the probability of burnout. In summary, the quality of leadership of the head of department was responsible for 47% of physician satisfaction.[27] These data clearly demonstrate the importance of effective leadership in the satisfaction and well-being of hospital physicians. In 2013, although the frequency of burnout among Mayo Clinic physicians was higher than the national average, the launching of the abovementioned burnout prevention program was able to gradually reduce the frequency of this work-related illness. In 2015, the clinic burnout rate reached approximately two-thirds of the national level. The authors underlined the importance of promoting physician leaders able to recognize the unique talent of their professional or in-training colleagues. For coaches active in the hospital setting, such analysis indicates the effectiveness of these measures and should encourage them to offer an active and targeted assistance of care providers suffering from burnout.

The *cares provider responsibilities* are also important. She is responsible for taking active measures to take care of herself in the context of her work environment and outside the hospital as in the following:

- To organize and control her activities within the limits of her possibilities. For medical heads, this goal includes controlling schedules, developing priorities, delegating tasks, promoting teamwork, and cooperating with colleagues when overloaded or overwhelmed. In addition, they should prioritize a portion of time on leisure tasks.
- To allocate time for herself in the hospital and at home. Family life, especially husband or spouse support, provides psychological stability and comfort that play a protective role against burnout. When analyzing the activities of healthcare professional clients, coaches noted preserving "time for oneself," even in the most overcrowded departments is fairly possible. This option can be a real challenge for care providers suffering from burnout because of their ambiguous relationship with their work, their fear of not being up to the job, and their difficulty to say no.
- To participate in team life: sharing, debriefing, mentoring, and developing social activities. Despite the medical profession's poor reputation for

helping one another, various surveys showed that support or mentoring by experienced colleagues improves the well-being of physicians. Therefore, organizing a support system at the hospital and at the level of major departments is worthwhile.[27]

- To become aware of the deleterious effect of tension and conflicts with colleagues, which play a key role in the process of exhaustion.
- To remember that the patient–doctor relationship promotes one of the most important factors of satisfaction to the doctor at work given that the relationship is positive. This notion contrasts with the deleterious effect of a heavy or frankly negative relationship, which induces stress.
- To maintain a healthy lifestyle, which contributes significantly to the prevention of burnout, although it is often neglected by care providers.

The *well-being of care providers* at work has been the subject of an abundant literature in recent years. It highlights their difficulty in caring for themselves contrary to what they do daily and effectively for patients. Studies showed the reluctance of hospital physicians to consult their doctor, especially in terms of psychic or psychosomatic diseases, such as burnout.[22,28] The American Medical Association emphasizes that every physician is responsible for maintaining his health and well-being, as well as for consulting with a personal physician whose objectivity is not compromised.[29]

- The general factors of well-being are simple and similar to those described outside the hospital setting: take the time to eat, if possible a hot meal, at noon, thus avoiding the daily sandwiches swallowed in speed; workout (i.e., outdoor and sports); reserve time for rest; and emphasize the importance of regular sleep. Furthermore, a balanced family life with a supportive and listening partner is a significant factor for preventing burnout.
- The literature in the previous ten years showed interest in care providers who wish to improve their well-being to practice "mindfulness-based stress reduction."[30] Other similar methods for relaxing or mind–body work, such as yoga, and tai-chi, are also well accepted. Mindfulness meditation is the best studied and probably the most effective.[7] Its purpose is precisely to develop the capacity for mindfulness, which enables one to be present and to live the present moment without prejudice or judgment.[30,31] Several studies attested to its effectiveness in the prevention and treatment of burnout among doctors, nurses, and medical and nursing students.[7] In addition, mindfulness meditation seems to stimulate interest in the other person and seems to increase the capacity for compassion.[31,32] A study conducted among pre-graduate students showed that a 10-minute exercise of "meditation of love and benevolence," which is centered on other people, was able to induce an improvement of the well-being and feelings of social connection. Such feelings are associated with a decline in self-centeredness.[33]

Another North American study combined a variety of approaches, such as mindfulness meditation, self-awareness exercises, narrative exercises about key clinical experiences, appreciative inter-views, and group discussions among 70 primary care physicians in a postgraduate training program.[31] The results are impressive: improved well-being, improvement in the MBI in all areas, and improved overall empathy and mood.

Mindfulness meditation training is part of an eight-week program; however, a shortened training has been developed and validated. These results have led various hospitals to urge their care providers to follow such training.

René Chioléro (like many other coaches) regularly uses a simplified technique of mindful meditation with his clients interested in this approach. It consists of doing a sitting meditation of 10–15 minutes with the client during coaching to develop self-awareness and live in the present moment. The coach proposes that the client resumes the exercise every day at work and possibly at home at convenient times. The feedback thus far has been favorable.

Conclusion

The hospital work of care providers is considered particularly difficult. This heaviness mainly affects physicians and nurses active in the advanced fields of acute medicine, who are subject to very busy work schedules and associated with extreme and repeated stress. Their consequences are psychological and even mental health issues, which are more frequent in the medical profession than in other professions. Burnout, for example, can reach as high as 50% in certain medical specialties. The symptoms are frequently underestimated or ignored by those who are affected. This chapter described in detail this work disease, which is common among healthcare professionals. Exhaustion and burnout in low and moderate intensities can be reduced by coaching. When severe, however, it requires medical care. The coaching of these exhausted care providers involves specific knowledge and skills as well as sufficient experience. Today, preventing burnout is considered an essential mission of hospital healthcare executives and managers. Prevention is the responsibility of the hospital managers and healthcare professionals themselves.

Bibliography

1 Shanafelt TD, Boone S, Tan L, *et al.* Burnout and satisfaction with work-life balance among US physicians relative to the general US population. *Arch Intern Med* 2012; 172(18): 1377.

2 Printzen G. La profession de médecin: rêve ou cauchemar ? *Bull Med Suisses* 2010; 91(43): 1677.

3 Tyssen R. Health problems and the use of health services among physicians: a review article with particular emphasis on Norwegian studies. *Ind Health* 2007; 45(5): 599–610.

4 McClafferty H, Brown OW. Physician health and wellness. *Pediatrics* 2014; 134(4): 835–835.

5 Miller NM, McGowen RK. The painful truth: physicians are not invincible. *South Med J* 2000; 93(10): 966–973.

6 Zwyssig I. Les médecins devraient prendre soin de leur santé. *Bull Med Suisses* 2016: 412–413.

7 Irving JA, Dobkin PL, Park J. Cultivating mindfulness in health care professionals: a review of empirical studies of mindfulness-based stress reduction (MBSR). *Complement Ther Clin Pract* 2009; 15(2): 61–66.

8 Alspach G. When your work conditions are sicker than your patients. *Crit Care Nurse* 2005; 25(3): 11–14.

9 Moss M, Good VS, Gozal D, Kleinpell R, Sessler CN. An official critical care societies collaborative statement: burnout syndrome in critical care healthcare professionals: a call for action. *Crit Care Med* 2016; 44(7): 1414–1421.

10 Poncet MC, Toullic P, Papazian L, *et al*. Burnout syndrome in critical care nursing staff. *Am J Respir Crit Care Med* 2007; 175(7): 698–704.

11 Shanafelt TD, Sloan JA, Habermann TM. The well-being of physicians. *Am J Med* 2003; 114(6): 513–519.

12 Shanafelt TD, Noseworthy JH. Executive leadership and physician well-being. *Mayo Clin Proc* 2017; 92(1): 129–146.

13 Shanafelt TD. Enhancing meaning in work: a prescription for preventing physician burnout and promoting patient-centered care. *JAMA* 2009; 302(12): 1338–1340.

14 Shanafelt TD, West CP, Sloan JA, *et al*. Career fit and burnout among academic faculty. *Arch Intern Med* 2009; 169(10): 990–995.

15 McMurray JE, Williams E, Schwartz MD, *et al*. Physician job satisfaction: developing a model using qualitative data. *J Gen Intern Med* 1997; 12(11): 711–714.

16 Maslach C, Jackson SE, Leiter MP. *Maslach Burnout Inventory Manual*. 3rd ed. Consulting Psychologists Press, Paolo Alto, CA; 1996.

17 Biaggi P, Peter S, Ulich E. Stressors, emotional exhaustion and aversion to patients in residents and chief residents – what can be done? *Swiss Med Wkly* 2008; 133: 339–346.

18 Rotenstein L, Torre M, Ramos MA, *et al*. Prevalence of burnout among physicians: a systematic review. *JAMA* 2018; 320(11): 1131–1150.

19 Kristensen TS, Borritz M, Villadsen E, Christensen KB. The Copenhagen Burnout Inventory: a new tool for the assessment of burnout. *Work Stress* 2005; 19(3): 192–207.

20 Trockel M, Bohman B, Lesure E, *et al*. A brief instrument to assess both burnout and professional fulfillment in physicians: reliability and validity, including correlation with self-reported medical errors, in a sample of resident and practicing physicians. *Acad Psychiatry* 2018; 42(1): 11–24.

21 Saleh KJ. The prevalence and severity of burnout among academic orthopaedic departmental leaders. *J Bone Jt Surg Am* 2007; 89(4): 896.

22 Doppia MA, Lieutaud T, Mertes PM, Arzalier-Daret S. Congrès EAPH: le CFAR et la campagne #DIDOC récompensés au niveau européen [Internet]. *CFAR*. Available from: https://cfar.org/congres-eaph-le-cfar-et-la-campagne-didoc-recompenses-au-niveau-europeen/

23 Gazelle G, Liebschutz JM, Riess H. Physician burnout: coaching a way out. *J Gen Intern Med* 2015; 30(4): 508–513.

24 Berg IK, Szabó P. *Brief Coaching for Lasting Solutions*. 1st ed. W.W. Norton, New York; 2005.

25 O'Connell B, Palmer S, Williams H. An overview of solution focused coaching. *In*: O'Connell B, Palmer S, Williams H. *Solution Focused Coaching in Practice*. Routledge, London; 2012, pp. 13–36.

26 Dilts RM. *From Coach to Awakener*. Meta Publications, Capitola, CA; 2003.

27 Shanafelt TD, Hasan O, Dyrbye LN, *et al*. Changes in burnout and satisfaction with work-life balance in physicians and the general US working population between 2011 and 2014. *Mayo Clin Proc* 2015; 90(12): 1600–1613.

28 Wallace JE, Lemaire J. On physician well-being – You'll get by with a little help from your friends. *Soc Sci Med* 2007; 64(12): 2565–2577.

29 Taub S, Morin K, Goldrich MS, Ray P, Benjamin R. Physician health and wellness. *Occup Med* 2006; 56(2): 77–82.

30 Kabat-Zinn J. *Full Catastrophe Living. Using the Wisdom of Your Body and Mind to Face Stress, Pain and Illness*. Bantam Books Trade Paperbacks, New York; 2013.

31 Krasner MS, Epstein RM, Beckman H, *et al*. Association of an educational program in mindful communication with burnout, empathy, and attitudes among primary care physicians. *JAMA* 2009; 302(12): 1284–1293.

32 Boellinghaus I, Jones FW, Hutton J. The role of mindfulness and loving-kindness meditation in cultivating self-compassion and other-focused concern in health care professionals. *Mindfulness* 2014; 5(2): 129–138.

33 Seppala EM, Hutcherson CA, Nguyen DT, Doty JR, Gross JJ. Loving-kindness meditation: a tool to improve healthcare provider compassion, resilience, and patient care. *J Compassionate Health Care* 2014; 1: 5.

Further readings

Dilts R. *From Coach to Awakener*. Meta Publications, Capitola, CA; 2003.

Kabat Zinn J. *Full Catastrophe Living. Using the Wisdom of Your Body and Mind to Face Stress, Pain, and Illness*. Revised ed. Bantam Books Trade Paperbacks, New York; 2013.

O'Connell B, Palmer S, Williams H. *Solution Focused Coaching in Practice*. Routledge, London; 2012.

11 Conflicts and violence in hospitals

René Chioléro

"You don't see the world as it is, but as you are."
—Anaïs Nin, *Seduction of the Minotaur*, 1961

Introduction

Contrary to expectations, conflicts frequently occur in all areas of hospital activity. They concern the contacts of care providers with patients and their relatives, relations between colleagues, within care teams, interdisciplinary relationships, as well as the often difficult relations with the administration. With appropriate management, conflicts can become opportunities for change, improvement, and growth. Training in conflict management is currently a component of the panoply of leaders and coaches worthy of the name.

Violence at work affects not only care activities but also medical–nursing relationships and can also be observed in the academic setting. Its repercussions on the functioning of the hospital and well-being of care providers are notable. In other words, it is a cause of suffering for personnel and a major source of malfunction in teams. When violence is related to problems internal to departments and conflicts between care professionals, such violence is typically hidden and difficult to discern from outside. In recent years, the impact of violence against medical and nursing students as well as in-training physicians has been exposed by the media and efforts are being made to make it disappear. Conflicts and, rarely, violence between care providers concern the hospital coach and represent a significant source of activity. Therefore, the coach should become familiar with specific aspects of conflicts and violence.

The general purpose of the chapter is to present the main aspects of hospital conflicts. A special emphasis is placed on situations observed during the coaching of medical teams. In addition, certain aspects of hospital violence that may be of significance to the coach are presented.

General considerations

If medical and nursing leaders are asked about common difficulties in work, conflict management certainly belongs among the top five. Many medical

DOI: 10.4324/9781003291831-14

personnel admit that they experience difficulty in managing daily dissensions, which cost a substantial amount of energy and are recurring sources of concern. Prolonged interpersonal dissension and team conflict disrupt not only team operations but also interactions with patients and families to a certain extent as well as the quality of care. In the United States, various studies illustrated that time spent by hospital staff managing conflicts of any kind varies from 1 to more than 3 hours per week per person with annual costs (related to lost time and energy) estimated at $300 billions.[1] In the most serious cases, the entire operation of a division, department, or even more can be affected. At the beginning of his career, one of the authors experienced conflict in a hospital department that lasted several years, which led to the departure of senior doctors and dismissal of the head of department. The heads of hospital administration, human resources, and other non-caring sectors of the hospital cannot escape this reality.

Prolonged conflict between senior physicians

A medical division in a university hospital is disrupted by a long-standing antagonism between two senior physicians. This conflict overflows into the functioning of the medical team, which has split into two opposing groups around two protagonists, namely, doctors N and W. The division head, Joann, admits to being powerless to calm dissent and restore peace. The medical director failed twice to mediate. The consequences are significant: the nursing team complains about the lack of collaboration of a few physicians, which complicates the care of patients; secretaries regret the difficulty in allocating consultations; and handling of emergencies during the working hours suffers from lack of cooperation of doctors. The medical director offers coaching for Joann, which she accepts.

At first, the coach meets the head of division who describes her repeated failures to pacify the medical team.

Joann: The story is impossible because it is worse than a class of kids. I do not understand why I cannot calm the team down. In addition, I think that for a woman, interfering in conflicts between colleagues is nearly impossible because I lack authority.

Coach: What have you done so far?

Joann: For the conflict between the two attendings, I met each of them several times to assess what I can do. I asked the medical director to mediate but nothing worked. Both accuse the other of not wanting to collaborate and prevent one from working. Finally, the medical director suggested that I should undertake coaching.

Coach: Well, I see that it is really difficult. What are other repercussions on the medical team?

Joann: Well, the team split into two opposing groups, which complicates the entirety of the division and collaboration with the nursing team. The care plan of the patients is difficult to finalize, and the management of emergencies suffers from the lack of cooperation among doctors. Moreover, reaching an agreement with all medical staff to apply good practice recommendations is difficult.

Coach: How do you relate to the two clans?

Joann: Actually, I am closer to Dr. N and her supporters.

Coach: And ...?

Joann: This closeness is making things more difficult because this preference is known to everyone.

As agreed with the medical director and division head, the coach meets each of the senior doctors and chief residents, who confirm the malfunctions of the medical team and underline the difficulty of the leader to impose herself. Thus, group coaching is initiated.

This vignette reveals the adverse consequences at multiple levels with regard to the inability of a department head (who is also an excellent clinician) to manage her medical team. Joann's lack of competence in managing and leading the team is certainly the most important factor that can explain such a situation.

Conflicts in the hospital: frequency, causes, and contributing factors

Conflict management is part of the core of key competencies that every leader must have, especially in today's institutions. A survey of 461 North American nurses in a hospital group found that more than 90% had been verbally abused in the previous month. Doctors were primarily responsible, followed by patients and their relatives, supervisors, and subordinates.[2] Many factors favor conflict, particularly the high stress of the care environment, overwork, failure in leadership, inadequacy of organization and management, and inappropriate behaviors of several care providers.[2,3] The cumulation of such factors in the operating theater and intensive care unit explains why these hospital environments are particularly prone to all forms of confrontation.

The operating theater as an example

The operating room is a classic example of a conflict-prone environment.[4] Within a limited space, it concentrates the various professionals necessary for managing surgical interventions, such as surgeons, anesthetists (physicians and nurses), doctors-in-training, instrumentalists, technical staff, and assistants. Each professional body has a proper organization and its culture and professional values. The work atmosphere is frequently stressed and tense. As a result, the execution of tasks and interrelationships between various stakeholders trigger clashes. One study reported that task-related quarrels occur between one and four times per surgical operation[4]; two other studies cited that two-thirds of anesthesiologists regularly came into conflict with surgeons one to four times a month, and even more for a minority of them.[5] These studies also illustrated that task conflicts easily overlap with relationship problems.

Such fights are caused by misunderstanding and rivalries, and rarely by clashes between difficult personalities. Fatigue and stress, which are associated with frequent delays in the operating theater, also play a role. The emotional component, which is perceptible, provokes verbal abuse. Physical violence, which is severely sanctioned in the present, is less common. In a coaching, we encountered the case of an irritated anesthesiologist who had slapped an instrumentalist. He was initially suspended by management, then fired. Among the physicians, surgeons often have the reputation of indulging in inappropriate behavior more often than colleagues in other specialties.

Difficult people

These disruptive or even destructive and "toxic" behaviors disturb the entire operating team. A toxic behavior may destabilize the individuals present, the functioning of the teams, and, ultimately, the entire organization.[1] In other words, mean, abusive, and disruptive behavior among medical professionals interferes with the cooperation, teamwork, and communication necessary to work efficiently and operate safely on the patients.[6] These behaviors occur not only in the operating room but also in other areas of the hospital where such behaviors can be observed. Unfortunately, initially turning a blind eye to the misconduct of physicians in high academic positions or who actively contribute to recruit patients to the hospital is common among hospital managers.

Disruptive behavior is divided into two categories, namely, aggressive, dominant, and occasional violence (i.e., those who impose their views and demands on employees), and passive and withdrawn (i.e., leaders who are unwilling to cooperate). Such behaviors are less tolerated. In general, we are moving toward zero tolerance of such attitudes in public hospitals, such as when they are initiated by superiors and higher-ups. An abundant literature demonstrated the negative effects of high-intensity conflicts, such as fatigue, increased stress, decreased care provider satisfaction, resignation, reduced quality, and increased number of surgical complications.[2]

A chief resident in a bad mood

During a morning report in the intensive care unit (ICU), I heard that the ICU chief resident had been insulted the previous night by John, a surgeon in a bad mood. John insulted her because he disapproved of the antibiotic treatment that she prescribed to his patient at admission to ICU.

The following day, I summoned the surgeon, whom I knew (a former resident), and asked him to tell me the event.

John:	This bitch did not want to listen to me. It is true; I was tired, and I let myself go and insulted her, but it was not very bad.
René Chioléro:	Do you have any regrets about the incident?
John:	No. Sincerely, no. I was tired and she looked for me.
René Chioléro:	Well, I find that this behavior is unacceptable, especially since I have received complaints about you from other senior physicians. I ask you to apologize; otherwise, I will notify you in writing of my disapproval.
John:	You can say what you want. My boss also gets upset from time to time and does the same or worse. So I do not see …
René Chioléro:	Well, I will write to inform you of my disapproval and, next time, I will send a copy to the medical director.

This exchange ends the episode without recurrence to the best of my knowledge.

Although the confrontations and conflicts between nurses and anesthesiologists have largely diminished, the same is not true of the quarrels between surgeons, who are known as "the kings of the operating theater," and anesthetists. Although surgeons are frequently worried about being able to operate on their patients as soon as possible, anesthesiologists are confronted with numerous safety rules and activities in the recovery room, which can lead to delays in the procedure of the operating program, which are poorly tolerated by surgeons.

Preventing the emergence of conflicts in an operating theater is possible using the following measures that have been proven useful:

- appropriate organization with sufficient staffing and day-to-day management of the operating program;
- intervention by the heads whenever a dissension increases or relates an entire team or several teams;

- particular attention to repeated oppositions, which must be dealt with accordingly by the various heads concerned; preventive measures are typically necessary;
- appropriate leadership, which includes (brief) training in conflict management and non-violent communication. This training should involve all heads of instrumentalists, nurses, and anesthesiologists. Ideally, such an incentive should also involve surgeons. Although all clashes cannot be prevented, solving them in a simple manner is possible. The ability to hold difficult conversations, as well as acquiring conflict management skills, should be part of the background of these leaders;
- brief training for all staff, including the basics of non-violent communication and a module dedicated to appropriate behavior in the specific environment of the operating theater. This measure has proven effective in a troubled environment[1] of emergency medicine, where staff are trained to act effectively;
- help from an external speaker, such as a coach, in protracted confrontations involving several professional categories.

Finally, we summarize several basic principles of conflict management in hospitals as proposed by Overton et al.[2]

1   Conflicts are inevitable and can have positive consequences if well managed.
2   Active strategies produce better outcomes than avoidance strategies, except for everyday petty quarrels.
3   Managers should be motivated to intervene in a sufficiently quick manner before radicalization.
4   Promoting respectful behaviors and practicing emotional self-control during tense situations are abilities that can be acquired. Compromise and collaboration favor the development of win–win solutions, whereas active opposition is inappropriate.
5   Emotional management requires personal awareness. The first step is that everyone should be able to recognize his reaction (see information on emotional intelligence; chapters 2 and 7). Human beings are naturally destabilized by tension when they exceed a certain threshold. The two previous vignettes illustrated this aspect.
6   The environment should be capable of providing a secure, conflict-resolution solution. Indeed, when stakeholders are aware that they are safe and respected, expressing oneself and disagreeing are possible.

Example of intensive care

The ICU is one of the hubs of the hospital. It is a highly stressful workplace for many reasons: a high concentration of care providers who retain multiple interactions with external care providers; the intensity of work is particularly high; and the permanent contact with suffering and death and oftentimes difficult interactions with families affects the staff, especially at end-of-life situations. These conditions result in a high level of conflicts of all forms, most of which are resolved easily by care providers themselves (Tables 11.1 and 11.2). Examples include the following:

- the selection of patients for admission (triage), specifically, refusal of admission related to the shortage of beds ("How can you refuse the admission of my patient that I operated yesterday?");
- end-of-life decisions, where active treatments are reduced or stopped and which can be a source of disagreement with relatives ("They plan to unplug my father, I am outraged!");
- antagonisms between the medical and nursing teams, which is frequently linked to power relationships in which physicians engage in domination and non-collaborative behaviors ("I want my patient to be up three times a day despite shortage of staff"); and
- disagreements with the medical teams of other departments, such as anesthesiologists, surgeons, cardiologists, and transplant physicians, to name a few. These arguments most likely relate to power relations concerning the treatment of patients ("I do not want my patient to be extubated today because I am in the operating room all day long") and disputes with patients and their families ("your parent is a little agitated today, so we had to limit visits to two people").

Table 11.1 Hospital conflicts: multiple aspects

Type and category	Examples
Severity	
• **Minor conflicts**: part of everyday life, little or no impact	• Finalizing the doctors' plan of calls for Christmas
• **Moderate intensity**: significant impact, no vital threat, and resolution within the unit (i.e., division and department)	• Disagreement between two medical attendings with repercussions on medico-administrative tasks
• **Serious conflict**: serious repercussions for care providers, functioning of the unit, patients, care, and interdisciplinary relationships, requires the intervention of the division or department head or medical director depending on extent and severity	• Tension between a surgical team and intensive care medical team with repercussions on patient care, information of families, work of nurses, and training of residents
Type of conflicts	
• **Interpersonal (relationships)**: between two or several persons, within the team, and between two teams	• Conflict between two attendings who covet the direction of clinical research
• **Task-related (cognitive)**: differing opinions on performing tasks	• Lack of agreement on the role of hypothermia in the treatment of cardiac arrest
• **Process-related**: poor organization of work (i.e., time of clinical rounds, supervision of in training doctors), and delegation of tasks	• Change of treatment and therapeutic project following executive rotation and delay in the execution of delegated tasks

Table 11.2 Interpersonal conflicts

Type of healthcare provider	Possible solutions
Medical team	
• Between two or several residents	• Commonplace, regulated by the residents or chief residents themselves, and rarely by senior physicians
• Between two senior physicians (or chief residents)	• May require the intervention of the head of department but rarely a mediation
• Between the head of division and one senior attending	• Danger to be regulated by the chief and his subordinate; if necessary, intervention of the head of department or of medical director, more rarely a mediation
• Within the team and between two clans	• Danger to be imperatively settled by the head of department and if necessary, intervention of the head of department. Coaching can be offered
Nursing team	
• Between two nurses	• May require the intervention of the head nurse
• Between the head nurse and a member of the team	• To be settled directly by the persons or by hierarchy
• Within the team and between two clans	• Danger to be settled by nursing hierarchy. Coaching can be offered
Physician–nurse conflicts	
• Interpersonal	• To be settled by head physicians and nurses
• Inter-team conflicts	• Danger to be imperatively settled by head physicians and head nurses
Conflicts with members of other divisions and departments	
• Between senior physicians or department chiefs	• High-risk situation, to be imperatively settled by the head of division or department or by the medical director
Conflicts with patients or relatives	
• With patients or relatives	• High-risk situation, requiring the intervention of the division head or medical hierarchy (medical director)

"As long as your patient is not in cardiac arrest ..."

Charlie is chief resident in the ICU at a university hospital. The head of department receives a complaint from a head nurse regarding an incident during the previous night of duty: a student nurse complains that Charlie called at 2 am and did not respond to her request for a patient whose condition worried her. Instead, he answered, "I am busy now; is the patient dying?" The nurse answered no; he did not move for 30 minutes, which made the young nurse very anxious.

The department head and the head nurse decided to meet Charlie and clear the case. After explaining the complaint, they made him understand why they took the incident very seriously. Then, they questioned him.

Head of department:	Explain what happened.
Charlie:	Well, I was busy at the computer preparing a conference when the nurse bothered me unexpectedly. I knew that the patient was stable 2 hours before.
Head of department:	So what?
Charlie:	I did not mind immediately, and I was right because the patient did not have any complications.
Head of department:	But the nurse was worried?
Charlie:	Yes, that was not my problem, but she certainly went to talk to her colleagues.
Head of department:	Do you regret what happened?
Charlie:	No, it is difficult for everyone.

A few weeks later, Charlie relapsed with the assistant on call. This scenario motivated the management to dismiss him. Two years later, he was fired again from another hospital due to inappropriate behavior.

A survey was conducted in 2008 in 323 European ICUs on conflicts perceived by care providers for seven consecutive days. 7,358 providers from 24 countries took part to the survey and answered a questionnaire. Conflicts as perceived by care providers over seven consecutive days were assessed using a questionnaire.[7] Of providers, 72% reported at least one conflict, 6% more than one, whereas 28% reported none. One-third of the clashes involved care provider–family relationships and two-thirds pertained to relationships within care teams. Dissent was perceived by care providers as serious and dangerous in more than 50% of cases and harmful and not useful in more than 80%. The main effects identified were a disruption of interindividual relationships and quality of care. Conflicts were significantly associated with hard work with two main causes, namely, (1) behavior of people, especially animosity, lack of trust, and poor communication; and (2) end-of-life care, especially decision-making processes and lack of communication between medical teams and nurses. Two-thirds of the care providers perceived that the clashes could have been prevented.

Another study showed that senior physicians and nurses and families perceive the frequency of end-of-life clashes differently: doctors underestimate it (approximately 15% of cases), whereas nurses and families were more sensitive (up to 80% of cases).[8] This observation indicates that the perception of conflicts varies across professional categories, that is, managers who stay away from care more frequently underestimate it in comparison with the perception of nurses or families.

When end of life is inescapable

A 38-year-old patient is transferred from a regional hospital to the ICU of a university hospital. She has severe necrotizing pneumonia with destruction of a large part of the lungs associated with extreme respiratory failure. The patient is a mother of two children aged 4 and 6 years old. The entire family is mobilized and hopes for a favorable outcome in a climate of increasing anxiety. The initial therapeutic project, which is aimed at the patient's survival, offered two options, namely, a favorable evolution under maximal medical treatment (i.e., artificial ventilation and antibiotics) or an unfavorable outcome leading to consideration of a lung transplant.

The evolution is unfortunately catastrophic, and the patient suffers a cardiac arrest; this event modifies the care project toward palliative treatment. Relationships with the family become difficult. Relatives are convinced that they are not receiving complete information and that the care providers are hiding things. They ask many questions and even check care sheets every day. After four weeks of hopeless maximal treatment, the family is exhausted; the care providers wonder about the therapeutic project; a few of them talk about "futile treatments," which will lead to a fatal outcome regardless of evolution.

The solution finally comes after the change of the attending physician responsible for the patient. The new doctor assisted by the nurse takes up contact with the family he already knows using a listening strategy.

Attending: I am the doctor responsible for leading the therapy of your relative for one week. You know her situation is particularly serious, with little hope of survival. I would first like to summarize the current situation and all that has been undertaken. Then, I would like to hear your opinion on the evolution.

The husband is the spokesperson of the family:

Husband: Contrary to what some of your colleagues imagine, we realize that the situation is virtually hopeless. What do you have to propose in such condition?

Attending: In a dead-end situation, we usually start a palliative treatment after obtaining the family's consent. This treatment is centered on the comfort of the patient and support. It ensures a peaceful and painless end of life. What do you think?

Husband: Well, I believe that as of today, we are ready for this issue because we do not want her to suffer unnecessarily. As you can imagine, it is painful for all of us. However, we do not want to experience such a situation any longer if it does not make sense.

Attending: This statement corresponds to that of the healthcare team. The nurse acknowledges.

Husband: Therefore, we agree to follow you on this path. I will talk with my family and I will come back to inform you.

Two days later, the patient dies surrounded by family. The nursing team is appeased despite the inevitable outcome.

Obtaining consent from the family is oftentimes more difficult when they are not ready to accept the death of their beloved. Frequently, disagreements on end-of-life care between families and care providers diminish over time. When it continues, seeking external help is necessary, for example, from a chaplain or hospital ethicist if relatives rely on religious beliefs to postpone an inevitable palliative project. The increasing inclusion of relatives in decision-making processes during the previous years and constant weakening of medical authority occasionally lead to heated discussions and disputes over treatment.

Taking care of a patient with major burns: how to convince the family?

The patient has severe burns, which requires staying in a specialized burn station. The family has long opposed scientific medicine and preferred alternative care, which was evident in their refusal of certain antibiotics that inhibit immunity and artificial nutrition with commercial products. The son of the burned patient asks the care providers to apply a new healing treatment from a naturopathic center. No information in the medical literature is found on this therapy, and the drug has never been tested on burned humans. Thus, the senior physician (rightly) denies this request. The tone escalates, and the son stands by his request. A meeting is organized between the wife and son of the patient, the attending in charge of the patient, a nurse, and head of department, in addition to the hospital medical director. The latter, after listening to the son's request, quickly takes a stand against the proposed treatment: "Administering a treatment that has not been previously tested in humans is not allowed."

The relationships with the family remain difficult until the end of stay.

When relations between care providers and patients or their relatives become negative and necessitate external intervention, it is usually conducted by a hospital mediator, who helps to calm the conflict.

Interpersonal conflicts

Interpersonal antagonisms are frequent, particularly among mid- and end-of-career executive physicians. The accumulation of frustrations related to hospital and academic life, frequent power contests between colleagues, repeated burnout episodes, and inadequate leadership foster tension and arguments. The presence of professionals with difficult behaviors also plays a significant role.

Prolonged conflict between senior physicians

Two attendings have been competing for several years. Dr. N (Nancy) does not bear the behavior of a young colleague, Dr. W (William). She sharply criticizes his professional and general misbehavior. William, despite several conciliation attempts, also openly criticizes his colleague in the department and often counters her vigorously during discussions of the medical team. The head of the department is attempting to calm the situation but seems to support Nancy, as observed by the medical team.

The coach proposes to organize a mediation to develop a common solution, which is accepted by Nancy and William. They express their preference for mediation to be conducted by a coach they know. The latter accepts reluctantly because he fears a confusion of role.

Mediation is difficult because the two doctors have no common project and seem to share nothing. The only favorable element is awareness, as admitted by the two protagonists, that their quarrels, which have been transmitted to hospital management, weaken them and ultimately expose them to sanctions. They finally agree to define a minimum relational framework that they commit to respect, that is, say hello, talk to each other, give their opinion, and avoid criticism of each other. A written commitment defining the relational modes and certain codes of conduct is signed in front of the head of department. The effect appears positive for a short period of approximately three months. Afterward, the conflict starts again, but less virulently.

This vignette highlights the difficulty of the coexistence of "seemingly incompatible personalities" when opposed by a long history of confrontations. The responsibility of the head of department, who has allowed the situation to continue and rot for a few years, is obvious. After several years, such a situation can permanently affect team dynamics. We encountered two similar situations in our hospital coaching practice. In both cases, we emphasize that the team had accommodated this situation, as well as the head of department, who sometimes "played" a role in fueling the conflict. He said: "Their constant quarrels have led the team to malfunction despite all my efforts; we have been poorly quoted by doctors in training for three years because of them ... ."

Difficulty in collaborating with old senior physicians

A strong antagonism pits two senior physicians (Drs. C and D) for several years, which was tolerated, even sometimes encouraged by the head of department. A new department head with little experience of team leadership is appointed. He rapidly shows difficulty in leading the department, particularly the medical team. In addition, he struggles to delegate tasks. He repeatedly complains about the conflict he inherited, which in his opinion rots the functioning of the medical team. A coaching is offered to him.

The coach individually meets the senior physicians and quickly takes note of the difficulty of the situation. The head seems unable to lead his team and gradually becoming exhausted despite the strong motivation. An interview with the two protagonists also indicates the heavy consequences of an unresolved conflict: repeated absenteeism and an episode of burnout in one and extreme loneliness and feelings of "persecution" in the other.

An afternoon of teamwork is organized, which is focused on the organization of the department, thus bringing together the medical and nursing staff. This meeting is the coach's first contact with the team. The two antagonist doctors are present. On this day, the coach observes that C quickly puts himself in a disruptive role: he openly criticizes his boss and his "hand-off leadership," suggests that his colleague Dr. D had failures in the last weeks. This contrasts with

Dr. D, who seems dismayed and almost unresponsive, as is the head
of the department. The coach interrupts the interactions and reframes
the transaction: "This is a conflict that has been neglected for several
years; it has to be solved once and for all." He points out that in
addition to the three directly opposing people (i.e., Drs. C, D, and the
department head), the team is also directly impacted by the situation.
During the discussion, a proposal that the coach will meet the head of
the department and the two attendings is proposed to address the
conflict and identify possible solutions to be transmitted to the group.
This proposal helps calm the situation, and the team resumes its work.
However, the coach notices that mobilizing the remainder of the
participants is difficult, with the exception of the chief residents who
are less concerned by the conflicts of the elders.

This vignette relates in another form to the serious consequences of
an unresolved conflict between two senior doctors who have been in the
department for a long time. It also points out the inability of two consecutive department heads to manage the issue despite the support of the
medical director.

Finally, it illustrates a typical element of the dynamics of protracted conflicts
called the "drama triangle of Karpman." According to the author, lasting
conflicts typically take place in the context of a psychological "game" that is
totally unconscious to the protagonists. Such a game is played frequently by
three or more people and enables the installation of stable dynamics that can
last for years. The "players" take on the defined roles of a *persecutor, victim,* or
savior.[9] A characteristic feature of this game's dynamics is the change in roles
played by the protagonists during the game. For example, the victim turns
against the persecutor or savior and vice versa. This case is true of Dr. C that
day, which came out of his typical attitude as a victim to attack his colleague
and boss. For the coach, the first step is detecting the presence of a game and
avoid taking an active part. Indeed, the coach would easily adopt that of the
savior and rarely that of the persecutor or victim. In group coaching, the coach
has to be especially aware and attentive to this unconscious but frequent
phenomenon given the importance of parallel processes.

Two chief physicians unwilling to cooperate

An uncontrollable conflict disrupts the operation of a department headed
by two chief physicians in a regional hospital. This opposition started
two years ago when Georgia was appointed to replace a sick colleague.

The other chief, Christian, who had been in office for five years, strongly opposed Georgia's appointment but in vain. Christian said, "She is not a reliable person, I have had problems with her during my years of training, I know I will not get along with her." However, the nominating committee did not heed his request. Thus, collaboration was difficult on the first days. A hostile relationship was established, which worsened and resulted in the lack of any collaboration. The nursing team complained about the difficulty of working with two senior doctors who do not communicate with each other and fail sometimes to pass on information required for patient care during the night and weekend. On two occasions, the medical director warned the two protagonists that sanctions would be taken if they did not remedy the situation. He also carried out mediation unsuccessfully. Finally, the management of the hospital-imposed coaching.

The coach quickly notices the severity of the situation. The two physicians clash regularly and ignore each other for the remainder of the time. In this context, properly treating patients is impossible. However, the coach observes that the doctors get along relatively well with other physicians of this and other external departments. The assessment of the nursing team differs: a few appreciate the spontaneous behavior of Georgia, whereas others prefer the reserved behavior of Christian. Interviews with the head physicians confirm this reality.

Coach: What prevents you from collaborating with your colleague?
Georgia: Christian did not welcome me, and I immediately felt hostility. I do not know what he thinks because he ignores me, and I know he criticizes me in front of the nurses. How should I communicate with him?
Coach: Are you ready to make an effort?
Georgia: Yes, I can try, but I am pessimistic about the outcome.
Coach: What does that mean and what are the possible consequences for yourself?
Georgia: It means they will eventually realize that they have to fire my colleague … .

The discussion with Christian further confirms this impossible relationship.

Coach: What is preventing you from working with your colleague and collaborating with her?

> *Christian:*   She does not respect me, is arrogant, and oftentimes dominant. I have attempted to improve our communication several times. For example, I invited her to coffee to establish a better relationship. Each time, however, she does not understand what I say and even makes offensive remarks about me.
> *Coach:*   What should you do?
> *Christian:*   I think she has to leave. I said it to the Nominating Committee but failed to make myself heard.

The two head physicians have been fighting for two years despite all the attempts from their colleagues and the hospital management to make them listen to reason. They co-direct the department in a system of horizontal hierarchy, which requires sufficient agreement between the leaders to ensure the function of the structure throughout the year. Despite their understanding of the need to cooperate to care for patients, their antagonism is stronger than their desire to collaborate. This contradiction urges the director of the hospital to impose coaching.

Conflicts within teams

In our experience, antagonisms in medical teams are common and can have serious consequences because medical practice and care are usually performed in teams. When addressed in an appropriate setting, conflicts within teams can be a source of development and learning.[10]

An appropriate discussion framework should be implemented to enable a return to a reassuring atmosphere, which usually require the following conditions:

- The discussion is conducted by a neutral and benevolent person who is uninvolved in the conflict.
- Time should be sufficient.
- Enable the possibility of an open discussion to allow the expression of feelings.
- Clear rules of communication that ensure respect from each person should be provided. The speakers should not interrupt each other and display intolerance to aggressive, domineering, and violent behavior; proper management of emotions should be observed.

Establishing such a framework helps build trust among team members, which is an essential ingredient of emerging from long-term conflicts. Once installed, such a framework allows people to voice their thoughts, express disagreement, and address inconvenience without restraint but with respect to identify solutions that can satisfy the majority of the team.[10] For the coach, working with a dysfunctional group (i.e., oppositional, closed, and passive) is a delicate and often difficult task. Tuckman's classic rule, which describes the evolution of groups into four stages, namely, training stage, storming stage, normalization and equilibrium step, and performance stage (i.e., forming, storming, norming, and performing[11]) is relevant. In this approach, the presence of repeated divergences often indicates that the group is constituted and feels sufficiently safe to dare to confront each other. The coach must be aware of this reality when beginning coaching in a conflict.

Conflicts that occur in the hospital setting are categorized into three, namely *person-related* (between two people or factions in a team or between a person and a group), *task-related* (cognitive conflicts, usually related to performing tasks linked to care and hospital life), and those related to *work processes and work organization*, in particular, the delegation of tasks. These causes can be intertwined. For example, management and organizational failures favor discord in tasks and people.

In our experience, the most frequent conflicts affecting medical teams have four main causes, which can be cumulated as follows:

- Weak or inappropriate leadership.
- Presence of difficult personalities among team members.
- Presence of factions in the team.
- Weak management, especially in the organization of processes and tasks.

Inefficiency of leadership is one of the leading causes of prolonged and seemingly insoluble antagonisms in medical teams. We emphasize that managing a group of doctors is difficult. These teams are often individualistic, non-accepting of team life, and reluctant to build a balanced working relationship with nurses. In academic hospitals, hierarchical and academic rivalries further complicate the dynamics of the medical team. For these reasons, the frequency of tension and fights within medical teams is particularly high. The mode of head leadership also plays a contributing role in this type of conflict. That is, the authoritarian type of leadership, which many leaders continue to employ, is poorly accepted by doctors. The same is true for weak or *laissez faire* leadership.

Weak leadership

Emily is head of a division at a large regional hospital. She worked for nearly 15 years in a university center, where she gained extensive clinical experience and recognized academic skills. Appointed to her new position two years ago, she regularly complains to the medical director about certain difficulties with her colleagues. Leading the team is a big challenge for her, which she finds unlikeable. She admits to lacking authority and complains that her colleagues do not comply with delegated tasks. In addition, a conflict between two executives, which began before her arrival, rots the dynamics of the medical team. She has attempted several times to resolve such a conflict and threatened her colleagues of sanction to no avail. The medical director offers coaching. The tripartite meeting enables the elaboration of two work goals, namely, strengthening the leadership of the division head and improving team dynamics. Upon agreement, the coaching started with individual sessions with Emily. Team coaching was then undertaken as soon as possible. The medical director remains ready whenever necessary to get involved in the resolution of the conflict.

The start of coaching is painstaking, especially during the preparation of work objectives, because Emily does not know what aspects should be changed and admits that she has adapted to the current situation.

A team meeting for an entire day is organized, which brought together medical and nursing executives. The opposition between the two senior doctors is weighing on others all day and disrupts teamwork despite the efforts of Emily and the coach. The other executives are passive and intervene in a limited manner. At the end of the meeting, another agreement was reached, that is, coaching of the medical team in parallel with the coaching of the head of department is initiated. However, outlining the initial goals of work remains impossible.

The division head, although competent in the clinical, teaching, and research aspects, has displayed a weak and ineffective leadership. In contrast to many of her colleagues, she was trained in management. However, her lack of self-confidence and difficulty in managing group processes prevent her from exercising the authority required by her position and thus compliance.

Authoritarian leadership unappreciated by executives

George is a department head in a large regional hospital. Appointed two years ago, he is a leader in a medical specialty that he has envisioned to develop in his department. Very committed to clinical work, he positions himself as an authoritarian leader who wants to devote as little time as possible to his tasks as head and delegates numerous tasks to his colleagues. Team meetings are rare (once a month), which are devolved mainly to the transmission of information and management of the department but not team life. For more than a year, the medical team has been suffering from all forms of conflict. However, George disengages from this field and says, "They are adults. Solving their futile problems is up to them. If necessary, however, I will take sanctions."

The medical director proposes coaching to improve George's leadership and the dynamics of the medical team, which he accepted.

The coach quickly realizes that George is a novice in most of his tasks as leader.

George: I have other things to do in this hospital than spend time leading the attendings. I have no interest in this endeavor.
Coach: How much time do you spend doing your management and chief tasks?
George: Approximately 10% of my time is considered excessive.
Coach: Do you want to keep your hierarchical position and department direction?
George: Of course. How can you imagine the opposite?
Coach: The job of a head does not happen by itself. You have to learn the fundamentals of management and team conduct. How satisfied are you with the functioning of your team?
George: I would like a high-performance team that supports me in developing the department. But ... what do you want me to do with passive and less committed colleagues?
Coach: If you stay there, what is going to happen?
George: Well .... Deep down I know I have to do something. I know I have to change things now. The medical director warned me because he thinks that if I do not change my leadership style, then it will end badly.
Coach: And you, what is your appreciation?
George: I do not have a choice. I have to jump into the water, although I would have preferred the opposite.

Three months later, George progresses in his objectives and agrees to progress to group coaching with the medical team. Twelve months later, a participatory system is set up, and the coach notes an improvement in the dynamics of the team.

Understanding of the hospital environment and the professional culture of various groups of care providers is necessary to intervene in hospital conflicts. We recently had the opportunity to work in a department in which physicians and nurses collaborate daily with non-care providers. Interestingly, each professional category adhered to its work culture, which remained unshared by other professionals. This reality rendered communication and collaboration difficult in multidisciplinary tasks. For the coach, working in such a context requires mobilizing intercultural skills to effectively support such a group.

The presence of *difficult personalities* among team members, as described previously, favors recurring interindividual skirmishes, especially when there is associated weakness of leadership. This process can produce prolonged dysfunction in the team dynamics and disrupt interdisciplinary relationships.

My colleague is suffering from paranoia

The medical team of a hospital department is experiencing a long-standing conflict. Two consecutive department heads ran out and left, thus leaving the position open. The general director requests a coach to undertake an assessment of the situation to prepare for the arrival of a new head of department. A coaching of the latter is envisioned as soon as he takes office.

The interview of the hospital management, nursing staff, as well as senior doctors and chief residents (three division heads, four attendings, and four chief residents) quickly highlights the following factors:

- Weak leadership of the previous two department heads, poor communication, and weak collaboration with the three division heads.
- Three division heads who do not communicate with each other and manage their sectors without collaborating with others.
- Repeated conflicts within the medical team.
- Structural weakness that encourages discord and prevents resolution. The organization is inadequate and provokes exhaustion and burnout, that is, five of the seven executives suffered from burnout during the previous two years with the prolonged absence of the ill medical director.
- Frequent triangulations with the General manager(administrative), who attempts in vain to interfere in interpersonal conflicts and to settle the conflicts of the medical team in the absence of the medical director.
- Strong rivalry between senior physicians for succession.

- Complaints from the nursing team with regard to the poor atmosphere and conflicts within the medical team that disrupt collaboration and care. The nursing team complains of the difficulty to develop therapeutic projects shared between doctors and nurses under such a system.

The coach concludes that a senior manager with affirmed leadership is needed to reorganize the department and lead the medical team. He observed inadequate behaviors several times during interviews with the division heads and senior physicians as in the following example:

Coach: I want to hear your opinion on the means to improve the functioning of the medical team.

Allan (head physician):   For me, this team has been neglected for a long time. You need a competent leader to do the housework.

Coach: What do you mean by that?

Allan: I have colleagues with whom collaboration is impossible. A colleague is hyper-sensitive, even with paranoid traits; thus, communicating with him is impossible. Another colleague is a manipulator who turns everything you do with him in his favor. How do you collaborate with these two personalities?

Coach: And you, what are you doing?

Allan: I think I am currently the only one of the three division heads with whom building something is possible. I intend to apply as soon as the position is open.

Coach: I am surprised by your critics about a few of your colleagues ....

Allan: I take note, but I keep my appreciation.

The coach is looking for information from his colleagues and the nursing team. In fact, Allan is portrayed as a difficult and slightly dominant person, especially during team meetings.

At the end of the assessment, the management decides to modify the structure of the department and create a medical council made up of all senior physicians, as well as introduce medical-nurse management. A system for the periodic medical evaluation is established (non-existent to date). The choice of the head of department is entrusted to an ad hoc committee, which is instructed to select a new department head external to the medical team and organize support by a coach as soon as the new head of department takes office.

The chief physician Allan appears to display egotistic traits and a domineering behavior that leads him to underestimate his colleagues and disrupt the dynamics of the team. The coach also underlines the inability of the two consecutive department heads to remedy the situation and the presence of external factors that favor dysfunction of the team, such as the absence of the medical director.

The scapegoat

If power struggles are common in teams of senior doctors, then the common presence of "scapegoats" who are responsible for *all the ills of the group* deserves attention. The scapegoat is one of the typical characters of group life, in which a propensity exists to attribute roles and labels to a number of members, such as the "leader," "expert" (the one who knows when others do not know), "protester," "bad guy (scapegoat)," and "king's madman."[12] This unspoken distribution of labels and roles in groups, which is mainly an unconscious phenomenon, also affects health care teams. It can be beneficial if it promotes good dynamics and distributes roles that match the profile of the designated people. That is, the elected expert is indeed an expert, or the contestant can counteract the authority of the leader. In the same manner, it can be negative or even catastrophic and lead to the mistreatment of members of the group, such as the scapegoat, as well as induce dysfunctions of the group if the roles are poorly distributed or stall the dynamics of the group. One can then make analogize with "the sick child" as a symptom of the family.

The presence of the scapegoat is not specific to groups of physicians of course, it can be observed in all groups. It often reinforces the cohesion of members against a "common enemy," where cynic leaders take advantage of this phenomenon to build up power similar to many populist politicians.

For the coach, detecting scapegoating is important to refrain from participating in this dynamics and specially to avoid reinforcing the stigmatization of this person.

A useful scapegoat

Group coaching is initiated in a hospital department. The main goal is to improve the functioning and cohesion of the medical team, which was shaken by long-term conflicts. Mention is also made of the weak leadership of the head of department, an assessment contested by the latter. As a first step, the coach is tasked to interview all medical and nursing staff to evaluate the functioning of the group and outline work objectives. The initial step highlights the conflicts between several senior doctors who disrupt the functioning of the division at all levels.

During the interviews, the coach is struck by the particularly negative attitude of one of the attendings who openly criticizes several colleagues as well as the head of division. The working sessions with the medical team confirm this observation. This particular attending is withdrawn, rarely intervenes in discussions except to criticize colleagues, and complains about the lack of discipline of the medical group. Her colleagues, ambiguously encouraged by the head of department, reciprocate and criticize her position and often hostile attitude with a low voice. Conversely, they recognize the excellence of her clinical practice.

The coach intervenes several times to address this situation and stimulates the group to talk about the issue openly. Each time, however, he is slowed down by the passivity and apparent disinterest of the entire group in this problem, including the attending concerned. The head of department declares that one should not put energy to solving this old and unsolvable problem. Nevertheless, team coaching is progressing as a *department project* is built without the conflict evolving. The coach gradually realizes that the withdrawn executive takes the role of a *scapegoat*, albeit in a nearly hidden form. This phenomenon suits everyone: the department head masks his weak leadership; the team members ostracize this unpleasant colleague, and even the attending plays the "victim," a role that she is familiar of playing.

Scapegoating is a process that belongs to systemic dynamics, as illustrated by this vignette: a careful observation of the team members indicates that the attending takes on the role of scapegoat, a role that she appears to accept. This case is also true for the department head and team members, who are accommodating of this situation. Such an unhealthy dynamics contributes to team functioning. That is, any change will destabilize balance, which will require the system to adapt and find a new (hopefully healthy) equilibrium with the contribution of the coach.

Clans

The presence of clans is common in large medical teams, as shown by our experience, being the source of patent dysfunctions in the team. Interestingly, this phenomenon frequently supports inadequate leadership. Indeed, the team leader typically directly enforces the formation of clans our indirectly by pretending ignorance of this anomaly. His attitude is, therefore, a symptom rather than a primary cause. Although detecting their presence is easy, clans are difficult to disband because their existence is based on many elements that reinforce them, such as professional and personal interests and agenda, parallel projects (unknown to other participants), emotional elements (i.e., anger, resentment, and rivalry), presence of a common enemy, and friendly relationships.

A multimodal strategy is often required to reduce the influence of clans, such as strengthening leadership, improving the overall dynamics of the group, organizing a transparent flow of information ("everything on the table"), and promoting the development of common objectives and joint projects. To improve group dynamics, we often use the Lencioni[13] model, which is based on the work on five fields related to team malfunctions as follows:

- *Lack of trust* in other members of the group or within the group as a whole.
- *Fear of conflict*, thus leading to the inability to voice opinions, which lead members of the group fail to take the floor or hold on to their opinion.
- *Lack of commitment* to the group and non-rallying to decisions made.
- *Lack of accountability*, which pertains to the absence of personal involvement.
- *Inattention to the results* of the group and colleagues.

This work model is easy to understand and use. In the presence of clans, the first three elements of the model (i.e., lack of trust, fear of conflict, and non-rallying) are present and actively contribute to reinforce the dynamics of clans. The first step then is to train the members of the group to take the floor as a person ("I think, I say ...") and not in the name of a subgroup and to speak up regarding differences and disagreements.

Two clans clash after the appointment of a department chief

The senior physicians of a large department, which was divided into three specialized divisions, have been suffering from conflicts for several years. The head of department who is also responsible for one of the divisions is overworked and spends little time on his duties as the head of department, such as managing tasks and team leadership. The medical team meets only once a month; the agenda is not distributed in advance; and no meeting minutes are noted. Dissent previously existed when he was appointed as the head of the department; thus, a true culture of confrontation is present in the medical team for a long time.

The arrival of a new division head is associated with an upsurge in conflicts. Local candidates were excluded from the outset by the nominating committee to avoid aggravating the current antagonisms.

The new leader is inexperienced but receives strong support from the department head. The division head and nursing executives set up a new organization of the structure. Other executives in place, who have found a new source of struggle, oppose it strongly. In response, the two clans reorganize. One carried by the new head of division is supported at a distance by the head of the department, whereas the other, which includes the three senior physicians, opposes the new head. Although the chief residents stand at a distance, they take sides with one or another of the clans. One virulent attending is thrown out. The head of the department attempts in vain to restore order in the team. Since then, the two clans have opposed each other for several months.

In response, the medical director proposes team coaching, which aims to improve the functioning of the medical team and settle all dissensions between the attendings. The head of department and the majority of medical and nursing executives approve the approach.

As illustrated, weakness in management is common in the medical field and can be observed at all levels of the department. Defects in management are thus associated with disturbances in functioning, which are sources of tension and disagreements. To avoid conflicts in tasks that are typically carried out by several stakeholders, a precise description of procedures related to specifying the delegation of tasks, for example, admission of patients, therapeutic protocols, and quality assessment, is necessary. Many medical fields (i.e., emergencies, intensive care, and surgery) have demonstrated the usefulness of this approach.

A study conducted on a management school in North America (MBA-type training) explored the relationship between the management strategies for several types of conflict and group performance of 57 autonomous teams (without a designated leader). Furthermore, the study assessed the satisfaction of group members.[14] The results suggested that teams that maintain or improve performance deploy three types of resolution, namely, (1) they focus on the content of interpersonal interactions, rather than the relationship style, during interpersonal conflicts; (2) all reasons determining the selection and distribution of tasks and mandates are discussed within the group; and lastly, (3) work and tasks are distributed after taking into account the expertise and skills of individuals, rather than only on the basis of volunteering, refusal, or suitability.

Conflicts between teams

Work in acute care departments (e.g., intensive care, cardiology, surgery) has demonstrated the importance of tension and dissension between teams of care providers of all kinds on a daily basis.

Responsibility belongs to the head nurse!

Anna is the head physician of the division of surgery in a large hospital. She has long complained that the medical–nursing collaboration is suboptimal. She admits to experiencing difficult relationships with the head nurse of the department of surgery who is open to collaboration with senior doctors. For the head nurse, the management of the nursing team is primary, whereas collaboration with the physician is secondary. She maintains a safe distance from the chiefs of divisions to avoid any medical intrusion into the management of nursing issues.

Anna has long expressed the wish to reassign a technician–nurse who is tasked with specialized medico-technical services. The head nurse objected, arguing that Anna lacks an objective reason for transferring this person. After an absence of more than six months, the technician–nurse resumes work without Anna's knowledge. She tries in vain to oppose, but the discussion with the head nurse slips quickly and the tone escalates. Anna expresses her frustration about being forced to collaborate with a technician she considers less competent and a difficult person. The head nurse calls on the HR management to resolve the situation. Anna finds herself in the presence of the general manager, the HRD, and the head nurse and is obliged to quickly retreat because regulation requires that nursing concerns are exclusively regulated by the hierarchy nurse without the interference of medical hierarchy. Anna takes note but leaves the office of the general manager with frustration. She has resolved to refrain from interfering in the nursing business and declares a loss of motivation to collaborate with the head nurse.

This vignette illustrates the oftentimes difficult relationships between medical and nursing hierarchies. The result is frankly bad as no resolution of the problem was reached because the person unwanted by the division head physician remained in place, which was associated with tension in the nursing team and disrupted the cooperation between the medical and nursing managers. In short, the conflict resulted in a "lose–lose" scenario.

Clashes between medical teams occur mainly in departments or divisions that require strong interdisciplinary collaboration to ensure the care of patients, such as intensive care, emergencies, organ transplant, and other or more areas of modern medicine. To raise the effectiveness of interdisciplinary activities, learning about interdisciplinary collaboration is necessary to determine the persons responsible for tasks in teams and to share the rules of communication and cooperation (chapter 2).

A clash between medical intensive care and neurosurgery teams

An 84-year-old patient fell from a bicycle, thus incurring severe brain trauma. Despite clinical and radiological signs indicating that the situation is hopeless, a young chief resident is attempting a "last chance" neurosurgical intervention (hematoma drainage). Three days later, although the patient receives maximal therapy in the ICU (i.e., artificial ventilation and vasopressors), he fails to wake up. The clinical and neurophysiological examinations show that the patient is in a deep unreactive coma of catastrophic prognosis. The discussion between medical intensive care and neurosurgery teams is challenging, whereas the two medical attendings responsible for the day treatments are in a clash. The result points to impossibilities in deciding under quiet and calm conditions and giving coherent explanations to the extremely worried family. The evolution quickly becomes unfavorable and takes a few days to ease the tension between the medical teams.

This scenario illustrates to see the difficulty of establishing effective communication in a complicated situation in the middle of a clash between two senior physicians. This result is truthfully detrimental with many inconveniences, such as tension between the teams, inability to define a coherent therapeutic project, and difficulty in informing the family. This type of conflict can disrupt cooperation between the medical staff for several days. In other words, we again present a "lose–lose" scenario.

Academic conflicts

Although protected by a thick curtain of silence, conflicts and even violence are also commonplace in the academic medical world. In particular, oppositions between teachers and students (i.e., abuse, harassment, mobbing, and aggression), which are painful and unacceptable, but outside the scope of coaching and thus will not be discussed. However, antagonisms between academic doctors at all levels are common even if they are hidden. On many occasions, doctors are coached at the request of the "victims." Three main factors are considered as source of these conflicts, namely, the very lively rivalry that reigns in this environment, clannish manner of functioning in the academic world, and the often-opaque management of promotions in medical management teams.

Rivalry is a source of stimulation and progression when contained; however, it is a source of destructive fights when excessive or manipulated by others. Although considerable literature has been published on the issue of conflicts of interest in academic medicine, that concerning conflicts among individuals is limited despite their frequency.

We present a few examples of our experiences in our university hospital.

1   Conflicts related to the selection and choice of academic promotions (common):

- between two senior physician candidates for succession;
- between two clans of senior physicians during a joint succession carrying two internal candidates;
- between a senior doctor recently promoted to an academic position and his colleagues (dismissed).

2   Eviction of a professor by one of the subordinate colleagues who organizes a smear campaign to have him fired and replaced.

3   Exclusion or firing of a colleague or a group of colleagues opposed to other colleagues who are supported by higher-ups in the faculty (we have experienced several cases).

4   Conflicts related to the emergence of new medical specialties (i.e., frequent given the hyper-specialization of modern medicine). We experienced this type with the emergence of intensive care medicine, which pitted ICU physicians against colleagues in anesthesiology, internal medicine, and surgery. Resentments and enmities remained prevalent for many years.

5   Disagreements and oppositions in the context of the Dean Council (probably common but hidden and difficult to identify).

The presence of clans is common in the academic medical world (similar to other leading circles). If we analyze the criteria for appointing professors of clinical medicine, a disgraced favoritism may be observed, which may lead to appointing doctors with weight support rather than with an excellent CV and outstanding skills.

Pressure builds up between candidates for succession

A professor who is a head of department must leave his position because of a disease that prevents him from maintaining his managerial position. An interim of more than two years follows. The senior physicians' team is torn apart quickly as two candidates (Professors A and B) are lining up for the succession despite calls from the medical director suggesting that preference will be given to an external candidate. Others who are close to the former leader also support the decision of the hospital general manager and a small group of executives to hire an external candidate. A turbulent period then ensues, and internal struggles take hold, which permanently disrupt the cohesion and cooperation of attendings. The consequences are dire: a significant drop in research activities, decline in the quality of medical training, and deterioration of the image of the department. The bad reputation of the department is spreading throughout the country, which provokes a prolonged crisis in the recruitment of physicians in training and in academic succession.

The consequences of a series of chain conflicts subsequent to the departure of a sick department head are serious. The situation is further aggravated by the lack of neutrality of the general manager and inaction of the Dean. The result is a prolonged crisis, a broken department, and several departures of experienced senior doctors.

A difficult succession

The succession of a professor is opened. The professor is a world-class specialist in a leading-edge field and surrounded by a team of senior doctors trained in various fields of the specialty. Two internal candidates apply, namely, Professors X and Y. X is a world-renowned physician and very experienced in a field of advanced specialty. Y is also a professor but less known and has acquired good management training. In addition, he benefits from several influential supporters at the local medical faculty and management of the university hospital center. The hospital management appoints Y as ad interim head of department, which results in many inconveniences for his colleague X, such as remonstrances in front of other colleagues, vexation, stalling of appointments with scientific collaborators essential to the pursuit of research, and delegation of uninteresting tasks.

X hesitates because she is unsure of what to do. Should she seek an academic position elsewhere? Should she withdraw, stand back, and wait for better days? Should she adopt a more assertive attitude and seek support? Advised by a friend, she decides to start coaching to prepare her application, manage unavoidable conflicts with Y, and to bear the stress of her situation.

The vignette describes another difficulty in academic life, that is, the inconveniences imposed on a senior executive related to rivalry and cronyism. In this case, the coach has assisted the client to enable her to analyze the situation with realism, manage emotions, develop appropriate defensive strategies, and avoid reacting to the provocations of her colleague at all costs.

Violence and harassment

Violence is concurrent with the use of force or power to aggress, dominate, coerce, conquer, hurt, or destroy. Surprisingly, it is frequent in the context of the hospital, particularly in exposed areas, such as the emergency, ICU, and psychogeriatric divisions. A survey conducted in four hospitals in the United States with more than 2,000 nurses found that 30% recently experienced various forms of violence, such as physical (19.4%), psychological, and verbal (19.9%).[15] The persons responsible for physical aggression were mainly patients (10%) and their relatives (7.6%), physicians (rarely; 1.5%), and supervisors (1.7%). The verbal and psychological forms of abuse were commonly initiated by patients (54%) and their families (34%). Approximately one-third of care providers reported psychological abuse caused by a colleague, who is typically a doctor. These figures illustrate the reality of hospital work and necessity to take measures to reduce violence in patient care and between care providers, which is often hidden. Coaching is usually not requested for such situations.

Hard to get worse

A chief physician retires and leaves behind a medical-nurse team with whom he has been working very closely. Nurses and physicians are collaborating smoothly and effectively. The head nurse of the well-knit team is highly respected, knowledgeable, and has a long history of working in the field.

An inexperienced head physician is promoted and takes her months to begin working with nurses in the clinical field because she prefers medical activities and teaching. At one of the first medical-nurse meetings that finally takes place, the head nurse intervenes as he used to ..., after which the head physician stands up and, with a gesture of an infantilizing hand and scornful mimicry, addresses him with "You, first of all, you shut up!" The team is dumbfounded.

What was the chief thinking: that an authoritarian, contemptuous, and coarse attitude toward the "de facto leader" would give her a place on this team; that she would thus mark her superiority? Had she planned and orchestrated the aftermath of her action: the breakdown of employees and her ability to recruit care providers "devoted" to her? In any case, the unfortunate consequences to care providers and patients have been serious because of a basic lack of sense of group management. A few years later, she was fired when the head of department (possibly her lover) transferred to another hospital. This scenario is also a sad example of a rather typical hospital way of life.

Violence and harassment among in-training nurses and physicians

Contrary to expectations, training at the hospital may be a particularly painful ordeal. A book published in France in 2017 entitled *Omerta at hospital* confirms the difficult situation experienced by French medical nurses and assistant nurse students during training at the hospital. The book contains the testimony of 130 students, which was collected by a general practitioner (active in an academic political science department). The picture is edifying: stress, humiliation, lack of daily respect, verbal abuse, sexist remarks, and even moral harassment.[16] Asked about this violence by a journalist from the newspaper *Le Monde*, Prof. Jean-Louis Dubois Randé, Dean of the medical school of the University Paris-Est-Créteil commented that

> "The world of the hospital is in general brutal, particularly in its relationships with human beings. It is a place of competition and suffering, facing the disease and a hierarchy that often remains hard and elitist. It is a difficult environment for the fragile persons, humiliation is frequent and has long been accepted, not to mention the still widespread machisme".[a]

Such comment is indicative of an unacceptable situation, which should be taken seriously and corrected rapidly as supported by numerous recommendations from the medical literature.

Assessment of a young physician by a malevolent professor

Christine is a young physician at end-of-training. During the first four years of training, she had to change hospitals three times. She reports a difficult relationship with trainers despite her efforts. She is now a senior resident at a regional hospital, but even this situation is precarious. The head of department regularly gives her devaluating remarks, tends to ignore her, interrupts her when she speaks or takes a stand. She became very disturbed about a recent evaluation from this well-known teacher, who even said "I don't appreciate you, I dislike working with you. You have no future in my department, and you are not made for this job." One of the attendings suggested that she undertake coaching, "to improve the relationship with her trainers and stop them from getting upset." She makes an appointment and comes to the first session scheduled at the end of the week.

Coach: Please explain your request and what you expect from coaching.

Christine: I need help because I cannot adapt to the hospital medical world. I work in a department for training and experience repeated failures. "It is hopeless." She tells her story and the importance of training to obtain the title of a specialist. At the onset, she complains of a lack of self-confidence but misunderstands her failures.

Coach: How do you evaluate your relationships with other attending physicians? Are they tense, for example, with the Professor?

Christine: No, I do not think so. I get along well with colleague residents, chief residents, and the attendings, but not with the head of department who obviously depreciates me.

After explaining a few characteristics of coaching, the coach asks Christine if she has considered her work goals.

Christine: I thought of three goals. First, I need to understand what is going on and why I am not appreciated by my boss. Second, I would like to learn how to improve my relationship with him. Finally, I feel that I lack confidence in myself, which probably leads me to behave inappropriately.

Coach: Okay, this acknowledgment is a good starting point. We will get to work, but first we will have to review your goals to start coaching. For the next session, I propose you prepare operational goals. What does that mean for you?

Christine: Well, I had the opportunity to prepare goals during post-graduate training, but I have never worked on personal goals.

Coach: No problem, I will assist you.

Coaching: second session

Christine begins the session by saying that she is satisfied to be assisted by a coach to advance in this task, which she deems complicated. She has prepared goals, but they remain vague and difficult to measure.

Coach:	To move forward, I propose an exercise called "perceptual positions." It consists of a role play, in which you will successively take your character, "me, Christine," and that of your boss, "me, Professor X." The game is played on two chairs. Whenever you change character, you will change chairs. I lead the exercise and you start a discussion with your boss in your usual role. At the end, we will work on what you discovered, and I will provide feedback. Are you ready? Okay.
Christine:	Hello professor, I would like to discuss the situation of a patient with you because it is a complicated case. Are you available now?
Professor:	Okay. Let's talk now. I'm listening to you.
Christine:	At the medical round, we discussed the situation of patient D. You said that you thought he suffers from atypical multiple sclerosis. I wonder if we could consider another diagnosis?
Professor:	I'm surprised you challenged my diagnosis.
Christine:	This suggestion is not meant to contradict you, but I really think we can think of another neurological disease ... .
Professor:	Be careful. I already warned you: you start to take me away!
Christine:	(thinking, silent for some seconds ...)
Coach:	Stop, we stop here. What did you discover?
Christine:	I think I disturbed him because he has already told me that several times. I also realize that I sometimes interrupt him when he said he did not like that. It is true that I can learn to do better.
Coach:	Can you translate this realization into goals?
Christine:	Yes, I wonder if I should make a list of behaviors to avoid and to prefer? I can also undertake practical work with you as we did today.

The objectives are worked upon at the end of the session and finalized by the next session. After three months of work, Professor X gives Christine a positive feedback, saying "You have made progress. Working with you is easier."

Such repeated humiliation and rejection can occur in several hospital departments. Senior physicians tend to ignore this form of violence as they have had to deal with the same harshness during medical training and thereafter in the life of a senior physician. It is greatly underestimated by hospital managers and hidden by those who suffer because of shame and fear of retaliation. It seems less frequent in the nursing staff whose humanist values are more pronounced. Importantly, hospital managers must grasp this problem because it is intolerable, promotes burnout, and contributes to doctors' lack of empathy for patients (chapter 10).

Harassment is a particular form of mistreatment in inter-individual relationships, which is characterized by repeated hostile acts and practices that a person or group (in a high position) repeatedly commit to another person or persons (in a lower position) to belittle, weaken, humiliate, offend, and threaten. It takes various forms, such as words, writings, gestures, domination, threats, and sexual aggression, all of which aim to psychologically weaken or destroy the other and gain power and domination. Harassment occurs not only at work but also in the family and in all social relationships in general.

Workplace harassment can take many forms, which may be difficult for an external observer to observe, such as devaluation, non-recognition of work, malicious surveillance and criticism, unjustified punishment, repeated teasing, humiliation of the person in front of colleagues, verbal and non-verbal threat, ignorance or exclusion, and non-promotion.[17] It is often encountered not only in the context of hierarchical relations but also in horizontal relations between colleagues and marked by rivalry, envy, or spite. The hospital is no exception to this reality. Many studies illustrated that healthcare providers are victims of harassment in the course of their work. This case is particularly true for medical and nursing students as well as doctors in training. A multiple-question survey was administered to all residents who are training in accredited general surgery programs immediately after the January 2018 American Board of Surgery In-training Examination (paper published in the *New England Journal of Medicine*).[18] Data were collected from 7,409 residents (99% of the total collective). Out of this percentage, 32% complained of discrimination against gender, 17% of racial discrimination, 30% of verbal or physical abuse, and 10% of sexual harassment. The incidence of abuse was significantly higher in women than in men. A total of 65% of the women complained of gender discrimination (versus 10% in men) and 20% of sexual harassment (versus 4% in men). Verbal or emotional abuse was reported by 30% of all residents. Gender and racial discrimination were more frequently caused by patients and their relatives (44% and 47%, respectively). Surgeon-executive physicians were primarily responsible for the complaints of sexual harassment (27%) and abuse (52%). Residents exposed to such repeated mistreatments were more likely to experience symptoms of burnout than residents without reported mistreatment. Emphasis should be given to the notion that the frequency of mistreatments varied widely among national programs. For gender discrimination among women, the median was 67% ranging from 0% to 100%. Moreover, the media for racial discrimination reached 16% ranging from 0% to 46%. Data indicate that maltreatment and harassment in all forms are common in surgical training in the United States. Similar reports demonstrate that the same phenomena are observed in Europe and Switzerland. In the next vignette, we describe a recent case in a Swiss university hospital.

Resident or escort girl?

Laura is a third-year resident that requested for coaching. She was profoundly worried by sexual harassment at work in the department of surgery, which lasted several months in the previous year and left her full of fear in the pursuit of training. She aimed to analyze the occurrence and how she could have prevented it and searched for solutions in the case of new episodes of harassment in the future. Laura was working for a short 12-month course in surgery. During her previous training in internal medicine, the department head encouraged her to apply in surgery for a basic course. An interview with the head of department was planned, and she was hired.

Laura: Although I had not met the department head since the interview, I am now nearly daily in touch with him. After approximately a week, he assigned me almost systematically to assist him in his surgical operations. He started to make me sexual innuendos. He invited me to the next department evening. Typically, only older residents are invited to this type of event. He said he invited me "just to flirt with me." Subsequently, on several occasions, he adopted derogatory attitudes by asking me during a full operation what I do with the penis and how I deal with it. He even called me "the clitoris of his department" at the end of a meeting.

I notice that the majority of the allusions he addresses me took place in public and were never countered by the colleagues present. These instances even seemed to imply that I was privileged to receive "compliments" from the professor, whereas I felt injured and humiliated each time and bore the feeling that whatever amount of work I provide, my efforts will be reduced to nothing by these remarks, that reduce me to a "sex toy."

After several months of this "bad play" and lustful looks, Laura was given the opportunity to finish training elsewhere and decided to resign. When she informs the professor, he goes into a fit of rage and responds that he will ruin her career. Furthermore, he intimidates her by threatening to call her future boss.

Laura: I am lucky that the substitute of the professor in the surgery department supports me and calls my future head to recommend me.

So, she finished training year in this department. During the last month of work, the department head never spoke to her again.

Laura: I hesitated to legally complain about his attitude, but I was discouraged by his threats as well as by the risk of meeting him again in the future. Today, I feel shame and would probably do things differently.

The first stage of coaching was devoted to the first goal, that is, analysis of the incident and gaining acceptance of the shame of harassment in the face of her colleagues who stayed passive, at a distance, and reacted with fear of the power of the professor or even laughter for others. The following instances were easier for her, and she finally discovered that she was becoming a fully adult woman who is stronger, able to say no, and resist difficult men whenever necessary. This transformation is a true post-crisis growth (chapter 9).

A chief resident at a University Hospital in Switzerland working in the department of surgery recently complained on air at the Swiss French Radio regarding repeated episodes of harassment, such as the following.[b]

He took my hand and stuck it on the patient's penis

"In the operating room full of people and at the end of the operation, a surgeon asks me how I find the penis of a patient. I am stuck like marble because I could not move. I missed 2–3 heartbeats. The surgeon insists and pushes me to give an opinion. He took my hand and stuck it on the patient's penis. Laughing, he asked me 'Is it good like that?' It is a big humiliation. I pulled my hand away and left. I cried in the locker room". Understanding why such instances are tolerated is difficult to understand. No one reacted.

Clearly, the hospital management is responsible for initiating actions to such cases and to rapidly and without compromise eliminate such behaviors in hospital life. Solutions include education of healthcare professionals, particularly physicians, regulation of feedback, and implementation of a zero-tolerance policy, thereby ensuring respect, health, and the well-being of all categories of healthcare providers working in the hospital setting, particularly students and residents in training.[17]

Conclusion

Conflicts that lack appropriate handling from hospital hierarchies tend to remain and disrupt the functioning of healthcare professional teams and their health, well-being, and quality of care, as well as the satisfaction of patients. When treated successfully, conflicts become opportunities for change, improvement, development, and growth. Coaching offers perspectives for teams suffering from internal dissension. The beginning of coaching in such a context is generally difficult and frequently disrupted by internal conflicts and the presence of clans. Two particular environments that are conducive to multiple antagonisms are described as follows: the operating theater and ICU.

Violence and harassment, which are often hidden and undetectable, affect all areas of medical activity, such as training and academic activities. Numerous studies called for a rapid resolution of such unprofessional behaviors, which cause dissatisfaction, loss of empathy, and burnout among hospital staff.

Notes

a https://www.lemonde.fr/campus/article/2017/03/02/un-livre-denonce-les-maltraitances-dont-sont-victimes-les-etudiants-en-sante-a-l-hopital_5087849_4401467.html
b https://www.rts.ch/info/suisse/10882851--il-a-pris-ma-main-et-l-a-collee-sur-le-penis-du-patient-.htm

Bibliography

1 Sofield L, Salmond SW. Workplace violence. A focus on verbal abuse and intent to leave the organization. *Orthop Nurs* 2003; 22(4): 274–283.
2 Overton AR, Lowry AC. Conflict management: difficult conversations with difficult people. *Clin Colon Rectal Surg* 2013; 26(4): 259–264.
3 The Royal College of Physicians and Surgeons of Canada. Conflict Resolution. Available from: www.royalcollege.ca/rcsite/bioethics/primers/conflict-resolution-e [cited November 21, 2018].
4 Booij LH. Conflicts in the operative theatre. *Curr Opin Anesthesiol* 2007; 20(2): 152–156.
5 Pelavski AR, Rochera M, De Miguel M, *et al.* Conflicts between anesthetists and surgeons. *Eur J Anesthesiol* 2007; 24: 182.
6 Van Norman GA. Abusive and disruptive behavior in the surgical team. *AMA J Ethics* 2015; 17(3): 215–220.

7 Azoulay E, Timsit JF, Sprung CL, *et al.* Prevalence and factors of intensive care unit conflicts: the conflicus study. *Am J Respir Crit Care Med* 2009; 180(9): 853–860.

8 Prendergast TJ, Claessens MT, Luce JM. A national survey of end-of-life care for critically ill patients. *Am J Respir Crit Care Med* 1998; 158(4): 1163–1167.

9 Stewart I, Joines V. *TA Today: A New Introduction to Transactional Analysis.* Lifespace Publishing, England, 2012.

10 Thornton C. Groups that don't work: understanding and tackling dysfunctional patterns in group behaviour. *In: Group and Team Coaching. The Essential Guide.* Routledge, London; New York; 2010, pp. 214–232.

11 Tuckman BW. Developmental sequence in small groups. *Psychol Bull* 1965; 63(6): 384–399.

12 Thornton C. Eight group factors influencing learning and change. *In: Group and Team Coaching. The Essential Guide.* Routledge, London; New York; 2010, pp. 64–84.

13 Lencioni P. *Overcoming the Five Dysfunctions of a Team. A Field Guide for Leaders, Managers, and Facilitators.* Jossey-Bass, San Francisco; 2005.

14 Behfar KJ, Peterson RS, Mannix EA, Trochim WMK. The critical role of conflict resolution in teams: a close look at the links between conflict type, conflict management strategies, and team outcomes. *J Appl Psychol* 2008; 93(1): 170–188.

15 Campbell JC, Messing JT, Kub J, *et al.* Workplace violence: prevalence and risk factors in the safe at work study. *J Occup Environ Med* 2011; 53(1): 82–89.

16 Auslender V. *Omerta à l'hôpital. Le livre des maltraitances faites aux étudiants en santé.* Michalon, Paris; 2017.

17 Leisy HB, Ahmad M. Altering workplace attitudes for resident education (A.W.A.R.E.): discovering solutions for medical resident bullying through literature review. *BMC Med Educ* 2016; 16: 127.

18 Hu YY, Ellis RJ, Hewitt DB, *et al.* Discrimination, abuse, harassment, and burnout in surgical residency training. *N Engl J Med* 2019; 381(18): 1741–1752.

Further readings

Lencioni P. *Overcoming the Five Dysfunctions of a Team. A Field Guide.* Jossey-Bass (a Wiley imprint), San Francisco; 2005.

Runde CE, Flanagan T. *Developing Your Conflict Competence.* Jossey-Bass (a Wiley imprint), San Francisco; 2010.

Part III

Views on coaching learning and avenues to humanize the hospital environment

12 Discovering coaching, overcoming fundamental skills and gaining experience

Véronique Haynal and René Chioléro

Introduction

The practice of coaching typically follows the exercise of another profession; it is part of a professional course and a history rich of experiences. Such was the case of the two authors of this book, who have opted to practice coaching in addition to psychotherapy (Véronique) or after a career as a hospital physician (René). This chapter aims to present a degree of thought about the discovery of coaching and its practice from the perspective of the two aforementioned healthcare professionals. The significant experiences made during their training and beginning of their practice are reported. In particular, this aspect focuses on the learning of numerous specific competences and skills, and mastering of basic techniques, such as working with emotions, learning to use critical moments and to solve difficult decisions. Each major topic will be illustrated by practical examples.

Practice of coaching at the hospital: Véronique's point of view

Born in a physicians' family and married to one, I am soaked in the medical culture.

My great interest for communication guided my steps in my journey into psychology with a specialization in non-verbal communication and psychotherapy. Luck assisted me and I was able to explore this topic in psychotherapy in the context of mental health and in clinical research. Indeed, a "Laboratory Affect and Communication (LAC)" was created in the Department of Liaison Psychiatry at University Hospitals in Geneva. There I spent nearly two decades observing, dissecting, and analyzing the doctor–patient relationship. I was immersed in the hospital. At the same time, as a clinician, I practiced a body-oriented psychotherapy (especially with psychosomatic patients). I also provided weekly supervision to re-markable care providers in the psychiatric emergency unit. Teaching oc-cupied a part of my career, and I retained this activity in which I take great pleasure apart from coaching and psychotherapy.

DOI: 10.4324/9781003291831-16

How did I come to coaching? Obviously, some of my patients did not seem to need real psychotherapy, whereas others needed coaching in addition to psychotherapy. Therefore, I began an interesting coaching training after 30 years of therapy activity. I found myself the oldest in this group of students. The difference with the studies I previously conducted was mainly with regard to the style of teaching, that is, very practical and "hands-on" with little theory. In terms of content, I felt at home. Indeed, I was familiar with active listening, reformulating, and working with empathy. I remained stable despite unusual or emotional reactions from a few of my co-students. However, my difficulties in the new role appeared mainly in the *change in posture*, which leans toward a more structured and frequently more confrontational attitude than that practiced in psychotherapy. Thus, keeping discussion on track, without unduly impeding the free flow of ideas to reach the goals is necessary and challenging. Encouraging my co-student to set clear, concrete, and measurable goals in the exercises was definitely new and difficult for me. However, this notion is the basis on which the coaching process is built. Toward this end, coaches must avoid being distracted by associations of ideas that will lead us (the couple coach-coachee) to deviate from our goal. That was not my cup of tea. In my psychotherapeutic practice, I used these meanders to understand and explore the reasons why the client cannot move forward. In this field, the first goal is typically a vague "I want to feel better!" Although painful, we then follow the paths of sensations, feelings, and images that emerge at the moment in the hope of gaining a better understanding of the patient's psyche. However, the precise goal of the treatment may take weeks, months, and even years to emerge. In coaching, I needed to adjust, which took considerable time. I definitely had to become more assertive.

I enjoy coach's tasks, such as preparing sessions and bringing materials, ideas for exercises, games, and roleplaying, for the next meeting. I am particularly fond of the creative part.

Fortunately, in coaching, emotions also assume their place and should be welcome—I found myself comfortable in this regard. In fact, I had learned the Facial Action Coding System (FACS) for research about non-verbal communication, which requires observing and noting subtle and quick facial movements to understand the emotions and signals sent by the person viewed on a videotape. Practicing this observation for hundreds of hours trains the eye. Similar to psychotherapy, detecting the fleeting or subtle expressions of emotions exhibited by a client is crucial. Indeed, a client may only be partially aware of the situation being experienced. Several possible paths can be used to raise awareness, understanding, and management of emotions. Therefore, I have been working for years in this field, where psychosomatic therapies frequently take a large part. Experiencing and reflecting about the relationship between patient and therapist, which expresses itself through emotions, is a fundamental healing process in therapy.

This coaching training humbled me to a large extent because my knowledge was entirely overlooked. However, the experience enriched me and enabled me to reflect again on the modes of relationship from another point of view. I acquired a series of tools, which was my goal. I learned a more structured, dynamic, positive, and light working style with clients, who are mostly engaged in healthcare. For instance, during a coaching session, I might ask "How do you rate your happiness at work on a scale of 0 to 10?" The coachee might answer "2." I would then answer: Oh, good, how did you reach 2? What are the elements that led you to select 2? Now, how will you increase to 3? In psychotherapy, we consider 2 as a profoundly negative situation and reflect on why the patient is so unhappy.

My fundamental relational attitude, however, remains the same. I experience an exchange with coaching clients because they trust me and share their secrets, wishes, goals, and hopes. In return, I offer my feelings and my tools. Surely, unlike patients, coachees are feeling rather well; thus, we move together on the path they decide to follow at their unique pace.

The substantive pith of these meetings in coaching and supervision, such as the experiences we undergo together, the coachees, and myself, continuously nourishes the understanding of my life and that of other healthcare professionals. It allows me to improve professionally and personally. These clients and the healthcare providers I supervise have inspired my reflections and chapters in this book. I am grateful for them.

Practice of coaching at the hospital: René's point of view

The interest for human relations has been a red thread throughout my studies and subsequent professional activity. In terms of selecting a path of university training, I opted for medical studies with the goal of becoming a psychiatrist after being enthused by my readings of Freud, Jung, Adler, and many others. After three years of training in internal medicine and pediatrics, I was interested by an internship in pediatric intensive care unit (ICU), a field that was booming in the 1970s. I discovered a specialty that I immediately appreciated for its dynamic and committed side, which led me to forego clinical pediatrics and train as an anesthetist and critical care specialist instead. The intimate relationship that connects the intensive care physician to patients and relatives, especially in complicated evolution of the illness and at the end of life, has been a source of endless interest and questioning throughout my career. This questioning about uncertainties of medical practice and human condition has led me, similar to many of my critical care colleagues, to become increasingly interested in biomedical ethics and to actively participate in the clinical ethics committee of our university hospital. Medical ethics helped me answering the dilemmas of clinical practice and giving meaning to its successes and, occasionally, bitter failures.

This questioning can be illustrated by the current COVID-19 pandemic. The whole world witnesses the high scientific uncertainties about this new virus, capable of killing both patients and caregivers, against which no specific treatment is known, thus spreading fear and insecurity. In the whole field of care and medical practice difficult questions were raised, such as: How to practice an efficient medicine, respectful of patients, in an overwhelmed hospital system? How to organize the triage of patients requiring hospital care or intensive care admission? How to make end-of-life decisions in a realistic and respectful manner? How to treat fairly elderly patients in nursing homes? How to protect care providers' life?

At 36, as a young chief physician in a university hospital, I discovered the traps of team management and leadership, which encouraged me to resume my reading on psychology and develop my skills in human relations and team life.

Fifteen years later, I participated to a training in sophrology,[a] where the other students typically came from alternative medicine. They were concerned about health, diseases, and the human being but within alternative systems of thought and not centered on science. What an opening discovery for me, focused on the scientific thought and technical mastery of intensive care! Notably, I also discovered the importance of the body–mind relation in health and disease.

During the last years of my hospital career, I progressively discovered the world of mentoring and coaching after a few short training courses. This opportunity led me to assist colleagues applying for jobs or in their personal change projects and reinforced my goal of becoming a professional coach after retirement from the ICU. I was strongly motivated to train in this entirely new activity.

Becoming a student

Four weeks after retirement, I arrive in Geneva in a school specialized in the fields of neuro-linguistic programming (NLP) and coaching. At 65, I am the oldest student, whereas the youngest is only 28 years old. Highly motivated to begin this experience, I quickly realize that I am beginning a period of discovery, contrasts, and adaptation to my new condition. I undergo moments of pleasure and stimulation in the skin of a student, which alternate with other difficult experiments. I have to descend from my professor's pedestal to mold myself into the shoes of a student. This new role teaches me the value of restraint and silent observation, which are key skills in coaching.

Training imposes on me a deep personal work with challenges even for the experienced care provider that I was. I have to unlearn many of the certainties acquired in my profession and modify entire elements of my cognition, behavior, and professional identity to replace them with those in relation to the coaching profession. I discover the position of a coach in front of a client as one that is a fair distance and in a respectful posture that excludes a high and dominant position. This notion contrasts with that of a doctor with a patient, which is a marked asymmetrical relation: one is ill and solicits consult for cure and healing, whereas the other is healthy and provides therapy. Indeed, the relationship between a coach and a "client" requires a markedly different positioning from that of a doctor and a patient. In coaching, the client is a unique person that the coach assists in the pursuit of objectives, she is the master of her life and decisions, she is standing. Furthermore, she has her own map of the world, a proper system of values and beliefs. Such a relationship implies that the coach learns to be fully available and attentive, focused on the other person, should devote sufficient time and space to support the coachee toward her goals. Such abilities are little developed in physicians, who treat patients, that is, sick people who are suffering and waiting for the doctor to care for them until recovery. The doctor, who is in a high position, dominates the relationship, although he shares information and decisions with the patient.

I love you, but not all the time

A sociologist and coaching student Lucy performs a brief 45-minute coaching exercise with me. She selects "to clarify expectations with my son, who wants to leave the maternal home" as a work objective. The 22-year-old young man has not finished his studies but found a job and wants to become independent and live his life. The mother–son relationship is difficult with not only few common activities, many tense encounters, and daily conflicts but also intervals of tenderness.

Lucy: I am disappointed, I find myself frequently overwhelmed and unable to answer him without getting angry. He can be charming, especially when he expects something from me. At other times, he is awful and does not care about my face.

Coach: I understand, it must be difficult …

Lucy: Yes, worse than that, oftentimes unbearable … I feel fooled, I even have times of desperation when he leaves home without saying a word …

Coach: Would you like to work about your relationship with him in search of solutions? I propose the exercise of perceptual positions, a role play in which you will alternately perform your role and that of your son.

Lucy: Okay, let's go for it.

The exercise of perceptual positions elicits a wave of emotions: anger first, then rage for short moments, silence for a few minutes, and finally a river of tears flows. I stay at a distance, feel embarrassed and stumped. Finally, I call a teacher who comes to help me comfort the mother and ease the situation.

This vignette took place at the beginning of coaching training and reflected my limited experience of coaching despite 40 years of medical practice. The result was suboptimal: insufficient listening, lack of time and space, inappropriate management of emotions, discomfort, and lack of self-confidence as a coach. That day, I was reassured to have the teacher by my side, who helped me finish coaching and regain footing. The conclusion seemed obvious: being an effective coach requires mastery of the positioning and coaching relationship. However, gaining such experience necessitates time, extensive assistance activities, personal development, and supervision once training is completed.

Teachers in medical training often misuse feedback, which can be a process of development and progression. They typically tend to assess activities through criticism, possible improvement, and correction, rather than through feedback as a learning process. In fact, feedback can promote self-discovery of areas that could be beneficial for improvement and additional training to achieve objectives. Honestly, I learned during my coaching training how to provide feedback that is truly useful to the person receiving it.

Being a professional coach: difficulties, surprises, and rewards

I began my activity step by step as a professional coach, starting, as said, with assisting head physicians, which was a familiar field for me after more than 40 years of hospital life. Addressing the coaching of heads in crisis was a difficult hurdle, which required me to question my practice and obtain supervision. I present here a few examples and questions:

- How will a coach assist a young physiotherapist who is currently in a catastrophic family situation, undergoing separation, away from her children, and paying exorbitant alimony to her former husband but eager to start life coaching to improve her confidence and autonomy in the relationship with her ex-husband?
- How will a coach assist a disunited team, composed of perpetually conflicting doctors and reluctant to work together? When I started coaching, I had a solid experience of teamwork and healthy level of self-confidence for this type of activity. However, contrary to expectations, the role of a coach in such a context is markedly different from that of a department head. Widening my experience took several years of learning to manage this type of situation and avoid its pitfalls, such as taking a position too close or far from the leader or team and playing the expert or frequently "playing the head of department" in the case of a weak leadership.
- How will a coach work effectively with a client who wishes to undertake coaching, although he is trapped in a prolonged crisis that is affecting all aspects of his life and admits being incapable of directing his hospital division, suffers from severe insomnia, and being treated by a psychiatrist? Will making useful assistance under such conditions be possible?

- How will a coach manage coaching sessions when the paces of the coach and client are a mismatch, the client does not seem to progress, and the coach becomes impatient and further increases the rhythm of work? I remember the painstaking start of life coaching with a doctor in his fifties who wanted to "work less to have the time to find a stable partner."

No time to find a partner!

During the first four sessions with this physician, we went around in circles to prepare defined, precise, and achievable goals. Each time the client took a step forward, he recoiled minutes after, for example, he would say "yes, but … ," thus returning to the starting point. I felt uncomfortable and many times irritated by this inability to move forward that I did not know how to approach. After four sessions, I proposed an assessment in a straightforward manner, with the aim of interrupting the coaching. I was surprised to find that the client quickly woke up at this moment. At the end of the session, he finally found his first goal, that is, "work less to have more time for me." After being questioned about the possibility of advancing a first step, he decided to block his agenda on Wednesdays afternoon to play sports and take care of the children's homework. Thereafter, the assistance revealed that the quest to find a partner reminded him of the bad memories of divorce; thus, he was unable to associate free time with finding a partner. The obstacle was lifted, and he managed to reduce working time without problems. Three months later, he found a new partner.

- How will a coach collaborate with impossible clients, such as those intolerants to the coaching process, fixed in their projects, or presenting behavioral problems? This difficulty may also be related to the coach's inexperience, for example, struggling to establish a relationship of trust with the coachee, using an inadequate work strategy unsuited for promoting the advance of the client's goals, or inattentive to parallel processes. I worked with clients who seemed intolerant of coaching. In general, I begin with the idea that undertaking a "coaching test" of two to four sessions is nearly always possible. We then make an initial assessment to determine the effect of coaching in the given situation. The following vignette describes a typical example, which may be more frequent during the first year of practice because of the coach's inexperience.

Coaching makes me anxious

I received a request from a client who has been unsuccessful for over 20 years in her goal to improve her self-confidence and develop balanced relationships with her family. She had previously undertaken many steps of all types (i.e., body–mind work, spiritual development, and psychotherapy) without considerable success. Despite my reluctance, she insisted on undertaking a coaching session while recognizing from the outset that it could fail: "Why not try? I still progressed in recent years. With you by my side, we may succeed at something." For three sessions, we aimed to develop valid goals. However, I noticed an increase in her anxiety, which prevented any progress. After a prolonged discussion, she agreed to continue the assistance with a psychiatrist we have chosen together. She sent me a note six months later telling me that she was feeling better and that she would contact me if necessary. I have never heard of her again.

Clearly, this client cannot tolerate coaching. Her ability to step out of her comfort zone may be limited. However, another angle cannot be ruled out. That is, she would have benefitted from coaching if another coach with more experience was able to establish a stable coaching relationship and use gentler and more responsive working strategies.

In other situations, the coach receives beautiful surprises and real rewards, which can bring tremendous encouragement.

I see you from the top

I received a request for coaching from Martina, a head of department in a university center, to prepare for her retirement[b]: "I'm not ready, I feel anxious and I go around in loops." This transition is a difficult task because she has been managing a medical division for over 20 years and the department for ten years. She has extensive professional activities in many fields, such as clinical, research, teaching, speaking at international meetings, and participating in scientific societies.

In the first two sessions, I note that she refers several times to the changes in the relationship that she perceived with her closest associate, a head of division in the department. For several years, the two doctors held brief meetings over coffee and met once a week to discuss the problems of the department in an open and constructive manner. For three months, this relation has been disturbed as they no longer shared discussions, coffee, or meals together. In addition, the head of division decided to apply to succeed Martina without her knowledge. This difficulty was not highlighted during the initiation of coaching despite several questions from the coach. For the first three sessions, Martina tackled this question, without integrating it into the objectives of the session. Finally, the coach insisted that she spend a few minutes to find a solution to the seemingly innocuous problem considered minor up to that moment.

The development of a goal is laborious. In fact, Martina is unsure about her purpose and what she wants to achieve. She identifies the goal as mostly to "find a normal and relaxed relationship with her colleague." However, she immediately says that she does not intend to leave her position as head and that taking a step toward her is the colleague's duty. After approximately 30 minutes of procrastination and the intention of progressing quickly, the coach offers a conditioning exercise that *Martina* accepts. The coach makes her stand on a chair while he remains seated and asks her to describe what she envisions.

Martina: I see your office, your library ...
Coach: What else do you see?
Martina: ... nothing really.

The coach repeats the same question twice without change. On the third attempt, after a few minutes of reflection, *Martina* lets go of her inhibition:

Martina: There is one more thing to say. As I am standing, I see you from above.
Coach: And how do you see your colleague? You can go back down as you think about this question.

The coach notes a lightning flash in her eyes and a broad smile on her face. I call this moment "the insight."

Martina: I think I understand. I also see him from the top ... maybe I should get off my pedestal to initiate contact with him?

The remainder of the story is similar to an American movie. The next day, *Martina* approaches her colleague, drinks a coffee with him, and they decide to share a lunch meeting on the following week.

The next session, I receive an extremely positive feedback on the result of this work. Moreover, we resume our retirement coaching in a more dynamic and relaxed setting.

This observation stresses the importance of selecting effective strategies for coaching to open the consciousness and to reframe a stalled situation. It also shows the weight of medical hierarchies and difficulty of head physicians in giving up their high and dominant positions in exchange for the relationships with colleagues even at the end of their careers. Such positioning complicates transition during retirement, which requires letting go and a grieving work, which is frequently difficult for medical leaders.

A comparative perspective about basic techniques, emotional work, critical moments, and decision-making

Working with emotions

Life in all aspects is colored by the complex world of sensations, feelings, and emotions. That said, such a case is true for the practice of coaching, which includes a rich and varied emotional dimension as recognized by all coaches. This emotional dimension is concerned not only with coachee(s) but also with the coach and their interactions. All clients come to the session with a basic emotional state, which may be favorable or unfavorable to the job. The coach is tasked to detect this aspect in himself and in the client(s) and to integrate it into the assistance.

The ability to manage the emotions that emerge during coaching should be part of the core skill set of the coach, similar to other helping relationship activities. Thus, how do we become aware of our emotions? How do we perceive them? How do we notice emotions appearing and how do we address them when overwhelmed? Which emotion triggers us most and when is it elicited in us? How is the environment coping with our emotional behavior? Notably, the coach is just as likely to experience emotions as the client is. However, the coach first has to learn how to appropriately regulate emotions.

Acknowledging, accepting, and addressing emotions grounds us in the face of intense feelings wherever it happens, be it in crisis and life coaching or conflicting teams. Otherwise, emotion may seriously complicate the course of coaching. For example, how do you develop work goals with a client in crisis who is on the verge of tears or hopelessness midway through a session? Finalizing goals is difficult for a major change in a career without naming and talking about affects and updating the feelings of the client attached to them, such as previous experiences, positive and negative memories, assessment of the current and desired states, and perceived "ideal future." Thus, how does a coach work with a medical attending in a difficult relationship with his manager without taking into account the fear or anger felt?

Notably, however, in the current practice of coaching, many experts consider the strong and "difficult" emotions that can emerge during sessions counterproductive. Many coaches observe that the work on strong emotions is difficult to conduct and believe that such emotions interfere with rationality and should be muted during coaching or reserved for psychotherapy.[1] In response to these coaches, accepting and addressing affects in coaching is indeed difficult. However, science illustrates that rationality without integrating and managing emotions is non-existent. On the footpath of Damasio's book *Descartes's Error* in 1994,[2] abundant literature focused on emotional intelligence in the present context and enhanced the understanding of the necessity of taking emotions into account.

In addition, when a client has developed *a good relationship* with a coach, her coach, she *will refrain* from switching to a psychotherapist to "treat her emotions" similar to visiting another store to buy another product. Indeed, coaching is a *relational* process, as is psychotherapy, which makes changing persons difficult.

However, the truth is that dealing with emotions begins with the coaches themselves, who can opt to learn this competence (at this point, however, this aspect is usually taught outside coaching training). Much of the coaching reference material contains little information on this important facet of the practice. Cox and Bachkirova explored the importance of "disturbing" emotions in their practice among 39 experienced British coaches (executive and life coaching specialists).[1] The authors assessed the manner in which coaches cope with emotionally charged situations and how they integrated them into the coaching relationship. The results show that coaches have different points of view on this topic. With regard to clients' emotions, four response modes are observed, namely, (1) use of reflection either personal or via supervision, (2) avoidance of a difficult situation, which must remain client-specific, (3) active work with the client on the situation in question, and (4) transferring the client to a psychotherapist or stopping coaching. For the sake of their emotions, coaches point out that certain emotions exhibited by clients are likely to mirror emotions in the coach and thus exert an impact on his ability to lead the work. This case is particularly true for strong, disturbing, and negative emotions that cause the coach to feel uncomfortable emotions, such as anger, fear, and despair. States such as apathy and resignation are also troubling for coaches. We note that coaches use four main modes to deal with the emotional responses of their clients, namely, processing alone or during supervision, active exploration of the situation with the client, ending the coaching or referring the client to another professional, and through supervisory work.

Véronique's point of view is that engaging in a relationship of support requires a constantly improving knowledge of oneself to remain sufficiently strong and grounded to manage the relationship smoothly, adequately, and with compassion. Practicing teaches her more and questions her differently on a daily basis. The coaching training placed her in a new environment to learn about herself and helped her become more assertive and confrontational. She heard new viewpoints that she could reflect on by herself, in groups, or under supervision.

Outbursts of emotions should first be recognized, labeled, and discussed. After an emotional expression in a team, everybody may react according to their own feelings, which can be considerably varied. Stating and explaining the state of each member of the group and exchanging discussions about it is important for *understanding one another*. In this manner, the group can feel stronger ties and improve collaboration. Otherwise, if not addressed, the member who expressed a strong emotion will feel terrible, and the group subdued, impressed, or contemptuous, may secretly (or overtly) criticize this member.

During his work as head of department, *René* was confronted with emotionally charged situations on a daily basis, especially in terms of relationships with patients and their relatives, other department heads, colleagues, as well as during conflicts between medical teams and nursing teams. These experiences gave him the opportunity to gradually learn to deal with the individual and collective emotions of others, as well as to master his own, although sometimes with difficulty. In the clinical setting, he felt at ease with emotions from the outside, even in the most extreme situations related to uncertainty, suffering, and end of life.

How can you tell this story without shame?

A 43-year-old man is treated in the intensive care unit after a difficult cardiac surgery operation. Upon leaving the operating room, he undergoes a state of deep shock and requires mechanical circulatory assistance. After a few days, the situation improves, and withdrawing the circulatory assistance device became possible. The next day, however, the patient suddenly has a cardiac arrest that causes irreparable brain damage. He dies a few days later in deep coma. Data analysis reveals that the cause of the cardiac arrest is related to a nurse's error: the patient inadvertently received a rapid infusion of a drug that produced cardiac arrest. Therefore, informing the family of the error is necessary shortly after death. I am assisted by the surgeon and another nurse. We meet the wife and the two young adult sons. We carry out the conversation step by step to explain the terrible news. The wife is speechless; one of the sons sobs and the other takes us to an aggressive party. Nearly shouting, he said: "I was sad, now I'm more angry. How dare you tell us in this way this terrible story?" We explain that informing them was our duty and that we are very sorry to have added pain to their plight. Two months later, the family makes an appointment with me and I wonder if they came to inform me that they will sue me. However, they appear calm and apparently soothed. I am relieved to hear that they are doing better and that life is resuming. I was very surprised to hear that they are thanking the ICU team, whose honesty they salute.

This vignette illustrates the importance of accepting, taking into account, and addressing emotions that belong to life and its events. It helps overcome the crisis, and we see that the abovementioned family is making large strides in managing grief. The situation underlines the ability of the physicians and nurses to handle the situation. Such a capacity is also necessary for the good practice of coaching.

From the beginning of his coaching training, René discovered other aspects of human emotions during coaching exercises. Such emotions can be felt when one is within the open and safe framework of coaching. Here, we develop a special relationship with the client that consists of common experiences and sharing with greater proximity than that in medical practice, where the expression of emotions is in principle reserved for patients and relatives. Such a space of emotional freedom concerns not only the coachee but also the coach, albeit in a tenuous manner.

Work on the wheel of life (René)

At the end of training as a coach, I take part in a course devoted to tools to explore the fields of life of the coachee: health, work, spouse–partner, family, finances, and leisure. On this day, the program introduces the "wheel of life" tool. We participate in a workshop with practical exercises, which are performed in teams of two students. At the medium of each exercise, the roles of the coach and client are reversed. I start by playing the role of a coach, whereas a student colleague was the client. I am surprised to find that the colleague carried an evaluation of 1/10 for the spouse–partner section. Although I question him with restraint, he refuses to answer. After approximately 2 minutes, I ask him again. This time, he answers, "Let me breathe. I need to think before answering." After a few minutes, he said, "My partner left me three months ago. It was a painful experience. A week ago, I learned that she committed suicide." I do my best to comfort him and put my hand on his shoulder.

Tears appear on his face, and he cries silently. During the feedback, he tells me that he is feeling better, but he has not yet recovered from the incident. Moreover, he tells me that my hand on his shoulder initiated the tears and that he would have preferred that I did not touch him.

This vignette illustrates the emergence of a strong emotion during a coaching exercise, which surprises the young coach. He observes that, with adequate space (and permission) for the coachee, emotions can emerge and express themselves freely during the exchange. We note the emotional reaction mirrored by the coach, who tries a gesture of appeasement, which is refused by the coachee who does not bear this sign of intimacy because it intrudes into his safe space at the wrong time in the context of group learning.

I discovered the importance of empathy from the coach, who perceives the emotion of the other and the need to assist him in a sensitive and attentive manner. Although I often kept emotions in check during my hospital practice, I found that this aspect of the interindividual relationship was more difficult to manage in the context of the coaching relationship because it requires learning and mobilizes the coach's attention. In addition, surprisingly, I discovered that empathy and compassion are more likely expressed in the practice of coaching than in medical practice. As a witness, I note the frequent complaints of patients and their relatives about the apparent lack of empathy and compassion from many hospital doctors[3].

A teacher overwhelmed by emotions

A real-life coaching exercise is organized during a training session for coaching. Each student came on the day with a companion, who played the role of a volunteer client for one of the students of the group. The exercise, which was carried out in front of the class, consists of elaborating a general goal of working with the client and leading him to sketch the first step toward a solution. One of my colleagues begins with his client, who immediately presents himself as a problem person. The work is laborious, and the client clearly suffers from exhaustion at work and complains repeatedly about his boss and colleagues. He fails to move forward or find a coaching goal. The student coach is obviously uncomfortable and overwhelmed. At the end of the session time, everything appears stalled. During the evaluation of the work that follows, the teacher is very critical.

Teacher: Work in this manner is impossible because you do not know your fundamentals.

Student: I tried to follow the method we learned. In my opinion, the client was having a bad day, and his situation may have worsened since the day I offered him to come for the exercise ....

Teacher: The method you applied is certainly not the method I taught. You lack empathy, fail to reassure the client, ask the right questions, and lead the job. In addition, you must learn to develop your self-critical sense. Otherwise, you will have difficulty developing your expertise. I maintain my point of view: the session is clearly insufficient.

Two students who attended the session show up to strongly challenge the teacher's evaluation. However, the teacher remains obstinate and affirms that he is the expert and maintains all of his critics in the class. As the students also maintain their point of view, the tone of the conversation escalates. Suddenly, the teacher becomes angry, crashes, and cries .... The group is stupefied. After 10 minutes, work resumes slowly but lacks true discussion or feedback about the event. The session ends with a dull and restrained atmosphere.

This vignette illustrates the emotions that can emerge when an unsecure "expert" feels challenged in his field. This scenario constitutes a true example of a *critical event* during a teaching session (see later). Notably, the scene was held in front of a group of students in coaching that disapproved the teacher's attitude. Such circumstances, which may be associated with the emotional tone of the teacher on that day, spark an emotional overflow. The inability of the teacher to request a feedback at the end of the work underlines the loss of control of himself and the group. In such situations, we believe that supervision is mandatory.

With years of practice and concomitant experience, we (*Véronique* and *René*) find that feeling at ease in most individual coaching situations is possible, that is, able to cope with the emotions of the client and in general use them to advance the process. However, this feeling can be more difficult in the coaching of problematic groups, who are conflictual or closed off in their interactions. In any case, introspection and supervision frequently render possible the search for a solution for the advancement of the coaching process and growth of the coach.

Critical moments in coaching

As previously mentioned, the coaching relationship is considered a co-construction within a common field of interaction and sharing, in which the client and coach are active participants.[3] Moments of tension or relationship breakdown can be observed during the course, which can be perceived as a difficulty or, in another setting, opportunities for advancement, thus unlocking development and growth. Although its detection is typically difficult, perceiving these moments is important for the coach to enable working with the client in the *here and now* and advance in the coaching process. These moments are characterized by a qualitative change in the behavior of the client and in the relationship, whose intensity, form, rhythm, and emotional content also change. Day et al. observed 28 experienced professional coaches and analyzed 51 critical moments.[4] The authors observed six common characteristics from these moments, which were expressed at varying degrees of intensity, namely, (1) intense emotions from the client; (2) intense emotions from the coach; (3) tension in the relationship between the two; (4) tension influencing the boundaries of the relationship, such as respect of confidentiality, limits of coaching, need to refer the client to a psychotherapist, relationship of the coach with the client's head or other third parties, and special requests of the client; (5) unexpected nature of the event; and (6) qualitative change in the coaching relationship. The majority of coaches express doubts and anxiety about responding to critical moments partly because of the unexpected nature of these moments. Such a scenario puts into question their role, manner of conduct, desire for satisfaction in the activities, the requirement to be up to the task, and the possibility of following their intuition.

The effects of critical incidents on the coaching process are complex and varied, such as an immediate and impulsive response from the client or coach; a change in the coaching relationship, such as a reinforcement or an increase in distance or rarely, a break in the relationship; joint reflections by the coach and client; unexpected client changes, such as discovering new items or changing the collaboration with the coach.

Numerous vignettes described the occurrence of critical moments in this book. Here is an example during a prescribed coaching.

I need you but I am unsure I can trust you

Louise, a new medical specialist, is imposed a coaching by the hospital's management. The hospital director criticizes her lack of experience in multiple areas of management, such as organization of the division, leadership of the medical team, and quality assurance, although her clinical performance is reliable. The beginning of the coaching is painstaking because Louise is convinced that she is unsupported by the hospital management, whereas she considers not to demerit in her management. The relationship with the coach is rather distant and laden with mistrust and reserve. However, the finalization of the coaching project makes a warm-up of the working atmosphere possible to a certain extent.

A few days before the fourth work session, Louise calls the coach. She seems tense and nervous and explains that she has an appointment with the management to carry out her annual assessment. She admits to being anxious. A one-hour work session is organized with the coach at the end of the day to prepare for the said meeting. After defining the objective of the session, the coach questions Louise about the reason for her fear. After 3 minutes of silence, she burst into tears and takes another 2–3 minutes to recover.

Louise: Many people scare me, such as the director and you, the coach.

Coach: Can you tell me more?

Louise: I will start with you. In the initial meeting with the director, I noted that you seem to have a good relationship with him and I wonder if I can trust you?

Coach: I understand your doubt, which actually makes me feel uncomfortable because I obviously have failed to establish a relationship of trust with you. In fact, as you have seen, I have known the hospital director for a number of years because he has already given me mandates in this hospital before. However, our relationship does not mean that I won't be doing my coaching job with benevolence or that I have a conflict of interest about you. From my point of view, you are my client with all her rights. What do you think?

Louise: This question is important for me because I have reached my limit in terms of difficult relationships with the management. I cannot stand it anymore, and I really need support from someone I trust.

Coach: How about giving ourselves the time to answer this question? You know, trust is a key element in coaching.

The discussion that follows renders addressing several important points for Louise possible, such as being informed of all discussions in the first interview between the director and coach, in particular, the points of reproach for her. How then could she be sure that confidentiality is guaranteed? How does the coach respond to information requests from the management? Eventually, a decision was reached, that is, Louise will have access to all exchanges between the coach and the management.

The remainder of the work is more peaceful and productive. Louise decides to prepare a summary of the learning she has undertaken in the division since the beginning of coaching. Afterward, the coach notes a change in work dynamics; the atmosphere relaxes. Louise expresses herself more freely, evokes her worries, successes, and questions about the management of the division.

This vignette illustrates the sudden occurrence of a critical incident in the course of coaching, namely, the invitation to the management for its annual assessment precipitates Louise in a crisis. Her hidden and muted expression bursts out suddenly in the presence of the coach with an emotional storm. This confrontation leads to a feeling of discomfort in the coach because he learns that the client has a strong doubt about the amount of trust she can give him. The joint work, recognition of each emotion that they underwent, and capacity of the coach to assist with restraint enable a real change of state in the relationship in the client, which is favorable to the continuation of coaching.

Difficulty in the decision-making process

Difficulties and inability to make decisions hinder many clients to reach their objectives. This situation, which is relatively common in all assistance, reflects the complex factors that influence a person's ability to decide at a given time:

- The client's ability to make a decision is often reduced during emotional overflow, crisis, or mental health impairment (typically burnout), like anyone. Awareness of resistances and possible obstructions have to be checked. Special attention is given to quick and impulsive decisions. Repeated avoidance of decision-making may be a form of defense expressed during coaching.
- *Analysis of stakes.* How important is the decision, whether good or bad, its consequences? This question necessitates the performance of ecological analysis in terms of personal, finances, family, benefits, and disadvantages in the present and future.
- *Responsibility of the decision-maker.* Who makes the decision? Who will endorse the consequences of this decision? Is it the client, another person (delegation of decision), or the coach (according to the client's views)?

The delegation of the decision to the coach, typically in a hidden manner, is one of the pitfalls of coaching, which can become difficult to resist when a young coach.

- *Emotional aspects of decisions.* These aspects require careful exploration. Anger, sadness, and guilt must be identified, recognized, and discussed openly as appropriate because they may blur the decision-making process.
- *Ability to develop a clear view of the situation.* If this ability is not acquired, the entire decision-making process will be disturbed. A powerful questioning to determine and clarify various elements will frequently elicit a decision.
- *Undetermined needs.* Analysis of the desires governing the goals of the client is required. Furthermore, considering the updating of possible elements that obscure the process is necessary.

These difficulties in decision-making can typically be solved using several propositions or actions from the coach. Oftentimes, simply reframing a decision helps increase the awareness of the coachee about its consequences and purpose.

We certainly significantly improved support by acquiring know-how and experience in the conduct of coaching.

Leave my husband or my lover?

Alice, 63, requests a coaching to "try one more time to make a decision concerning my conjugal situation." Married for more than 25 years, she has been involved in an extramarital relationship for four years, which remains undisclosed to her husband. Each time she made the decision to leave, she gave up at the last moment. Presently, the situation is focused on taking a stand because the lover gave her a deadline that seems definitive and considered a genuine ultimatum: "You leave him, or I will break up our relationship."

Once again, Alice feels unable to make a decision, which disturbs her. She has consulted a psychiatrist twice to try to solve her problem without success. The coach questions her about the key elements of the situation. She responds at ease: "I love my husband whom I respect, but I need Peter, my lover, to feel completely a woman, to exist. In fact, I live well and do not want to change my situation." Her coaching objectives seem clear: "Discover the elements to consider, to make a good decision; this time I cannot go back." To promote the process, the coach urges her to prepare an "ecological analysis" of the situation for the next session: to identify loss and gain, responsibility and non-responsibility, and repercussions of the situation on her life and proxies.

At the next session, Alice arrives with a big smile.

Alice: I think I am going forward in my problem ... .

Coach: Explain that to me.

Alice: Actually, I am currently living a very pleasant life. My husband and I are at ease and we get along well, who in my opinion is turning a blind eye to the situation. Conversely, my friend is nice, but I do not see myself living with him every day. In addition, he has a modest situation, which would force me to change my lifestyle and I cannot consider this option.

Coach: And ...?

Alice: Contrary to what I imagined, I am going to interrupt my relationship with Peter and probably without much regret. Now, it is time to finish this story.

A simple ecological analysis of a situation carried out at the right time led to a new perspective, thus promoting the decision process. The goals were achieved after only two sessions in a sustainable manner. I received a message from Alice at the end of the year telling me that everything was fine and that she was satisfied and thanked me.

Coaching at hospital: using a wide approach and various techniques

The hospital environment offers a particularly wide field of accompaniment demands, according to the needs of physicians and nurses. As said, this support can take many forms. Notably, there is no clear boundary among these practices. The client's needs and the coach's training determine the method and strategy of support. It is important though to be clear about the method used and to mention it to coachees. Although some coaching experts recommend a practice strictly based on a pure coaching approach (which excludes any mentoring or expert advice), others believe that as long as the coach's skills and experience are sufficient, he may expand the support according to the needs of the beneficiary and circumstances. We do use such extended practice, attempting to enlarge the method, when justified, as in the support of people suffering from crisis or burnout, in whom the capacities of adaptation and change are initially reduced. Notably, a return to a practice based on the classic coaching-type relationship should be adopted as soon as possible. Such wide approach of coaching depends on the training and experience of coaches, provided that they know and respect their limits and benefit from supervision.

Conclusion

We have illustrated the entirely diverse paths of the two authors toward the practice of coaching. Although each author has been in the health care environment for the majority of their lives, their trajectory has been completely unique. They were exposed to questions of a different order. Indeed, an easy and natural scenario for one called for questioning for the other. We are describing a few stumbling blocks in learning in this new profession and our points of view today.

We mentioned a non-dominant posture, which is the attitude of the coach in front of the coachee with nuances of distance and rhythm. It is a key point in the establishment of a genuine coaching relationship, which can be rather difficult for a doctor. The need to structure coaching to progress effectively and achieve the client's goal without getting lost in the meanders of free associations was challenging. We also struggled with the hurdles of several coachees in terms of making either the right decision or no decision at all.

We address the important question of the emergence of emotions during a session whether as a group or an individual and how coaches should react to and use them to advance the process of assistance. This theme could be largely developed in the world of coaching in general and during training in particular; naturally, as it is a delicate topic, it requires time.

Notes

a Sophrology is defined as the science of consciousness, which promotes harmony of body and mind. It is based on methods of relaxation and works on the body and mind.
b Where she lives, retirement is compulsory at the age of 64 or 65 when working in a public institution.

Bibliography

1 Cox E, Bachkirova T. Coaching with emotion: how coaches deal with difficult emotional situations. *Int Coach Psychol Rev* 2007; 2: 2.
2 Damasio A. *Descartes' Error: Emotion, Reason, and the Human Brain.* Putnam, New York; 1994.
3 Hadi MA, Alldred DP, Briggs M, Marczewski K, Closs SJ. "Treated as a number, not treated as a person": a qualitative exploration of the perceived barriers to effective pain management of patients with chronic pain. *BMJ Open* 2017; 7(6): e016454.
4 Day A, Haan ED, Sills C, Bertie C, Blass E. Coaches' experience of critical moments in the coaching. *Int Coach Psychol Rev* 2008; 3(3): 13.

Further readings

McMahon G. *Coaching Strategies and Techniques*. Routledge, Hove East and New York, 2010.

National Geographic Your Emotions. Single Issue Magazine, 2020; ISBN-13 978-1547852543.

Whitmore J. *Coaching for Performance: The Principles and Practice of Coaching and Leadership*. 5th ed. Nicholas Brealey Publishing, Boston and London; 2017.

13 Viewpoints, perspectives, and conclusion

René Chioléro and Véronique Haynal

Introduction

In this book, we share our hospital experience, with a focus on the coaching of physicians, nurses, and medical teams. The content is a critical view of the functioning of medical organizations and hierarchies, largely explained by the type of requests for coaching interventions, usually related to inefficient leaders, teams' dysfunctions, and crises. Even if this vision is, in essence, biased because of its context, our experience clearly demonstrates the need to realize major changes in hospital organization and operation, to increase such institutions' concern with the well-being and health of their care providers, resulting in the patients' benefit.

This chapter aims to consider the hospital through two perspectives: long-time, experienced health care professionals and coaches who have observed hospital care providers during a decade of coaching practice. We then formulate some proposals to improve the quality of hospital governance, leadership, functioning of teams, and health care hierarchies; changes are also proposed to improve the health and well-being of hospital health care providers.

The hospital, viewpoints of psychologist and coach

For many years as research psychologist and supervisor, I experienced from the inside the joys and sorrows of university health care institutions. Of course, for me, I was immersed in another context and culture than René because I worked mostly, but not exclusively, in psychiatry. In all the professions I have supported, I met remarkable individuals, with their skills, dedication, and tact. I supported them, as supervisor, during their doubts, fatigue, and successes. I have worked under leaders who can fill with enthusiasm the teams around them and propel them into excellence. I have observed that the secretaries, receptionists and telephone operators play a leading role in welcoming patients and in the group's atmosphere.

I had the opportunity to experience several successions of leaders, often delicate disruptions—some happy, others catastrophic. For example, a new

DOI: 10.4324/9781003291831-17

executive physician had "no time" to meet one of his nursing teams for six months. Three months later, the head nurse left, followed by ten nurses who requested their transfer, reducing to nothing this team of great human quality, welded, and extremely powerful. I also lived through other emblematic stories, such as that of this other well-established and well-reputed psychiatric unit that was in crisis because its budget was decreased by half and a geographical shift had occurred. There was this department head who was treated in psychotherapy, and would also have benefitted so much from coaching. He actually motivated me to undertake a coach training.

My position as a research psychologist, studying the relationship between therapist and patient, especially in terms of nonverbal communication, offered me a position of choice to observe the diversity of care providers' relationship skills; this observation also underlined the requirement of some doctors to be trained in this field, sometimes starting with the basics as mere politeness (e.g., how to greet or to introduce themselves)!

For me, adopting the role of a coach after being a therapist, researcher, and supervisor did not require a great change of attitude, other than being more concrete and structured with individuals wishing to drive changes and develop projects.

In my opinion, René Chioléro considers the doctors' world from a unique perspective: he was part of this world, this culture, of this ruling aristocracy; he was *soaked* in it, felt the joys and the sorrows, felt the incredible pressure, and lived its tensions, great satisfactions, and also privileges. Then, he went through a revolving door. When he returns, he has a new perspective and sometimes speaks to his old professional family in a critical tone. We describe realities that could be considered taboo. We discuss the dark sides, for example, workplace violence. We describe common work ethics that can be exhausting because illness develops day and night; thus, how can care providers be entitled to another schedule? Can they leave the fight? Additionally, some doctors commit suicide, and little is done to remedy this situation. As Adam Kay[a] writes:

> ... In any other profession, if someone's job drove them to attempt suicide, you'd expect some kind of inquiry into what happened and a concerted effort to make sure it never happens again. Yet nobody said anything—we all just heard from friends, like we were in the school playground. I doubt we'd have got so much as an email if she'd died. I'm pretty unshockable, but I'll never cease to be amazed by hospitals' willful ineptitude when it comes to caring for their own staff.[1]

In response to our descriptions, will we be excluded from this particular coterie? Will the ranks of this elite tighten up to refuse, as has often been the case for so many years, in our experience, any change to a broader level of selection, basic training, and team management, institutions? Or do physicians really have to incur a serious illness or disabling accident to understand, as did

BJ Miller, that health care facilities are intended to treat illnesses, not sick individuals ("[health care] was designed with diseases, not individuals, at its center"[2]). Have these doctors forgotten the modern version of the Hippocratic Oath written in 1964 by Louis Lasagna (Tufts University): "I will remember that I don't treat a fever chart, a cancerous growth, but a sick human being, whose illness may affect the person's family and economic stability?"[b] No. We have noticed a reform movement emerging. This movement is reflected in a worldwide revision of the Geneva Declaration, that is, the "Oath of Hippocrates," to which some paragraphs have just been added or deleted. New requirements concern the patient: "I will respect the autonomy and dignity of my patient," and others address the doctors: "I will attend to my own health, well-being, and abilities to provide care of the highest standard."[c]

On a regional level, in March 2018, *Swiss Medical Journal* published the article "As colleagues, what are we doing to protect doctors from burnout?" citing the worrisome results of a survey of 24 young medical assistants at Geneva University Hospitals.[3] In 2020, there have been protests against sexism at the Lausanne University Hospital Center, initiated by physicians in training, who report that their trainers have unacceptable attitudes. Notably, across Europe, Canada, and the United States, these complaints have been recorded and studied for more than 20 years. A possibility is that the new culture of abuse intolerance may help in this case too. We hope that by revealing the violence publicly there will be positive consequences, at the Lausanne University Hospital and everywhere.[4] Measures must be taken to promote a change in culture through reforms, for example, increasing awareness and disseminating disturbing information. However, the task is so vast that the movement requires all the available resources.

The hospital, viewpoints of doctor and coach

After a prolonged career as a hospital physician and head of department, I have practiced the coaching for more than ten years, mainly in the hospital setting. I have noted the evolving hospital environment and system: clinical practice, teaching, research, and hospital management have all undergone rapid, significant change. As a coach, I discovered realities that I was unlikely to perceive when I was a physician. To discern them, I had first to put on my new glasses of coach, which revealed many hidden aspects of the care providers' behaviors: for example, many facets of the relationships that bind a doctor to her patients and their relatives, her colleagues, all types of care providers, and also members of the administration.

From this new perspective of a hospital coach, I also observed many aspects of the behaviors and professional culture of the care providers, which significantly influence the practice of coaching. I particularly noted the management of emotions, markedly different in the contexts of the coaching and care relationship. I was also touched by certain dark aspects of the hospital world, for example, the sad reality of conflicts, violence, and harassment among care providers and the male dominance of academic medicine, often ignored by the individuals in charge, which all contribute to the common occurrence of exhaustion at work among health care professionals.

Such experience was not perceptible from the inside of the hospital: the perception of a coach highlights images different from those of a hospital perspective. Some striking examples are described as follows:

- In my experience in intensive care, I have often lamented the power struggles and the harshness of interdisciplinary relationships, which are indispensable to effectively treat most of the patients, especially for end-of-life decisions.
- When I started my coaching practice and supported my former colleagues, I quickly observed other aspects of their person and their identity, as if discovering *the hidden side of the moon*. Once the reluctance related to a coaching prescription is overcome, the coach is commonly privy to the secrets hidden deep in the soul of the client, in this case, a doctor. The physician then often describes with restraint her solitude and suffering related to her practice, the insufficient institutional recognition, and the difficulties encountered in the context of team life. As soon as the relationship of trust is established with the coach, she and her client often prove to be active partners, strongly involved in the coaching process, able to progress and learn.
- The hospital medical world in Europe has evolved slowly over the last three decades, compared with other types of service companies. This sluggishness is particularly the case in the areas of department management and team leading. Although modern management has gradually been chosen in other types of companies, the hospital—until recently—has preserved obsolete management strategies, particularly in department and care management. From the beginning of my coaching activity, I discovered the sometimes-catastrophic effects of the management of the medical department and teams by untrained, incompetent, and inexperienced leaders. If this reality was already perceptible at the time when I was running a department, I only had the opportunity to meet it with full force, when I was a coach supporting medical leaders to correct their difficulties and failures.
- The academic commissions are responsible for the choice of medical professors and are more inclined to choose senior physicians with a high academic level than those competent in management. Unfortunately, academic excellence and the ability to develop high-level research do not necessarily go hand in hand with the ability to lead a division or a department. In Switzerland, the cumulation of medical, academic, and managerial responsibilities of most heads of university departments remains the rule, a reality that many of them cannot master. This finding often negatively affects the organization and functioning of such structures. The consequences can be dramatic. Some years ago, the

professors, heads of intensive care departments at two Swiss university hospitals, have retired and were replaced by two high-level academic physicians with poor management and team leadership experience. In both cases, this resulted in a prolonged crisis, with striking consequences: conflicts in medical teams, dismissal of senior doctors, and disorganization of training. The same phenomenon led to the dismissal of a professor of cardiology, replaced by a senior physician with high skills in medical management. This observation relates mainly to the European situation.

- The contact with death was a daily occurrence in the intensive care department, in which there were approximately 300 deaths per year. As a physician, this experience did not pose an intractable problem for me, probably because of the sufficiently distant relationship I had with dying patients and their relatives. The nurses, however, who assist the patients until their last breath, feel death differently.

Contrary to my expectations, the practice of coaching led me to approach death in other contexts, as demonstrated in the following example. During a six-month work period with a client, I noted several mentions of death during consecutive sessions: the passing of the client's ex-husband, two adult children with serious health problems, and unrealized dreams of having another child. The client then wished to prepare her "Living Well" paperwork to address her mortality. This work affected me deeply, leading me to ask for a supervision that allowed me to confront the reality of death, a concern of the given client, but also of coaches—even if it is a subconscious concern. On another occasion, I supported a colleague, a long-time friend, in assisted suicide because he suffered from a severe degenerative neurologic disease. This experience, new to me, was difficult and emotional, placed me much closer to death. I then sensed emotions and feelings more noticeably, and they differed from those I experienced in intensive care. I rediscovered on these two occasions how physicians protect themselves from death by placing sufficient emotional distance between them and their dying patients, sometimes even losing all empathy.

- Violence among care providers far exceeds what I imagined when I was running a medical department. It is often hidden by the hierarchies, in relation to the sociocultural characteristics of these professionals. Surprisingly, I discovered a magnitude of violence I did not expect against medical and nursing students, as well as doctors in training, endured from their trainers and, more rarely, their colleagues. This violence has been frequently denounced during the past ten years in the media. How can we imagine that a teacher, a long-time trainer, could begin the assessment of a young novice physician with the following speech: "Hello Dr. X, you have come today for your evaluation. I will start by saying that I neither like working nor collaborating with you in the department. Notably, to be honest, I don't appreciate you … ?"

- The expression of feelings and emotions in care providers is most often contained, sometimes blocked, as aforementioned, to control the relationship with patients and relatives and the course of care. In coaching, encounters with the authentic and sometimes strong emotions of the other confront a coach with a different experience. A coach should respond with empathy and compassion to the emotions that occur during the work, to exploit them to allow the client to advance in his coaching project.
- We have repeatedly stressed the difficulties of starting a coaching prescribed by the hospital hierarchy. If the physician in such a context is initially a difficult client, the situation changes as soon as the coach develops a genuine relationship with her, based on mutual trust. This client often turns into a motivated individual who wants to achieve her goals.

Promoting systemic changes to prepare the hospital of tomorrow

This book highlights many situations where a coach is responsible for supporting a department head to improve her leadership, to disentangle the functioning of a team, to manage a crisis, and to help find solutions to conflicts. There are institutions led by competent leaders, with teams that collaborate effectively and can build a common mandated culture and strong shared values. In addition, the available data show that the satisfaction and well-being of care providers are higher in such a context, and the prevalence of burnout is lower. However, in other places, when a director or a committee takes the decision (sometimes long overdue) to spend the money and mandates a coach, the problems are sufficiently serious to necessitate an intervention. Thus, coaches have a biased view of the operation of the hospital because they are called only when the difficulty or complexity exceeds the capacity of its internal resolution system. Today's hospitals therefore include an inhomogeneous set of medical units: some of which correspond to management standards, and others are unsuccessful in their organization and team leadership.

Working with an effective team: a particular case

We recently had the opportunity to coach a medical team composed of several senior physicians, in a truly participatory setting; all of them had been convinced to work together toward common goals. Their aim was to establish a system to ensure high-quality care for all patients, reinforce the supervision of doctors in training, and improve the management of the department and distribution of tasks between medical executives. The preparation of the department project offered them the opportunity to review all their areas of action: the domain devolved to the head of department, the organization of team meetings, the distribution of tasks, the organization of the training and supervision, the nurse–physician relationships, and so forth.

The coach's participation in the team meetings made it possible to approach interindividual relationships interactively in an open, permissive setting, promoting that *everything can be put on the table*, except for the confidential matters. The feedback from all senior physicians has always been favorable, promoting the continuation of the process to its end, despite the initial observation that the team was already working satisfactorily before coaching. Even in this situation, these doctors said that coaching offered them a unique opportunity to improve several aspects of their functioning:

- communication in the team and management of the flow of information: everything is discussed openly, there is no retention of information;
- shared management, especially in decision-making;
- distribution of tasks;
- trust between members, which increased during the process, allowing them to manage previously unaddressed hot topics and express their opinions and sometimes emotions; and
- the ability to manage disagreements at all levels, for example, those regarding the quality of care to patients, distribution of tasks, and the relations with physicians in training and nurses.

For the coach, this obviously was a "gift coaching!"

We had similar experiences with some department heads whom we meet once or twice per year to assess specific points in their management, reflect on particular situations, or discuss personal concerns, such as understanding failures or preparing transitions in their career. These department heads are most likely to be effective leaders, satisfied with their role, and confident that they should improve their style of leadership and their behavior throughout their career. Such a context merits assistance distinct from that intended to resolve serious leadership failures or long-standing conflicts, described throughout this book.

Proposals

After gathering the material to write this book and describing the various fields of activity of the hospital coach, we felt compelled to provide further thoughts on Western health care institutions in general, to promote changes and prepare the "hospital of tomorrow." Such a hospital would better fulfill the needs and expectations of patients and their families, health care professionals, and other staff of the institution. For hospital management, what should be established is a system of conduct promoting the satisfaction, well-being, and development of the care providers. This purpose implies a profound transformation of hospitals' cultures and their organization to improve their functioning and humanize them. Such a project has been initiated and implemented at the Mayo Clinic and some leading hospitals, whose administrative and health care management has been open to change and considered its benefit. Of course, we are proposing an ideal future for health care institutions that should be reached incrementally. From our point of view and in line with many studies on the matter, the changes should include all levels of the institution, from the bottom of the hierarchy to the top. This evolution should also embrace questions on the highest purpose of the hospital (e.g., vision, mission), down to the most common expectations.

Our propositions are the following:

- *Humanize the code of conduct at all levels in hospitals,* starting with the management and the high strata of the hierarchies, to obtain a ripple effect. Develop strong values such as benevolence and compassion and encourage all leaders and their collaborators to share them. From this perspective, the role model of management (e.g., general, medical, nursing, human resources, technical) should be emphasized and carefully determined.
- *Evaluating and promoting the well-being, as well as the psychological health,* of the whole staff. A policy should be established at the general-direction level. This evaluation involves setting up a test of these endpoints, as has been accomplished at the Mayo Clinic in the United States. As explained in detail in chapter 10, the first step at the Mayo Clinic was to recognize the importance of the problem and to evaluate it. Then, the general management (i.e., CEO, medical, and nurse directions) introduced nine categories of measures to promote the motivation and personal commitment of care providers, as well as reduce burnout. Among the measures advocated are leadership training, encouragement of team activities, use of incentives, promotion of shared values and culture, learning time management, prioritizing tasks, and preserving time away from work.[5] These measures should also be valid for academia, which suffers from the same failures and "illnesses" as health care institutions.

The organization of a common education for all managers, regardless of their professional category (e.g., physicians, nurses, administrators), is essential to promote interdisciplinarity, the recognition and collaboration of all, and the development of common values and a shared vision. Such a program has recently been initiated in several major hospitals.

- *Support for inexperienced leaders* should be established early. In our experience, the call for the coach or other types of consultants is often too late, namely, once problems have been so serious that they are identified and acknowledged by all levels of the hierarchy. At that point, the problem becomes more difficult to fix. A successful intervention is difficult in a department that has experienced more than two years of unresolved conflicts, which have led to several departures of senior physicians and eventually to the lay-off of the head of department. An easier and cheaper plan would have been to offer efficient support to the chief physician, to help her organize her management system during her first year of service. Therefore, we posit that coaching (or mentoring) should be offered to all senior medical and nursing leaders during the first months of their employment.
- *Participatory management* of medical units should be initiated and supported. This change involves appropriate training of managers and participants of all types in this form of leadership and encouraging leaders to establish such a system. The literature has demonstrated that this model of management improves the satisfaction of executives and collaborators and simultaneously reduces the conflicts. A hospital is similar to a living organism: in constant motion, always on alert, constantly adapting to new internal situations, and maintaining an ecological relationship with the outside. It is comparable to a human body, where organs as different from each other as neurons and bones, blood, and eyes do collaborate closely to maintain homeostasis and well-being. Health care institutions do not manufacture cars, whose parts are designed in advance, made by the hundreds, all identical and replaceable at will. In hospitals, emotionally gifted care providers work in continuously changing conditions. Each patient has a unique response, and each family has unique demands and expectations; this uniqueness also applies to the surrounding community and social environment. A medical facility should be imagined as a place where all employees of each unit, division, and department—from janitors to administrators, to technicians, IT specialists, and medical teams—are recognized as indispensable and unique. They collaborate in their team context, as they do at higher levels, intra- and extra-organically, in participatory management. The impact on the well-being of the members of the staff and the patients will greatly improve, as well as that of the surrounding community.
- *Expand the range of support and development incentives* for managers and employees by offering internal and external coaching, mentoring (most

often internal), and setting up speech groups and development groups similar to those found in some North American hospitals. These allow care providers to share their difficulties and sorrows with their colleagues, to solve them and provide meaning to their failures.

Regarding professional coaching, we want to emphasize that leadership failures, malfunctions of the medical and nursing teams, burnout, and pre-term departures of senior doctors as well as nurses have an incomparably higher cost than coaching. The validity of professional coaching in companies has been supported by many studies, as explained in chapter 1.

Developing internal mentoring allows the institution's executives to support and advise their young, inexperienced colleagues. This assistance from senior members is highly appreciated by young leaders, who emphasize the importance of benevolent, constructive help from a colleague who knows the environment and the functioning of the hospital. However, mentors require training and supervision in many fields, to understand, for example, the processes of the helping relationship, the risks of a breach of confidentiality, and the emergence of power relations.

- *Encourage the medical director to maintain clinical practice and teaching in addition to executive tasks*, as the Mayo Clinic does.[5] This type of work organization allows her to maintain her skills in managing clinical complexities and strengthen the closeness and complicity with her head of department colleagues. At the Mayo Clinic, a pilot hospital in many areas, the general director is always a former head of department or division, who maintains reduced clinical activity.
- *Value all areas of medicine and care*, especially in university hospitals, for example, clinical practice, teaching, research in all its forms, project management, and development. The devaluation of clinical practice in some of these hospitals hampers collaboration between clinicians and researchers and the development of joint projects and prevents the construction of a common vision of the hospital.

Final comments and conclusion

Throughout this book, we have described, explained, and illustrated the life of professionals in health care institutions, with their varied cultures, chronic overload, frequently insufficient preparation for certain executive positions, difficulty in being present on all fronts, and competent in the numerous tasks in their purview. In this context, coaching in its various forms is an effective driver of change and problem resolution. This contribution can be extended to larger projects of restructuring and reorganizing divisions, departments, or whole institutions. The favorable results, largely confirmed by our experiences and supported by studies, should facilitate a healthy, dynamic transformation of the hospital system.

However, this task is difficult, and there are requirements for coaches who undertake it. First, coaches must be familiar with the culture of the health care providers they support. In addition, they need solid professional foundations, for example, university-level training before their coaching training, combined with extensive field and life experience. These foundations allow coaches to put themselves in the roles of their clients and coachees, thus becoming better considered. The task is difficult.

The hospital of the twenty-first century is constantly changing and has not reached its "adult stage": its overall vision requires further adjustment to provide an appropriate work environment, promoting interdisciplinarity and quality care, as well as the well-being of all care providers. The medical, human, and administrative objectives should converge. Such changes cannot occur without extensive collegiality and collaboration, as well as a clear shared vision. In this manner, the hospital becomes a human and effective company. Coordination, cooperation, and a responsible attitude toward the health and well-being of health care providers are all included in the mission of the hospital of tomorrow. This vision may resemble an idealized image, "image by Épinal," but, with our coaching experience as a driver, it can be attained because it already exists and is replicable. We propose that our book provides vital information for the transformation of today's hospitals.

Notes

a Former senior registrar in obstetrics and gynecology in the UK, now writer.
b https://www.medicinenet.com/hippocratic_oath/definition.htm
c https://www.wma.net/policies-post/wma-declaration-of-geneva/

Bibliography

1 Kay A. *This Is Going to Hurt. Secret Diaries of a Junior Doctor.* Macmillan, London; 2017.
2 Miller BJ. What really matters at the end of life. Available from: www.youtube.com/watch?v=apbSsILLh28 [cited August 29, 2018].
3 Luthy C, Chytas V, Perrin E. En tant que collègues, que faisons-nous pour protéger les médecins de l'épuisement? *Rev Med Suisse* 2018; 14(957): 522.
4 Frank E, Carrera JS, Stratton T, Bickel J, Nora LM. Experiences of belittlement and harassment and their correlates among medical students in the United States: longitudinal survey. *BMJ* 2006; 333: 682.
5 Shanafelt TD, Noseworthy JH. Executive leadership and physician well-being. *Mayo Clin Proc* 2017; 92(1): 129–146.

Index

Printed in the United States
by Baker & Taylor Publisher Services